WITHDRAWN

THE NATURE OF

THE UNITY WE SEEK

THE NATURE OF
THE UNITY WE SEEK

Official Report of
The North American Conference
on Faith and Order
September 3-10, 1957
Oberlin, Ohio

Edited by Paul S. Minear

THE BETHANY PRESS, St. Louis

FOREWORD

This volume is designed to fulfill a triple function. (1) It is the official report of the North American Conference on Faith and Order which met at Oberlin College, September 3-10, 1957. As such, it provides basic information concerning the deliberations of that conference. (2) It is a method of delivering to the participating churches a series of messages from the sections and divisions of the conference. As such, it serves as an invitation to every church and congregation in North America to join in continuing study of the salient issues. (3) It places in the record a strong plea to existing ecumenical agencies in the United States that they establish a permanent program of Faith and Order Study which will be oriented toward the range of problems explored at Oberlin. As such, this volume may serve as a prelude to this future program.

The editor takes this opportunity to acknowledge two specific debts: to Darrell K. Wolfe and the Bethany Press for their help in transferring manuscript into printed pages in an unusually brief time; and to Samuel McCrea Cavert and Frances Maeda who together shared the heavy task of compiling and editing the materials.

November 1, 1957   PAUL S. MINEAR

CONTENTS

8 Contents

PART TWO

The Sections at Work

PART THREE

Appendixes

PART ONE

The Conference in Session

THE CONFERENCE IN CONTEXT

Paul S. Minear

An ecumenical conference is a baffling mixture of tangibles, such as persons and places, and of intangibles, such as fears and hopes. This was obviously true at Oberlin in September, 1957. More than a thousand churchmen in North America had been in one way or another involved in the preparations. At the conference itself more than four hundred churchmen engaged in the process of study and discussion, each contributing his own particular wisdom and experience, and each interpreting the conference in terms of his own expectations and discoveries. No single interpretation can therefore give an adequate epitome of the entire story. Nor can any essay which is prepared, as this one must be, without consultation with other participants, be in any sense offered as the authorized version of what happened. Nevertheless such an essay may help readers to set the work of the conference in its proper context. This at least is the major objective in what follows. In this context we may distinguish a background from a foreground, both of which are suggested by the official designation: *North American Faith and Order Study Conference*. The background is furnished by the Faith and Order Movement; the foreground by the North American scene. Let us glance first, then, at

The Faith and Order Background

The whole story of ecumenical movement is, of course, so long and so colorful that it defies any brief summary. Basically it is the story of all the efforts made by the people of God to bring their whole existence into obedience to the unity and wholeness intended for them by their Lord. The story begins therefore at the very beginning, when God called into existence his covenant people and gave to them a special mission. The events of the Exodus from Egypt and the revelation on Sinai thus belong within the story. Ever since then, God's calling of his people has been creative of their unity and of their mission. But there has also been disunity and rejection of this mission. The story will doubtless continue as long as this struggle continues, or until the full realization of God's kingdom on earth. According to the New Testament, such a full realization will be preceded by messianic wars

11

and woes in which the cosmic roots of division are laid bare and are overcome. Between this beginning and this end, the story tells of successive struggles in every province on the earth as well as in every heavenly realm where God battles unceasingly with "the prince of darkness grim." So extensive, so pervasive, so deceptive is this struggle that it is quite impossible for our limited imaginations to span its total compass.

What we call *the* ecumenical movement is, of course, a more limited phase of this history. It is primarily (though not exclusively) a twentieth-century development.[1] Thus far it has been restricted to non-Roman Christendom. Within these limitations, the movement has had only modest resources, vastly incommensurate with its task. It has developed only minimal organizational structures, vastly incommensurate with its impact on the mind of Christendom. Such structures as have emerged have come in response to the desires of those churches which wish to move toward one another, out of mutual ignorance into mutual understanding, out of isolation into co-operation, out of inherited antagonisms into reconciliation. The impetus for this centripetal movement has stemmed not from novel organizations but from the "pressure of our common calling" by the one Lord, Jesus Christ. It has become a movement through which the churches are enabled to worship, to work, to witness and to suffer together, looking forward in hope for that fullness which is in Christ their mutual inheritance. It is thus a movement forward into the world in response to Christ's commission and a movement forward into the future in response to Christ's promise. Engaged in such a movement, the churches have found themselves facing all sorts of countermovements, both within and among the various traditions. The phrase "ecumenical movement" thus covers a vast configuration of turbulent forces and counterforces. One measure of its vitality is the dynamic activity of these counterforces. The churches have in fact found themselves caught up in a revolution which began centuries ago and which will continue for centuries.

One central factor in the contemporary stage of this revolution has been the work of the Faith and Order Movement. Even this work is too extensive to be described here.[2] It has been punctuated by three world conferences (Lausanne, 1927; Edinburgh, 1937; Lund, 1952). Although in its origins it was quite independent,

---

[1] cf. R. Rouse & S. Neill, *A History of the Ecumenical Movement*, Westminster Press, Philadelphia, Pa., 1954.

[2] For a fuller suggestion of the work of Faith and Order see the addresses by the Rt. Rev. Angus Dun and Dean J. Robert Nelson, pp. 31-43 and 44-51.

since 1948 it has carried on its work as a department of the World Council of Churches. The punctuation must therefore be extended to include the two assemblies of this Council (Amsterdam, 1948; Evanston, 1954). For more than thirty years its distinctive task, according to its constitution, has been:

"to proclaim the essential oneness of the Church of Christ and to keep prominently before . . . the churches the obligation to manifest that unity and its urgency for the work of evangelism.

"to study questions of faith, order, and worship with the relevant social, cultural, political, racial and other factors in their bearing on the unity of the Church. . . .

"to study matters in the present relationships of the churches to one another which cause difficulties and need theological clarification. . . ."

For several decades ecumenical statesmen have been wrestling with these matters. Most of the wrestling until now has proceeded in the arena provided by delegated gatherings on a world scale. And to be sure the meeting of churches from many countries has had unique advantages. The proclamation of "the essential oneness" has been impressive, as has the recognition of its "urgency for the work of evangelism." But the platform of a world conclave has not been the best seminar room or laboratory for studying many of the factors which actually divide the churches in their day-by-day living. Churches whose representatives work together amicably in Lund or Geneva may be at swords' point in Topeka or Syracuse. It is often true that the most destructive and divisive forces are to be detected within the bounds of a single state or province. The complex configuration of cultural factors which decelerate or accelerate Christian unity often comes into clearest focus within a single city. Such considerations as these persuaded the Faith and Order Commission, both at Lund and at Evanston, to adopt a new policy. Henceforth it would encourage regional agencies to project their own programs of study in terms of that constellation of divisive forces which operates in each region. The North American agencies were among the first to respond to this encouragement. The two-year program of study concluding in the Oberlin Conference constitutes the first result in our region. If there was any conviction unanimously expressed at Oberlin, it was at this point: the wisdom of the new policy laid down by Faith and Order. This, in an all-too-brief sketch, is the broad background of the Oberlin story. We therefore turn to the

NORTH AMERICAN FOREGROUND

In this region, the initiative was quickly taken by the United States Conference for the World Council of Churches under the leadership of Dr. Samuel McCrea Cavert. On January 12, 1955, the Executive Committee of the U.S. Conference voted to hold a conference in America on "The Nature of the Unity We Seek," a theme suggested by Dr. Franklin Clark Fry. It was also agreed that the U.S. Conference should accept both administrative and financial responsibility for the program. The matters of administration were delegated to a Committee on Arrangements,[3] which first met on May 5, 1955. On this occasion the Commitee extended a cordial invitation to the Canadian Council of Churches (CCC) and to the National Council of the Churches of Christ in the U.S.A. (NCCC) to share in sponsoring the proposed conference. The response—as in all later operations—was enthusiastic and vigorous. A date was selected for the conference. There was ready agreement to accent *study* and to include in the process of study as many North American churches as possible. Thereafter the Committee on Arrangements met twice annually until its functions were transferred to the Steering Committee at Oberlin.

The summer and fall of 1955 were occupied chiefly with preliminary exploration of problem areas and with the planning of the studies. Several items call for more detailed mention.

(1) Various departments of the co-operating councils began at once to plan programs that would parallel and supplement the Faith and Order work. For example, the Interseminary Movement decided to hold its Triennial during an adjacent week and to carry on advance discussions on "The Nature of the Ministry We Seek." The United Student Christian Council began to orient its regional conferences around related themes. The Association of Council Secretaries began its far-reaching examination of the relation of local and state councils to the ecumenical objectives.

---

[3]This committee, when expanded to provide representation from all cooperating agencies, included the following:

The Rt. Rev. Angus Dun, Chairman	Professor T. A. Kantonen
Dr. Eugene C. Blake, Vice-Chairman	Mrs. W. Murdoch MacLeod
Miss Leila Anderson	Dr. Paul S. Minear
Miss Eleanor Kent Browne	Dean Walter G. Muelder
Dr. Samuel McCrea Cavert	Dr. Reuben E. Nelson
Professor Georges Florovsky	The Rev. William D. Powell
Dr. Franklin Clark Fry	Dr. Alexander Purdy
Dr. William J. Gallagher	Dr. John E. Skoglund
Dr. Perry E. Gresham	Dr. Theophilus M. Taylor
Bishop J. Arthur Hamlett	Professor Leonard J. Trinterud
Dr. David W. Hay	Dr. Justin Vander Kolk
Dr. Douglas Horton	

(2) The key religious journals in the region were apprised of the plans and began to project special series or issues which would bear on the major theme. There was a generous response on the part of editors, and a ready eagerness on the part of contributors from almost every segment of Christendom.[4]

(3) Already at work in North America were three theological commissions under the aegis of the Faith and Order Department of the World Council (a fourth was constituted in 1956). These commissions were put on the alert. They entered heartily into the planning and agreed immediately to devote some of their energies to the preparation of interim reports dealing with their several fields of exploration. It is difficult to say in retrospect whether the members of these commissions were more heartened by the conference's mature and enthusiastic response to their work or whether the members of the conference were more inspired and impressed by the depth and power of the Commissions' reports. In any case, all would agree that the interaction was extremely effective and profitable. (See below, the addresses by Robert L. Calhoun, Albert C. Outler, Walter G. Muelder, and Joseph Sittler.)

(4) The most strategic activity during the summer and autumn of 1955 was the planning of new studies. Imperative was the selection of those areas which would be most conducive to genuinely ecumenical explorations. Imperative, also, was the selection of personnel to conduct the explorations. In this dual selection, it was possible to apply, at least in limited fashion, a highly co-operative method. Christian leaders from many churches and regions were asked to suggest the areas of "consensus and conflict" where the unity of Christ's Church was being conspicuously tested in our day. These suggestions, totalling more than forty, were screened not by a single individual but by constant discussion across the boundaries of confession and region. This preliminary sifting left a residue of some eighteen important problem areas which appeared to affect vitally the movement toward unity and to be open to productive study by the churches in concert. These eighteen seemed to fall into three categories: Unity in Faith and Order, Unity in Order and Organization, Unity in Mission to the Local Community. At its meeting on September 6, 1955, the Committee on Arrangements gave to this list its sagacious scrutiny, and after

[4]The following journals deserve special commendation: *The Christian Century, Religion in Life, Theology Today, The Ecumenical Review, National Evangelical Action, Encounter.* A sampling of the best essays will be edited by J. Robert Nelson and published by Bethany Press under the title "Christian Unity in North America."

adding independent suggestions of its own approved the list as preliminary agenda for studies.

A similar procedure was followed in the formation of study groups to carry out the work. Wide consultation led gradually to the choice of sixteen cities of diverse size and type. In each of these, able leaders were found to serve as chairmen and secretaries. Chosen by the Committee on Arrangements with the approval of their denominations, these leaders, in turn, helped in the nomination of members for their study groups. The goal in each case was to enlist from ten to twenty individuals, each competent to deal with the subject at hand. In each study group we encouraged representation from as many diverse denominations as possible. One had as few as six, another as many as thirteen. Effort was taken to include both men and women; theologians, pastors and laymen. Many invitations were extended to competent spokesmen for some of the churches which do not normally co-operate in similar activities. As a result of these policies, a large majority of the study group members were virtual newcomers to ecumenical ventures.

By September, 1955, the process for selecting study group leaders had been established. By January, 1956, most of the study groups had begun their work. (For a list of these sixteen groups see Appendix III.) To each was assigned a list of five or six questions to initiate and to guide their studies. In addition, they were urged to relate all of their work as closely as possible to the general theme and to the biblical and theological grounds for all Christian thought and action. Each was urged to examine "the current centrifugal and centripetal forces in typical church life" in its own city, and in the light of these forces to clarify those dominant issues which characterize the contemporary church situation in North America. Each group proceeded to its task with a minimum of supervision and a maximum of independence. Some co-ordination was made possible by the circulation of a series of mimeographed releases called Study Grist and Gist. In this series were included the more significant essays produced by the various groups. Of great help was the trip of Dr. J. Robert Nelson, during the spring of 1956, in which he visited ten of the groups.

During the summer of 1956 two further steps were taken. The first represented an effort to extend the numbers of churchmen participating in preparations. The second was the crystallization of thinking on the shape of the conference program itself. A word about each of these.

At the outset it had been clear that literally thousands of Christians were eager to study the current obstacles to greater unity. It was therefore decided to prepare a brief pamphlet which would serve as an invitation and as a guide for such a study. This pamphlet, entitled *Ecumenical Conversations,* appeared in the spring of 1956. It was hoped that almost any group of interested churchmen would find it useful. Records indicate a wide use among four types of agency: local and state councils of churches, ministerial alliances, United Church Women, students in colleges and seminaries. No record could be kept of the number or the personnel of these groups. A conservative estimate would place the figure at three hundred and fifty groups. They were scattered, rather unevenly, over at least forty states of the United States and several provinces of Canada. More than fifty groups submitted formal reports of their work. Notable among these were the reports of the Central Study Group of the Massachusetts Council of Churches and the Southern California Council of Churches, both of which were of substantial help at Oberlin. Some of these conversations were so fruitful that members decided to stay at work during the year following the conference. Out of this experience emerged the demand at Oberlin for a more continuous and systematic program in the future, a program which would establish Faith and Order on the regular agenda of local, state and national councils.

To return now to the work of the sixteen official regional committees who had been charged with the task of exploration. By August, 1956, they had made steady progress. Some questions posed earlier had been eliminated. The importance of other questions had grown. Each group had begun to center down on a specific project in preparation for Oberlin. Each had prepared a simple summary of what it proposed to do. To enable each group to have a share in the final stages of planning, it was asked to send a representative to a two-day meeting at Dickinson College, Carlisle, Pennsylvania. Here, for the first time, each got a glimpse of all the studies and each gave a report on the peculiar opportunities and dilemmas which it faced. Out of this pooling of experience, the consultation arrived at the list of twelve topics proposed for the twelve sections at Oberlin. Here too the basic organization of these twelve sections into three divisions was achieved. Each study group now received its final assignment: to produce a working paper specifically designed for a section of the conference. Deadlines were fixed. Each group was given eight months to complete its job. Such was the faithful devotion of leaders and members that every group came through with its assignment on time. Rarely has any ecumenical conference been so appreciative of the "working papers" or made such thorough use of them as was true at Oberlin.[5]

At one point the Dickinson consultation disclosed an important area for which no preparatory group could accept responsibility. All agreed that the factor of mobility of population, with the consequent shifting of denominational affiliations, was of vital significance on the current scene. All agreed that the conference should consider this factor seriously. But such a consideration would be hopelessly vague apart from definite figures which would show the extent and directions of this mobility as it affected the life of local churches. Dr. J. Leslie Dunstan agreed to initiate this study by drawing up and circulating a questionnaire. As soon as the returns gave a basis for detailed planning, others joined in the preparation of orientation essays for Oberlin. On short notice a small committee managed to come through with valuable reports, demonstrating what close teamwork between theologians and expert sociologists can accomplish in blazing new trails for ecumenical advance. In addition to Dr. Dunstan, I should mention as members of this committee Dr. Lauris Whitman, the Rev. Meryl Ruoss, Dr. Ross Sanderson, the Rev. Yoshio Fukuyama and the Rev. Walter Kloetzli.

The sixteen study groups made such steady and dependable progress that the early months of 1957 could be devoted to another matter: the selection and briefing of the conference personnel. As soon as the member churches named their delegates, these delegates were invited to join in the processes of study, and most of them accepted. All received a bibliography and a copy of the Conference Profile which gave a summary of the situation in North American church life with which the various sections would deal, along with suggested objectives for each section. Some entered organized "Conversation Groups." A few were added to the rosters of the Sixteen. And soon after they had chosen a section of the conference and had been assigned to it, the orientation paper for that section reached them. Later the conference provided ample evidence that most delegates had taken seriously their "homework." This fact, combined with the fact that every study group was well represented at the conference in the section

---

[5]It has been impossible to print these sixteen papers. A sample, however, appears in the *Ecumenical Review* of January, 1958: the working paper produced by the Austin Study Group.

for which it had prepared the orientation paper, lifted the level of accomplishment in every section.

I may summarize the "North American Foreground" by listing several features which were relatively new to Faith and Order conferences. These are given not to exalt novelty for its own sake but to suggest, for the record, features which may prove valuable in subsequent ventures.

(1) The study of the ecumenical significance of local and state councils, together with the enlistment of these councils in the work of Faith and Order.

(2) The study of the life of local congregations, of prevalent lay ecclesiologies, of the issues which prevent unity in mission, together with the enlistment of congregations in self-study.

(3) The study of those barriers to ecumenicity which alienate denominations which normally cooperate with one another from denominations which do not, together with the enlistment in corporate study of churchmen from both sides of the line.

(4) The exploration of the distance in actual working faith between laymen of the various churches which confessionally have been estranged, together with the participation of these laymen in the study.

(5) The co-operation of expert sociologists and theologians to examine such concrete social phenomena as governmental pressures, mobility, and the ecclesiastical forms of institutionalism.

(6) The full participation of youth in the advance studies and as delegates and consultants in the conference, along with the study of the nature of the unity we should seek on the college campus.

(7) The teamwork between the ecumenical forces of the United States and Canada, both in study and in action. The situations are sufficiently similar to make communication easy, yet sufficiently distinct to enable churches of each country to make great contributions to churches across the border.

(8) The opening up of Faith and Order activity to large circles of churchmen, who in many new places can carry on work that is geared into situations for which they are immediately responsible.

THE STUDY CONFERENCE

We must now shift our attention from the period of preparations to the climactic week of intensive study at Oberlin. It was a week of *study,* and of *intensive* study. In fact, those responsible for planning the conference were surprised at the degree to which delegates eagerly welcomed the opportunity for sustained, continuous work on the complex problems which had been posed. Each delegate or consultant spent most of his time and energy within the confines of a small classroom. In almost every section participation in vigorous discussion was virtually unanimous. In fact, the Steering Committee was impelled to allow even more time than originally intended for the work of the sections, at the expense of time which had been assigned to the divisions. A total of at least fourteen hours was spent by every section on its assigned topic. It was aided in the preparation of its report by its own drafting committee which worked unnumbered hours, day and night, to keep pace with the demand. The major result of this concentrated work will be found in the section reports below. Readers must be aware, however, that probably no section was wholly content with the written product, and that the fruitfulness of ecumenical study is only partially reflected in such reports. There was no time for the plenary session to receive or to discuss these reports. They come therefore direct from the sections to the churches. They seek to convey to the churches the more important discoveries made by the sections, along with their basic convictions concerning the immediate opportunities for ecumenical action by the churches. Each report represents the best co-operative thinking of about 35 leaders, drawn from many diverse Christian traditions.

In addition to this report, each section participated in the shaping of the report from its division. Each division's report was presented to the plenary body in two separate stages. The final draft of the three division reports is included in this volume. Since many of the suggestions made in plenary sessions were incorporated into the final drafts, it is unnecessary in this volume to give in detail the proceedings in full of the plenary sessions.

The studies of the conference proceeded within the continuing context of corporate worship. Each day (except Sunday) began with morning prayers. Leaders again were drawn from diverse traditions and were given complete freedom in their choice of an order of service. For this leadership the conference was indebted to Dr. Wilfred C. Lockhart, the Very Rev. F-M Galdau, Dr. Cornelius Wierenga, Dr. W. O. Carrington, Dr. Carlyle Marney and Dr. Robert S. Bilheimer. These services were conducted in the First Church in Oberlin, whose pastor, Dr. Joseph King, served on many occasions as gracious host.

Immediately following the daily service of morning prayer, the conference joined in Bible study under the guidance of Dean Walter J. Harrelson. First Corinthians provided the basic material for an examination of "The Church at Corinth: Its Unity, Diversity and Divisions." Using the Old Testament (especially

Genesis, Exodus, Isaiah and Ezekiel) to illuminate Paul's vocabu-
lary, Dean Harrelson expounded the significance for Christian
thinking of the following images of the Church: "Called to Be
Saints," "Those Who Are Not," "All Things to All Men," "The
Body of Christ," "The Man of Dust and the Man of Heaven."
On the first day, when Dean Harrelson was unable to be present,
Dr. W. A. Visser 't Hooft presented an exposition of John 17.

Each evening, immediately following the plenary session in Hall
Auditorium, the entire conference joined in a service of evening
prayer. Here, too, the leaders represented diverse traditions and
utilized liturgical forms drawn from those traditions: The Rt.
Rev. Georges Florovsky, Dr. Eugene R. Fairweather, Dr. Nils
Ehrenstrom, Dr. Winthrop Hudson, Dr. Franklin Clark Fry.
Both in the work of these leaders and in the response of the community there could be no mistaking the reality of authentic fellowship in worship through the power of the Holy Spirit.

Other occasions of worship should be mentioned, although the
mention must be too brief. The service which opened the conference on September 3, with Dr. Eugene Carson Blake leading the
prayers and praise, set the mood for the entire week. Bishop Angus
Dun's address, which both actually and symbolically struck the
"keynote," is in the record. So also is the sermon with which Dr.
Blake brought the conference to a close on September 10. A Service of Ecumenical Worship, open to the general public, was held
on Sunday evening, September 8, at Finney Chapel. Bishop Johannes Lilje of Hanover, Germany, gave the main address with
some of the visitors from abroad assisting in the service. What is
not in the record about these services is written in the hearts of
those who participated, all too deeply to be described here.

As in all ecumenical gatherings, the desperate urgency of the
demand for unity and the difficulties encountered by those who
accept that demand were illustrated by the fact that there could
be no service of Holy Communion which could be considered
"official." Provision was made for all to celebrate the sacrament
in a way which did not compromise their own Christian convictions, but no provision could be made for all to share together at
the one table. So in the host church on Sunday morning all members were invited to participate by the celebrants, Dean Douglas
Horton and Dr. Joseph King, although not all could accept the
invitation. The sermon by Dr. Visser 't Hooft appears in the record. On Sunday morning also the Divine Liturgy of Saint John
Chrysostom was celebrated in the Church of Saint Nicholas in

Lorain, Ohio. Then on Tuesday morning, all members of the conference were made welcome at the Holy Communion celebrated in the Christ Church (Episcopal) in Oberlin. Thus the conference experienced anew the double reality of the unity which Christ has given and of the divisions among Christ's people at his own table. But this experience induced among the delegates not mutual protests and recriminations but mutual searching to uncover the obstacles to unity in ourselves and to mutual commitment to continuing ecumenical study.

Again I remind readers of the record that the inner life of the conference cannot be put on record. One thing was clear, however: no wall existed between the praying and the working, between devotional and theological activity, between the sacraments and the *koinonia*. As sections discussed various concrete issues, the discussions were permeated by echoes from Bible studies and theological addresses, from the liturgies of matins and compline, from sacrament and sermon. Conversely, when the company shifted from the classrooms of Peters Hall to the sanctuary of First Church, there was no sharp sense of shifting from one world to another.

Perhaps I can convey some sense of this spiritual integrity by commenting on the Message which the conference adopted at its closing plenary. It is often the case that a "message" fails to convey the intangibles of work and worship. In the nature of the situation, no message can convey with precision the burden of convictions and prayers which are so deeply felt that they can be expressed, if at all, only with awkwardness. Yet there are several notes in this Message whose accuracy should be underscored.

"We give thanks that the conference has been so inclusive in its membership. . . ." Rare indeed is there a Christian assembly with such wide diversities represented. And to this diversity the delegates responded with—gratitude. That in itself was remarkable. One might have expected quite different responses. Parallel to this gratitude was the deeply sensed sadness occasioned "by the absence of members of other churches" and the frank recognition that we ourselves share responsibility for this absence.

So great were the diversities represented that they might well have produced an uneasy confusion. Not at all. At every turn delegates discovered unsuspected "solidarities among Christians of the most varied inheritances." The greater the diversity the more deep-rooted the solidarity. This mutual discovery, growing more certain as the grueling pace of daily study continued, evoked an

almost explosive sense of joy, an awed and reverent silence before
the manifest presence of the one Lord, and a chastened sense of
the power which is intrinsic "in the unity we now possess." Out
of this vortex of emotions grew a virile confidence in the future.
"We do not see clearly the path that God has set before us, but
we are sure that He is leading us." The conference as a whole was
not disconcerted by its inability to achieve unanimity in defining
the *directions* for moving toward the "Unity We Seek." Why not?
Because it was basically and deeply united in its confidence of the
direction in which God is leading the churches. It had discovered
that this is a direction which will conserve a "rich variety in worship, life and organization." A company which had experienced
profound unity in diversity could hardly think of God as leading
us toward its elimination.

It had also reached a clear certainty at another point. The unity
we seek is "a unity in mission to the world, originating with, sustained by, and offered to the one Christ." Oberlin became for
many a striking episode in the renewal of the Church. And it did
this because it was an episode in the mission of the Church, the
mission in the home town, in the local congregation, in the armed
forces, on the college campus, and in communities in fratricidal
strife over racial integration. I do not mean to imply that Oberlin
was simply a pep-meeting for future missionaries who would now
bend to the task elsewhere. The conference itself was an example
of mission—for here the Gospel confronted our North American
culture (in us as well as around us) with the judging and redeeming Christ.

If I were to select one feature of the conference which most
clearly indicates its dominant thrust into the future, I would describe it thus: the radical telescoping of the distance between the
global and the local work of the Church. By this telescoping I do
not mean to refer to what has been made possible by the external
means of rapid transit or the instantaneous movement of news
broadcasts. Rather, I refer to what takes place within the Christian Church through increased participation in "the common life
in the Body of Christ." In him God acts to eliminate entirely the
distance between the global and the local. The more *his* ministry
to the world is accepted, the more solidarity is realized with every
congregation and its work in its home town. The more fully this
local ministry embodies the ministry of Christ, the more truly
global is its significance. In Christ the term "mission field" ceases
to be a geographical term. The life which a congregation has in

him it also shares with all other congregations, however distant
in space and time. The unity which God gives thus becomes a
living interdependence of ecumenicity and locality. It is the pro-
gressive discovery of this dimension which opens up vast horizons
for future work. Let me give a few clues to this discovery.

(1) The very fact that the conference was held is evidence that
shepherds of the world-wide Church are coming to realize that
concern for the Church's catholicity compels them to manifest this
oneness in the church local. Shepherds of local congregations, on
the other hand, are coming to realize that they cannot fulfill their
vocation at home unless their congregation participates fully in
the Church universal. Hence, the decision of the Faith and Order
Movement to organize regional work and to focus attention upon
the divisions of the Church within a single city. Hence, too, the
eager response of local leaders in North America to wrestle with
the most stubborn issues of Faith and Order, and to relate that
struggle to the routine work of congregations and local councils.

(2) We point also to the fact that concern for the Church's
mission is compelling Christian leaders to give increasing attention
to every parish situation. When our ministry is defined by reference to Christ's ministry, every town becomes a mission field, a
place where heaven touches earth and where the healing powers
of the kingdom encounter the demonic infections of the world.
This means that competition and rivalry among missioners in this
town represent demonic infection rather than healing power.
Whenever one Christian company is indifferent or antagonistic
to another, this may be one of the subtlest forms of treason and
heresy. For instance, the world Church may loudly declare racial
segregation within the Church to be sin, but so long as local congregations accept and defend the prevailing racial and economic
barriers, the resolutions of world bodies will offer at best a cheap
compensation and a costly self-deception. In Christ men are
neither black nor white, rich nor poor. But how is either the
Church or the world to know this apart from his manifest power
to destroy the walls that divide race from race and class from class
in the very town where such walls loom highest?

(3) We also point to the discovery that every congregation is
immediately involved in all problems of Faith and Order. In every
city today the Christian community is obviously and obstreper-
ously divided within itself. There is no fully mutual recognition of
all churches as truly churches, of all ministries as truly ministry,
of all sacraments as truly sacraments. This conflict is as destruc-

tive on the local as on the universal scene. To be sure, sometimes the range of recognition is broader on the local scene than on the world scene, although sometimes narrower. Sometimes a congregation moves faster, sometimes slower, than the denomination to which it belongs. Sometimes its movement is quite irresponsible, and is due to casual indifference or to a false sense of autonomy. In any case, local congregations are as deeply involved in this scandal as are the world confessional bodies. And to ignore this scandal is to deny the lordship of the one Lord. For example, if every celebration of the Lord's Supper is viewed as a token of the scandal of Christian divisions, should not every church at every celebration attend to Christ's judgment on this scandal? Should it not accept the constraint to remove these divisions? To be sure, we annually join in World Communion Sunday, but is that enough? Unless *every* Eucharist includes the world it is not truly Christ's table. And we shut out the world from our table as decisively by policies toward a neighboring congregation as by policies toward the Orthodox Church in Russia or toward some other denomination in North America. Many Christians realized for the first time at Oberlin both the necessity and the promise of continuous study on the local level of such issues as this.

(4) Finally we underscore the fact that pastors and laymen are coming to realize that no Christian parish can be exempt from continuous theological activity. There is no excuse for apathy, passivity or illiteracy in matters of faith, nor is there any escape from the obligation to relate this faith creatively to the concrete factors which operate in cultural and civic life. Too long has theology been isolated from the parish. Now few can doubt that the ecumenical movement is closely linked, through many causes and effects, to the revival of classical Christian theology. Even though the extent of this revival may be often exaggerated, it is clear that it has been confined too largely to a few centers, all quite remote from parish life. What became apparent at Oberlin was this, as pointed out by an astute European observer: there was a surprising though unobtrusive indication of a deep-going *de facto* recognition of the authority of the Bible; of an eager readiness to see the relevance of biblical theology to the "non-theological" issues which were studied. There was also heartening evidence that, in spite of great diversities in educational background, the thinking and speaking of American churchmen is steadily becoming more confidently and competently theological. For a long time, responsible theologians have known that all valid theology must make

sense of the ordinary life of the simplest congregation. There are now signs that responsible parish leaders are coming to realize that every opportunity and every dilemma in the life of the parish is to be correctly assessed only in terms of a biblically grounded and missionary-minded theology. And it is precisely this theology which eliminates the chasm between the continents, the centuries, and the churches.

These various clues to the emergence of a new sense of the nearness of the local and the global, of the solidarity in Christ of each congregation with the whole Church, point toward a renewal in our day of a long-neglected facet in the *apostolic* ministry. The first apostles were given the commission and the power to guide the urban and the universal companies of Christians toward the unity given in Christ. Their vocation was not only to call men into the one Church but also to remind every congregation that its existence was unthinkable apart from that of the one Body of Christ. The apostle was impelled to teach the congregation in Corinth or Ephesus that it was the people of God localized in Corinth or Ephesus, its fellowship a microcosm of the one fellowship in the Spirit. And he must teach the whole Church that members in Rome and Jerusalem were truly members one of another, as truly as if they belonged to the same local congregation. This vocation of the apostles was no easy task, because this conception of solidarity, of unity, is hard to understand and even harder to embody in action. In fact, there is abundant evidence of the failures of the apostles, notwithstanding their wisdom, authority and power. Yet to the extent that the Holy Catholic Church inherits the apostolic vocation it must carry on the work of manifesting the truth that oneness in the Body of Christ includes this interpenetration of universality and locality. The life of God's people has a double horizon: the trivial immediacies of daily routines and the cosmic immensities of world redemption. This people must therefore embody simultaneously the cosmic significance of every congregation and the congregation's self-abandonment in its loyalty to the Holy Catholic Church. The unity we seek lies here. The apostolic ministry lies here. And this is the point where converge many of the vitalities of the current scene.

This leads to a final comment on the Message sent from Oberlin to the churches. This Message, of course, is wholly misunderstood if readers assume that it was formulated by bureaucrats in distant headquarters and that it was dispatched by them across the intervening space to churches in general. No. Those who formulated the Message are members of local churches. They were thinking of these close-knit fellowships in specific towns. They were speaking of their own home-folks. They did not yield to the temptation to indulge in rhetorical verbosity, to seek some dramatic pose, or to claim some esoteric vision. As a result the Message is not as "impressive" as some would want. But it may thereby be more applicable to the actual possibilities in every parish.

"We invite all churches, aided by these reports and findings, to engage with us in bringing their present life under the judgment of the Lord of the whole Church as we struggle to understand the unity we seek.

"We call upon every local church and congregation to examine the way in which it makes visible the nature of the Church of Christ. It is not only our separations as churches and denominations but in our social stratification, our racial segregation, our introversion and self-content despite God's summons to our mission to the world, that we deny and refuse the unity He would offer us."[6]

This call was not motivated by any managerial afflatus on the part of "world figures" to start a crusade for which they could pipe the tune. It was not issued in the mood of petulant exhortation. If this were so, it would have belied the spirit of the conference. The motives were quite different.

"As we invite our brethren to engage in this task of study and self-examination we also covet for them the renewal of joy, expectancy and hope that has been ours in this conference."

For those who worked hard in preparing for the conference, and for those who, as delegates of their churches, entered wholeheartedly into the common worship, work and witness during the conference, the dominant discovery was this very "renewal of joy, expectancy and hope."

---

[6]To help churches who wish to accept this "call," a study guide is available which indicates some of the issues where the conference found discussion to be especially pertinent and fruitful. This guide is called "A Guide to Christian Unity" and is edited by the Rev. George L. Hunt.

A MESSAGE TO THE CHURCHES

We have been sent as representatives of our churches to the North American Conference on Faith and Order to study "The Nature of the Unity We Seek." The fact of our commissioning as delegates by our own communions has contributed immeasurably, we believe, to the productiveness of our labors. It has assured us that the search for ways in making manifest the unity of the people of God is acknowledged as belonging to the very life and mission of every part of the Church. In the work of this conference we have been disciplined by the remembrance of the representative trust imposed in us, and we have been upheld by the prayers and hopes of many fellow Christians.

Meeting at Oberlin for this week-long conference have been 274 representatives of thirty-eight Christian bodies, together with ninety-two consultants and thirty-six accredited observers. We give thanks that the conference has been so inclusive in its membership that all of us have been encouraged by solidarities among Christians of the most varied inheritances.

At the same time we are saddened by the absence of members of other churches whom we recognize as fellow Christians, and we ask forgiveness for any failure of charity or understanding in us which may have kept them apart from our fellowship.

Gathered to consider the nature of the unity we seek, we give thanks for the unity we have found. This unity not only exists but is entirely the gift of God's grace and love. We are claimed for this unity as we confess with one voice "while we were yet sinners, Christ died for us"; as we acknowledge Jesus Christ as Lord, and as we accept his commission to declare to all men the good news of his victory. This is the Gospel which has ultimate power to shatter the human heart with wonder and shake the world with hope.

As we have known a common joy in the unity we now possess, we have also felt a common sorrow over the continuing fact of our separations one from another. We acknowledge the one Lord; we also own the peril of calling him "Lord, Lord," and failing to do the things he has commanded. We cannot forget that his prayer for the unity of his followers remains unfulfilled. Although some of our divisions arise out of loyalty to truth that we now see, we must acknowledge that Christ calls us to a fuller comprehension of truth and more obedient service. To proclaim that Christ is the one Lord is to give him pre-eminence over all else—over our most cherished traditions. This we have not done.

Yet God gives us hope. We do not see clearly the path that God has set before us, but we are sure that he is leading us, and that at Oberlin he has given us new light.

In this light we see that the Church is God's Church and that the unity is his unity. This unity, we believe, is to be:

— A unity in Christ who died for us, is risen, regnant, and will come again to gather together all things in his judgment and grace;

— A unity in adoration of God—one offering of wonder, love and praise;

— A unity of declared faith, sounding the vast Amen of the whole Church's believing life through all the centuries;

— A unity of bearing one another's burdens and sharing one another's joys;

— A unity in which every ministry is a ministry of and for all the members, bound together in a worshiping and sacramental community;

— A unity in mission to the world, originating with, sustained by and offered to the one Christ, and conducted with such transparency of love and faithfulness that the world will believe on him;

— A unity possessing rich variety in worship, life and organization.

Our message to the churches is an expression of desire and hope that something of what we have thought, experienced and wrought during these days together may be shared widely with our fellow-Christians.

(1) We commend a study of the reports of this conference. We invite all churches, aided by these reports and findings, to engage with us in bringing their present life under the judgment of the Lord of the Whole Church as we struggle to understand the unity we seek.

(2) We call upon every local church and congregation to examine the way in which it makes visible the nature of the Church of Christ. It is not only our separations as churches and denominations but in our social stratification, our racial segregation, our introversion and self-content despite God's summons to our mission to the world, that we deny and refuse the unity he would offer us.

(3) We look for continuing advance in the practical unity of united action by churches and congregations, and, with the Lund Conference and the Evanston Assembly, we repeat to the churches the question "whether they should not act together in all matters except those in which deep differences of conviction compel them to act separately."

(4) We ask all Christians to pray unceasingly that the oneness of God's people may be manifest among men.

As we invite our brethren to engage in this task of study and self-examination, we also covet for them the renewal of joy, expectancy and hope that has been ours in this conference. We have known more surely that in Christ "are all the treasures of wisdom and knowledge hidden"—not alone for the life of the churches in their quest for unity but for all the people of God in their pilgrimage.

THE CONFERENCE ADDRESSES
The Purpose and Spirit of the Conference

ADDRESS AT OPENING PLENARY SESSION BY
THE RIGHT REVEREND ANGUS DUN, CHAIRMAN
SEPTEMBER 3, 1957

Dearly beloved brethren: I hope the spirit of these familiar words may control what I say at this time and may pervade the interminglings of our common life during the eight days we are together. We are "dearly beloved brethren," not in the first instance by reason of our so imperfect love for one another, but in the sight of the one Almighty Father whom we all confess, in the self-giving of the one Lord Jesus Christ, whom we all confess, and in the fellowship of the Holy Spirit, whom we all confess. Our calling is to manifest here together in these days our given being as "beloved brethren." That surely is foundational to any consideration of the unity we seek. It cannot be put off to another time. It asks of us simplicity, great openness towards one another, the will to understand, the putting aside of the will to score on one another, the bearing of one another's burdens of perplexity or fear lest any be unfaithful to the truth he has been given.

Our first act together has rightly been a common act of worship and of prayer. We have sought to turn away from ourselves to Him who is the ground of our being and the sovereign of our lives. In him is to be found the unity we have and any greater unity which may be given. In the first freshness of each morning we shall turn to him and then together we shall be led in a period of Bible study. For all of us in different ways the Holy Scriptures are normative for our discipleship and for the life of our separate churches. Together we shall listen to the Word of God and seek to hear what the Spirit is saying to the churches. May we be faithful and blessed in this shared listening. That can help us in our listening to one another.

Though I have begun in the mood of devotion, this is not to be a sermon—an unfolding or proclamation of the Word of God. My task is to provide an introduction to the program of the conference we shall undertake together, not as an advocate but as a commentator. This conference has been planned with the full endorsement of the Commission on Faith and Order of the World Council of Churches. It takes its place securely in the ongoing world-wide consultations on faith and order which began with the Lausanne Conference in 1927 and have been continued in the

31

conferences at Edinburgh and Lund. The more immediate responsibility for calling us together has rested with the United States Conference for the World Council of Churches, the Canadian Council of Churches and the National Council of Churches of Christ in the U.S.A. As Chairman of the Committee on Arrangements I want to welcome at this time the official delegations of some forty churches in the United States and Canada, the consultants, the youth delegates, the official and unofficial observers, our small group of overseas guests and the representatives of the church and the secular press. Very particularly we welcome the observers from those churches which on the basis of conscientious convictions have not been ready to participate officially in the membership of the World Council of Churches or of our sponsoring National Councils or of the Faith and Order Movement. In the spirit of our reconciling Lord we would respect fully the restraints which their own convictions place upon them, and be grateful that they are with us even in a quite informal and unofficial way.

This is an official conference of churches on faith and order. As such it is the heir of certain objectives, even of certain assumptions, of certain principles of procedure and of certain restraints.

From its beginning the Faith and Order Movement has sought to bring together churches which accept our Lord Jesus Christ as God and Savior for continuing the responsible conversations on the subject of unity. Accordingly, the basic and voting membership of all conferences has been made up of official delegates of the participating churches. It has been presumed that official delegates would represent not simply their own private opinions, but the standpoints of their churches, and that they would be in a position to report back to their churches the results of these conversations. This does not mean that the Faith and Order Movement is unconcerned with our personal relations, but it looks beyond that to the relations of our churches with one another.

GOD WILLS UNITY

Certainly this movement has assumed and repeatedly declared that God wills unity for his Church, without prejudging the question as to what the Church is or where it is to be found, or the question as to the nature of the unity which God wills. On this subject I shall say more presently in connection with our main theme. Suffice it to say now that there has been widespread agreement that the unity God wills for his Church is a *manifest* or visible unity, not something hidden. Some of you may be moved to challenge even that conviction. We have often been reminded that the Faith and Order Movement was rooted back in the International Missionary Conference at Edinburgh in 1910. In more recent years within the life of the World Council of Churches there has been a recognition that *mission* and *unity* are profoundly interrelated and form two major pillars of any movement which can claim the ambitious name of ecumenical. The Church, many of us have agreed, is commissioned to unity in witness and to witness to our unity in Christ by word and act.

With the recognition that God wills unity for his Church has gone the matching acknowledgment that the present relations of the existing churches do not manifest the unity which God wills for us. That leaves open the question as to what it is in our relations we are to repent of and from what we are to seek deliverance.

This is called a Conference on Faith and Order. That phrase comes to us from the founders of the movement within which we find ourselves. Those founders were convinced that the unity God wills for his Church involves some substantial unity in faith and order and that correspondingly our differences or divisions in faith and order present the most stubborn and crucial obstacles to be overcome.

That word, *faith,* is familiar and meaningful for us all. Probably we can all agree that faith in some sense of the word is constitutive of the Church, and that faith, therefore, is essentially bound up with any unity we have or might be granted. We may differ greatly about faith or the faith, but at least we have some common understanding of what we are talking about.

The same cannot be said for the term, *order*. That term is securely at home in the tradition of the Anglican Communion, namely, that family of Episcopal Churches stemming from the Church of England. I cannot say that we Episcopalians are always quite clear as to what we mean by it, but I am certain that it is a strange word, not at all native, among many of the traditions represented here at Oberlin.

THE MEANING OF "ORDER"

It is not my prerogative to tell you what you should mean by this word or how you should use it, but to provide if I can, an intelligible starting point. The word, *order,* as I understand it, refers to visible, identifiable structures within a community of Christians, which are held to belong to its being as a church, or its well-being, or fullness, or wholeness as a church. Most familiarly, the term, *order*, refers to the ordering of the ministry in one or three or more "orders of ministers" and to the basic polity or structure of government which determines where authority is centered in the matters most sensitively related to the Church's faith and worship. *Order* in this sense is clearly to be distinguished from what is often spoken of as "mere organization," the changing practical arrangements for getting things done. This is true even through "order" and "organization" inevitably interpenetrate each other.

Certain churches clearly hold that a particular, visible ordering of the ministry belongs to the essential order of the Church. Some Christian communions hold that the "congregation" as an identifiable structure is the visible locus of the Church and the seat of authority. That is a view of Church order. Many of the traditions represented here do not hold that any particular form of ministry or of government belongs to the essential order of the Church. Those standing within such traditions may be helped to appreciate the force of the term if they recall that major churches of the Reformation inheritance have held that a faithful preaching of the Word and a right use of the two sacraments of the Gospel are visible marks of the Church. These, then, belong to order. Even the place given to an identifiable book, the Holy Bible, and the use made of it, may be seen as a visible structure by which the Church is in part known to be present. If there are any who hold there are no visible structures which belong to the very being of the Church, or to its continuing well-being, then the term, *order*, in its historic sense is irrelevant for their conception of the Church.

The Faith and Order Movement has from its beginning been marked by a particular method and spirit. These are part of the good inheritance into which we enter. We are here to discuss our deepest bonds of unity and our honest differences in a spirit of frank Christian conference. Not to evade real differences is as important as to avoid the spirit and method of controversy. As was said in the opening sermon at Lausanne:

"Conference is a measure of peace; controversy a weapon of war. Conference is self-abasing; controversy exalts self. Conference in all lowliness strives to understand the viewpoint of others; controversy, to impose its views on all comers. Conference looks for unities; controversy exaggerates differences. Conference is a cooperative method . . . ; controversy, a divisive method."

To use again words I have written in another connection:

"We cannot understand others without imaginative sympathy. To understand others whose ways are alien or, even more, threatening to our own ways, requires a kind of love for our enemies by which we seek to appreciate from within how it feels to be in their position, what they live by, perhaps even what truth they apprehend to which we have been blind."

A restraint which the Faith and Order Movement has accepted is that we do not undertake to formulate schemes of reunion and recommend them to the participating churches. If, in our conference, we refer to any schemes of reunion or to any unions of churches achieved or in prospect, it will be only as these throw light on the nature of the unity we seek.

Our Committee on Arrangements has even recommended that we should not be under heavy pressure to produce any agreed-upon message to the churches beyond the record and interpretation of our conversations with one another. We shall leave that question for determination in the course of our meetings.

A REGIONAL APPROACH

This is a regional conference, a North American conference. As such it represents a new method of approach within the Faith and Order Movement. That movement has steadily sought to be as truly ecumenical as the responses of existing Churches would make possible. It has sought to draw together in brotherly conversation the world-wide Christian community within the limitations set by its doctrinal basis. Its conferences have been world-conferences. Major churches, notably the Roman Catholic Church, and numerous smaller churches, have excluded themselves on the ground that participation would obscure or contradict their witness to the truth about the Church or the Gospel as they conceive it. But in spite of these grave limitations, the world-wide perspective has steadily been sought.

To hold a regional North American conference is not to surrender this world-wide perspective. It is to recognize the fact that churches located within one great continental area, in the midst of one more or less homogeneous culture, have special responsibilities toward one another in their quest for unity. In world conferences, the issues are inevitably generalized. It is difficult to do justice to the very different balance of traditions found on major continents, and to the radically different cultural, social, and political settings which profoundly condition the life and thought of churches in every place and time.

The churches of the United States and Canada are all, with minor exceptions, English-speaking. Our memberships intermingle and intermarry within a society which has common characteristics. The "world" in which we are set is a special "world," the North American world. As always, that world is an invasive power, driving disruptive salients into the churches, and the field which the churches seek to infiltrate redemptively. From either angle we face special common problems and tasks which we cannot possibly solve separately. We face enormous population mobility. You, in that other church, pick up some of our drift and we pick up some of yours. That holds for all of us, including some of the churches which cannot be represented here.

The balance of church traditions among us is markedly different from Europe, or the United Kingdom, or the Near East, or Latin America. Our North American pilgrimage has done things to all of us. An English Bishop once remarked that all Americans are "congregationalists." Whatever the exaggeration, that says something. What may be called an "experiential" or experimental and a democratic approach to Christianity has been very influential among us in a unique measure.

These observations and many others which might be made fully justify a North American conference. But let us not forget the world perspective. Let us not forget our brothers in Europe, Western and Eastern, in the lands where the ancient Orthodox churches are dominant, and among the younger churches of Asia and Africa. The God who wills unity wills unity for them and for us with them. Many of us in our own communions here have special ties with them in world-embracing church families. We shall be helped to keep in mind these wider perspectives by the background addresses to be presented by representatives of the Study Commissions which have been set up to serve all the churches in the Faith and Order Movement.

I turn now to some introductory comments on the program of the particular conference before us. What I shall say is certainly not to be taken as authoritative or controlling. It is intended to help us see together what we are to discuss, to see the parts in relation to the whole, and perhaps to further initial understanding of the issues we shall confront and the terms we shall be using.

Those of us responsible for planning the conference have chosen as the main theme, "The Nature of the Unity We Seek." Even that title may awaken dissatisfaction or misgivings or misunderstandings. It may appear to some to carry hidden assumptions which are unacceptable.

THE MEANING OF "UNITY"

The nature of the unity *we* seek! Can it be said of us that we seek any unity with sacrificial intensity and persistence? Is not the real question, What is the nature of the unity God wills for us? "Not our will, but thine, be done." Surely all of us agree that we seek far too feebly a unity which is willed for us by our common Lord.

Does the title carry the assumption that the one Church is divided, and that we are to seek the restoration of its broken unity? Not necessarily. Our Orthodox brethren are bound to have deep misgivings at this point, and these may well be shared by others. They believe uncompromisingly that the outward and visible unity of the Church in faith and order and worship is of its very essence, and is guaranteed by the overruling power of the triune God who called it into being. Accordingly they cannot in good conscience join in the search for a lost unity. Nevertheless, I believe that they recognize the presence in the world of many Christian believers, in a significant sense, who stand outside that unbreakable unity. They can enter into brotherly conversation and personal fellowship with those others in the hope that those others may find their way into the unity which is given. I do not speak of this view with condescension. There is no place for condescension here. All of us have some basis for understanding our Orthodox brethren, for all of us hold that we are of the Church and in the Church. All of us treasure the assurance that "the gates of hell shall not prevail." Many traditions represented here surely carry the conviction, in less explicit or rigorous terms, that if all the others would walk in their way, they would find the unity we seek. We only have to search our own hearts to discover some such notion, although some of us are more explicit than others.

To be sure, many of the churches represented here recognize the presence of the Church in other churches. They can acknowledge that the Church is divided into churches, and talk intelligibly of how the churches might become the Church. And there are probably those among us who hold that beneath all the differences and divisions of the churches there is a spiritual unity among

Christ's people. That is something given. It need not be sought. It only needs to be acknowledged and perhaps made more manifest, possibly without altering radically the outward shape and relationships of the existing churches.

The very fact that our main theme immediately calls out such questions as these is its justification, for its purpose is to set us moving and to raise some of the right questions.

"The nature of the unity we seek" has not previously been a main theme or even an explicit subsidiary theme for a Faith and Order conference. We cannot seek unity effectively if we do not know its nature. We cannot seek it together or have substantial unity in the search if we differ radically as to what we seek.

The questions our theme presents to us lead straightway to all the other questions that confront us and draw them together: questions as to how the Church is to be recognized or whether it can be recognized by men; questions as to what the Church most surely needs to be, what it is founded to be and to do, what it is sent to do; questions as to its faith and sacraments or ordinances, as to its ministry and discipline and government.

There are current among us many conceptions of unity and many terms used with little uniformity of meaning. There is not just one thing we can mean by the words we choose to denote the singleness of the Church as something of which there is only one, and can be only one, or the relations of the parts, whether individual members or congregations or larger groupings, which constitute unity.

Let me try to offer something in the way of an analysis of the various conceptions and terms in the hope that it may be clarifying.

CHRISTIAN UNITY AND CHURCH UNITY

A first clarifying distinction we might make is between Christian unity and church unity, recognizing that the two are often used interchangeably. Christian unity refers to the broad community of faith and devotion and ethical norms common to professing Christians throughout the world, on the basis of which individuals coming out of widely separated churches can have fellowship with one another. A common participation in the experience of communion with God in Christ, in the faith of the heart, in basic Christian loyalties and convictions, all fed by the common use of the Scriptures, the Lord's Prayer, many shared hymns, et cetera, may provide a sense of kinship which transcends ecclesiastical boundaries. And this informal Christian unity may find outward expression in the visible acts of common prayer and fellowship and common work among individuals without regard to their denominational connections. Is such an undenominational or interdenominational unity, when cultivated or magnified, the unity we seek?

Church unity may be helpfully distinguished from Christian unity, in the sense in which I have used it, as referring to all forms of unity that involve the Church or the parts of a church or churches in their character as distinguishable communities with some institutional structures. Church unity might refer to the relations between the Church of Greece and the Ecumenical Patriarchate, or between the congregations of the American Baptist Convention, or between the bodies joined in the United Church of Canada, or between the Protestant Episcopal Church and the Polish National Catholic Church, or between the member churches of the National Council of the Churches of Christ in the U.S.A. All of these reflect different levels and forms of church unity.

What are the chief distinguishable levels and forms of church unity?

The most elementary level of church unity is the unity of mutual recognition. This underlies all other forms of church unity. It may be found in many degrees and has many expressions. As the late Paul Douglass pointed out many years ago, churches in contact with one another in one area or in a mission field can be observed to pass through gradual modifications of attitude toward one another, moving from active conflict where they seek to eliminate one another, to competition, where they strive for the occupation of the same field, passing on to accommodation, where they accept one another's existence, even though unenthusiastically, and finally reaching mutual recognition of many degrees. "At the point where compromise permits co-action, and the interacting bodies pass over from opposition to accommodation, unity movements begin."

Even to talk together officially involves a measure of mutual recognition. That is why we must say, I hope without bitterness, that a substantial number of important Christian bodies will not talk with us officially. The recognition may be no more than that those others are bodies of Christian folk with whom we have much in common. It may be a recognition that this other church has many of the essential marks of the Church, even though lacking some which are essential for full recognition. It may be a recognition that the other church possesses all that is essential for the Church, though not in the form we believe in or like.

Mutual recognition is implicit or explicit in the free inter-changeability of membership or of ministers or ministrations, and in intercommunion or open communion. Barriers at any of these points reflect limitations of mutual recognition, and open doors for traffic reveal mutual recognition, unofficial or official.

The unity of mutual recognition always involves some likeness, whatever it may be, on the basis of which the recognition is given —whether likeness of inner spiritual life or confession or form of ministry or government, or some combination of these. The unity of mutual recognition always involves two distinguishable churches standing over against one another and retaining full control over what would be generally acknowledged as the central sanctities of a church's life, its standards of faith, its worship, and especially its sacraments or ordinances, and its ministry. Full inter-communion is probably the most advanced form of the unity of mutual recognition, but it is still *inter*communion, not simply one communion, and it may exist without regular and constant con-sultation or mutual aid. Is this the unity we seek?

There is another form of unity resting back on various meas-ures of mutual recognition, but so highly developed as to deserve distinct attention. It is the unity of co-operative action. This may be occasional; it may take the form of co-operation among the agencies of independent churches, mission boards, educational boards, et cetera. Its most developed form is to be found in what we commonly call councils of churches, on a local, state-wide, national, or world scale. Is it fair to say of this form of unity, so familiar to us in the North American scene, that it usually pro-vides for co-operation in important but relatively peripheral ac-tivities of the churches, but does not directly touch the most sen-sitive areas, their faith and worship, their sacramental practice, their relations with their own members, their ministry? Paul Douglass concluded from a study of popular religious thinking that this is the dominant ideal of unity in American Protestantism. Is that still a valid judgment?

Corporate Unity

There is much evidence that many of the churches represented here and churches in other lands, notably in India, have been seeking and are seeking something more. There have been an im-portant number of actual church unions and negotiations for such unions are in progress.

The last form of unity of which I shall speak is variously labeled "union," "reunion," "organic unity," "corporate unity." What I am disposed to call corporate unity is found most unambiguously in a single church: in the Church of Norway, the United Church of Canada, the United Lutheran Church in America, and all the other churches represented in this conference. It is found in varying measures in those complexes of churches that we often speak of as church families or world-wide communions, such as the Orthodox Church, the Anglican Communion, World-Lutheranism, or Congregationalism. In naming these churches as examples, I recognize, of course, how very different they are.

The most general objective marks of corporate unity are behaving as a body, functioning as a living whole, maintaining recognizable identity in space and time, making a single history. In the clearest cases, there are some recognized agencies of common action, organs that shape the policy for the body as a whole, and agencies that carry out their functions. These serve as uniting symbols of the common life and instruments of its united life.

It is very important to note in the American scene that the corporate unity of a single church or communion may be maintained without a high measure of centralized governmental control. That is certainly the case with the Baptist Churches, or the Anglican Communion, or the Orthodox Church. A common tradition embodied in characteristic expression of faith, in ways of worship, in sacramental practice, in devotional inheritance, in the forms of ministry, in ways of dealing with one another, may keep the parts together and hold them true to type, without any visible, strong, centralized government.

Obviously the corporate unity found in existing churches and communions varies markedly in shape and content, but it has common marks.

Corporate church union is the achievement of corporate unity by hitherto separated churches. It takes place when independent and self-determining Christian bodies form one body where there were two or more previously. It occurs when churches that have behaved as two bodies begin to behave as one body. This is the most manifest form of unity. Is that the form of unity we seek? Even if we give an affirmative answer, we are still faced with the large question as to whether the resulting church would look very much like one of the existing churches or some combination of them.

CONCRETE ISSUES

I have given a major place in this address to the nature of the unity we seek just because it is our main theme. This is not to minimize the importance of the three main divisions and the twelve subsections into which our discussions are to be organized.

These are intended to give greater concreteness to our discussions, to provide more manageable subjects in terms of which we can draw together, and to enlist the interest and experience of those engaged in special areas of church life. The imaginative and devoted service of Dr. Paul S. Minear and the faithfulness of the sixteen regional study groups working during the past two years have put us all in their debt by preparing the material for these sectional discussions.

The sections grouped in Division I, under the heading, "The Nature of the Unity We Seek in Faithfulness to the Eternal Gospel," will be dealing with certain of the more specifically theological approaches to our problem. They will be talking together of the imperatives which come to us from the one Gospel to which we all seek to be faithful, and of the prudential and even unworthy motives which may draw churches together. They will be wrestling with the familiar question as to how much unity in doctrine we already possess, how much we need for the unity we seek, and whether the formalized doctrinal positions of our divided churches really correspond to the operative faith of their members. They will be considering "the one baptism," in which there is such a large measure of apparent mutual recognition, and at the same time such a stubborn cleavage between those who stress the objective meaning and effect of baptism and those who stress the conscious faith of the baptized believers. They will be facing again the scandal of our division at the table of the one Lord, and what it would mean to make manifest the one communion and fellowship.

Division II will approach our common theme, "In Terms of Organizational Structures," within churches and between churches. Here attention will be focussed initially on the local congregation, on what gives it such unity as it achieves, and how it is taken up into a larger unity. Those very characteristic North American institutions, state and local councils of churches, will be discussed. What are their strengths and limitations, and how are they related to the unity we seek? Thought will be given to the perennial problems of all civil and ecclesiastical governments, how to do justice to the claims of authority and order, on the one hand, and to freedom and spontaneity on the other, and how we deal with these in our separate churches. There will be some comparative study of our various denominational polities, with the question in mind as to how far these reflect what is believed to belong to the "essential order" of the Church, and how far they are simply matters of practical functioning, even though very heavily entrenched.

The subjects to be discussed by the sections in Division III come out of the recognition that the churches do not live and operate in a social vacuum. They are profoundly conditioned in their ways of thinking and acting by the society in which they are set. All of us are confronted by the mobility of population which stirs together in one "smelting pot" our constituencies, in the nature of a pressure cooker. Government gives us all a kind of recognition and almost compels us to a certain interchangeability of ministries and ministrations. The North American setting certainly encourages ecclesiastical "free enterprise"—and we make the most of it! Our colleges and universities collect in distinct communities of life and thought the actual young people and the potential young people of all our churches. The stresses of racial and economic division penetrate all our communions, and the struggle for integration in our society challenges us all. We are not here to discuss college work or race relations or population mobiltiy as such, but to consider how these illumine or condition or give urgency to the unity we seek.

You will agree that we have set ourselves to an ambitious and difficult undertaking. Being finite sinners, we shall doubtless disappoint ourselves and one another.

If the divided churches are to meet and draw together, they can only meet through persons, through imperfect persons such as we are. Each one of us represents unnamed and largely inarticulate multitudes with whom our lives are linked in faith and prayer. Each of us would say in his own way: "I am a member of the Lord's flock to whom his promises were made. How could I know him save through the continuing community of memory and of present communion and of hope, which he planted in the earth? I am forever a debtor to my Church for the Gospel which it has borne across the years and brought to me."

For at least thirty-five years I have been engaged in such conversations as we undertake here. If you are like me, you will find, as you meet your brothers and sisters coming out of their own particular households of faith, that you cannot think lightly or contemptuously of what has nurtured them, even though you could not be at home where they are at home. And you will experience afresh the sorrow of realizing that they go back and you go back into households or structures of faith and prayer and allegiance that in many ways separate you from them and fail grievously to make manifest our unity in Christ. This sorrow can turn you into a patient seeker for the household in which we could all be at home.

The Oberlin Conference in Ecumenical Perspective

ADDRESS BY DEAN J. ROBERT NELSON
SEPTEMBER 3, 1957

It is my privilege to speak briefly about the place of our conference in the ecumenical movement as a whole. I do not intend to plead the cause of Christian unity by deprecating the divisions among the churches nor to extol the blessings of unity which these divisions now obscure. But I wish to remind you that what is now taking place in Oberlin is no isolated event in time or in the world; rather it is the consummation of many antecedents and the anticipation of significant consequences. What these antecedents have been is known to us. As to the consequences we can only conjecture and hope. Because we are able to discern the work of God's hand in the multiform events and processes of the ecumenical movement which have led to this moment, we can assert with confidence that God has been disclosing to his people the shape and lineaments of the Church's true unity. Often our dimness of vision, our coldness of heart, or our lack of authentic faith, hope and love have prevented us from receiving this disclosure. And even now, when our spirits have become more willing and receptive, our flesh—that is, our carnal suspicion and self-satisfaction—is still weak. However negative may be the judgments of God against us Christians as perpetuators of division, we find strength in the knowledge that for more than a century he has been leading us towards that form of unity which we cannot yet discern, but which is the expression of his perfect will.

Within this great surge and flow of work and prayer for unity, the organized efforts of the World Conference on Faith and Order and the Commission on Faith and Order have been a main stream. Probably very few of us here are unacquainted with the story of this movement since the decisive work of Bishop Brent in 1910. His was actually not the first proposal for a world conference on Faith and Order. Before the middle of the 17th century, John Dury had suggested such a conference in Europe. Even the words "Faith and Order" are found in John Eliot's book, *Communion of Churches,* of 1665. But nearly 300 years were required to pass before the condition of the separate churches was congenial for the holding of such a conference.

44

Incidentally, we of this generation, who have become so thoroughly conditioned to the procedures of church conferences that we would do well to have our names and denominations embroidered on our left lapels, have hardly caught up to the wisdom of John Dury, when he wrote the following advice to contemporary and yet unborn delegates:

"Nor is there any one thing that doth more intangle and increase the multiplication of needless Debates, than the mistake of the points of difference either wilfully or ignorantly entertained. By this means Satan doth enable and engage men's spirits to make their contentions inextricable, endless and irreconcilable; for when the question is not distinctly stated, and men are entered upon controversy, they will rather alter the point of debate twenty times, than seem to be found in error once."[1]

He who has ears, let him hear!

A wholly new influence upon Christian churches of the world has been felt in this century because of the great Faith and Order conferences, with their preparatory studies, confrontations, discussions, reports, and personal experiences. The effects of these conferences have been threefold:

1. A growing number of Christians have been educated in the complexities of doctrine and order to be found in all the churches.

2. A continuing organization for the systematic study of all matters affecting the unity and division of the Church has been at work.

3. An extending and often revolutionary leaven of thought has gone abroad to remind Christians of their obligation to remove the hindrances to their oneness in Jesus Christ.

FAITH AND ORDER IN THE WORLD COUNCIL

Just 20 years ago this summer, when the Edinburgh and Oxford Conferences decided to merge their forces, it was agreed unconditionally that the working principles and purposes of the Faith and Order Movement would have to be preserved and continued in the new World Council of Churches.

Since 1948 the Commission on Faith and Order has been an integral and effective organ of the World Council. At the Third World Conference in Lund, 1952, it was decided that the Com-

---

[1]Quoted by Newman Smyth, *Constructive Quarterly*, 1916, p. 412.

mission, with a maximum of 100 members, should become a part of the World Council's proposed Division of Studies. This organizational adjustment was made at Evanston in 1954. When this step was taken, many a veteran's head wagged with disapproval. Faith and Order is finished, they said. It is boxed up in a bureaucratic department, subject to other authorities. Sing the Requiem for a lost cause.

I hope that by this time the developments of the faith and order work within the World Council have themselves assuaged the pessimism of persons who held such fears. As the Council has gone from strength to strength in recent years, so has the work for Christian unity. Let me suggest briefly what these developments have been.

1. There is now being carried forward an exceedingly important program of study of the major issues affecting the unity of the Church. With due respect to the great accomplishments of the Lausanne and Edinburgh period, we can say without boastfulness that today there are more of the world's leading Christian thinkers giving more time to the common study of more faith and order questions than ever before. Nearly one hundred prominent theologians in many countries are members of our eight theological commissions in North America, Europe and Asia. In addition there are varying numbers of participants in the Faith and Order committees and study groups appointed by the churches of different countries. The British Council of Churches has its Faith and Order group, as do similar bodies in Holland, Sweden, Australia and other lands. And here in North America we give due recognition to the numerous persons who have worked together in preparation for our present conference. These efforts in their entirety constitute the study work of faith and order.

During this week we shall enjoy the privilege of hearing reports on the four major areas of faith and order study as given by the chairmen of the respective theological commissions in North America.

FOUR THEOLOGICAL STUDIES

(1) Commanding much interest in theological circles today is the study which Prof. Calhoun will describe. The recognition of the Church as being wholly dependent upon Jesus Christ and inextricably related to him in its earthly life is not a novel discovery. It is the very presupposition of the New Testament witness that

the Messiah and his people, the Shepherd and his flock, the Head
of the Body and its members belong together. While acknowledg-
ing this relationship in our Bible study or theological reflection,
however, we have frequently in ecumenical discussion talked of
the Church as though our own denominational traditions and
teachings were, at best, the sufficient media of the life of Jesus
Christ in the Church, or, at worst, the substitute for the faithful
conforming of the Church's life to his life. Prof. Calhoun will tell
how theologians in his commission are facing together the wonder
of Jesus Christ, and, with the humility of those who know only in
part, are suspending for the time their confessional self-consciousness and seeking in common a clearer understanding of both the
nature of the Church and its unity given by and in our one Lord.

(2) The study to be explained tomorrow by Prof. Outler is
one of the most obvious relevance and yet one which has been
passed by until the present. It concerns the relation of the one
great Christian Tradition and the various confessional traditions
to the movement for unity. We all confess and teach the one central Tradition of the saving Gospel of Christ, and yet we inevitably
inherit and are influenced by the different historical traditions of
past centuries. By coming to a more adequate recognition of the
one great Tradition which gives the Church in all generations its
life and continuity, and by being able more objectively to judge
the validity of our separate traditions, may we not find the way to
closer concord in doctrine and church life less cluttered with obstacles than it now is? Moreover, can we not learn to regard the
"common history" of the people of God in all the centuries and
all countries to be a unitive, rather than a divisive, factor? To such
questions, and with much expectancy, the members of the Theological Commission on Tradition and Traditions address themselves.

(3) Our third report on faith and order studies will be given
by Dean Muelder. It concerns a question which will be encountered at many points during the course of this conference, for its
implications are nearly limitless in the relations of the denominations to each other and to the one Church. We are speaking about
what are often and erroneously called "the nontheological factors."
Since theology is also concerned with the common forms and structures of churches, however, we prefer to call these the "social and
cultural factors affecting unity and division." But to be more specific still, we are studying now the role of ecclesiastical institutionalism in the whole question of unity. Granted that churches cannot
exist as purely spiritual societies any more than we as persons can

live without bone and flesh, what are we to say when the institutional forms of the churches seem to become ends in themselves and so hinder both the unity and the mission of the churches? Just because any probing in this area comes very close to the sensitive nerves of ecclesiastical tissue, Dean Muelder's study commission will be dealing with some very lively and perhaps explosive issues. But such fact-facing and truth-seeking need not be feared or suppressed by Christians, whom the Apostle admonished as people who "can do nothing against the truth but only for the truth." (II Cor. 13:8.)

(4) The fourth area of study is that of Christian worship. The various ways of worship, as well as the differing theories and doctrines underlying these diverse ways, are being examined in ways which Prof. Sittler will describe. Few of us need to be reminded of the paradox of the relation of worship to unity. It is precisely in worship services that we may at times feel ourselves most distant from other churches; but it is also in the act of worship that we most genuinely apprehend our oneness as Christ's people. It is not enough for us in faith and order studies merely to describe and compare the visible and audible varieties of services. Again we must face the matter in common, and ask what is really constitutive and indispensable for the devotional and liturgical practices of the churches. Fortunately we shall hear also from Principal Chandran about the significant studies on worship which his Asian theological commission is pursuing.

Having heard these reports, you may well ask what these ten-year studies are likely to accomplish for Christian unity and church unity. Let me make two comments on this query.

THE NATURE OF OUR TASK

First, these theological commissions have not set out to solve problems, to balance complicated ecclesiological equations, to prescribe neat and painless resolutions of the existing tensions between churches. By this I do not mean that they are not expecting to discover new insights or record further progress in understanding. One of the most provocative assertions of the Lund Conference Report was this: "There are truths about the nature of God and His Church which will remain forever closed to us unless we act together in obedience to the unity which is already ours." These faith and order studies are just acts of obedience on the basis of this given unity. And though they are not expecting to untie a series of Gordian knots, the members of the eight commissions, having some of the best minds in the various confessions, will certainly give help and guidance to all the churches in their quest to understand God's will for the unity, life and mission of his Church.

The second and greater value of our studies lies in the influence they have upon the thinking of all who take part in any way. It may be true, as someone remarked, that intellectuals today are paid more and heeded less than ever before. Theologians are intellectuals. And a random sampling of sermons heard in any city may vindicate the latter part of that observation, although the professors may question the former. In any case, we may still assume that theologians have a distinctive influence upon Christians' thoughts and attitudes. And because of the recent spread of ecumenical studies, the men who teach on theological faculties, write books of scholarship and instruction, preach and lecture, study and ponder, are becoming less disposed than before to think, write and speak as though their own denomination or tradition or theological circle were the only sphere in which God's truth might be received. I recall a book by a famous German Lutheran theologian which purported to be a general systematic treatment of the whole Christian faith. In its four-page index of names cited I discovered only two Anglo-Saxons—Shakespeare and Milton. It is a refreshing contrast to note that at least two of the foremost interpreters of Luther are British Methodists. It is more promising still when Prof. Outler and Father Florovsky speak in agreement about their common history.

So much for the scope and import of these studies.

2. Another task in the development of the Faith and Order Commission is, in the words of its Constitution, "To proclaim the essential oneness of the Church of Christ and to keep prominently before the World Council and the churches the obligation to manifest that unity and its urgency for evangelism." We have an obligation to propagate the gospel of unity in the organized work of the World Council and in the churches which are its members. Clearly we have small resources for mass propaganda, and this is not to be deplored. There is a better means of making it known that practical co-operation alone is not sufficient, and that the preaching of genuine reconciliation by Jesus Christ is sabotaged by the resistance of the denominations and parties to his reconciling work among themselves. We rely upon the experiences of many Christians in ecumenical conferences of all kinds to turn them into veritable "apostles of unity." And we count upon such

persons as you who are gathered here at Oberlin to preach the sermons, make the speeches, write the articles and books, plan the agenda, and offer the prayers which will further the movement for unity.

PROGRESS TOWARD UNITY

3. A third and often fascinating task we have is to trace the astonishing progress in the direction of intercommunion and church union. The plain facts contradict all notions that the urge for unity has spent its force. Are you Lutheran, Anglican, Baptist, Presbyterian-Reformed, Disciple, Methodist, Quaker, Mennonite, Moravian, or already partly United? Are you from Canada, the United States, Mexico, Jamaica, Uruguay or Argentina; from Great Britain, Holland, Germany, Poland, Italy or Spain; from Ghana, Nigeria, Kenya, Northern Rhodesia, South Africa, or Madagascar; from Pakistan, India, Ceylon, Indonesia, Japan, Australia or New Zealand? Then you may know that in at least one of these countries there are churches of your own confessional family which are now engaged in serious official negotiations which lead towards a relationship of intercommunion or even organic merger. Church history provides no record of times even comparable to this one. And we of the Faith and Order Commission, without violating our necessary neutrality towards particular schemes of union, do three things. We publish surveys and information and make the hard-to-find documents available. We hold periodic consultations on church union, as at Yale Divinity School this summer, to enable participants in negotiations to share their problems and insights. And we study the schemes and plans themselves, to see how the issues involved in particular ones are of general importance for all the churches. We should not forget, therefore, that this conference on "The Nature of the Unity We Seek," while it is not a conference on church union, is yet taking place in the context and time of an unprecedented proliferation of union movements throughout the world.

4. Finally, this conference in North America should be seen as one among several efforts to bring the discussion of Christian unity down from the awesome level of world-wide representation to regional, national and local soil. It has not yet been determined when or whether there will be held a Fourth World Conference on Faith and Order, in succession to Lund. Meanwhile we are asking the churches to wrestle with these problems in their own back yards. In 1955 an exceedingly fruitful conference was held in New Zealand; in May of this year a smaller, yet important, one, in

India. Since 1955 studies have been progressing in Europe in anticipation of a major consultation involving only the Lutheran and the Reformed confessions. And plans are now being made for a conference in Australia in 1959. You may all be sure that our brethren in these other lands are watching with keen interest and expectation what we do here at Oberlin. And the fruits of this conference will become a part of the resources of the whole ecumenical movement in the years ahead.

About these and other conferences some may be tempted to think cynically. They may share the disdain of Martin Luther, who, when invited to the colloquy at Regensburg, muttered "that a man would lose time, waste money, and miss everything at home" by attending. Nevertheless, in our time we have learned the value, indeed the necessity, of drawing the separate churches and their leaders out of physical, intellectual and spiritual isolation into encounter and communion with their brethren in Christ. This is the work of the ecumenical movement generally and the Faith and Order Commission in particular. So here we are, gathered to listen to one another, and thus to hear what the one Spirit of God says to the churches.

Christ and the Church

ADDRESS BY PROFESSOR ROBERT L. CALHOUN
SEPTEMBER 3, 1957

We have come to Oberlin because, with millions of fellow Christians, we crave fuller realization of the unity that properly belongs to the Church of Jesus Christ. Many of us would agree that "The Unity We Seek" is in some sense already real, else we could not all seek it. But if we should try, one by one, to tell one another more precisely what it is we are seeking, it would soon be evident that we have come with many different ideas of unity, some clear, some vague, some compatible and some incompatible with one another. A part of our task here is to explore together a fresh approach to the basic question, What kind of unity can and ought we to seek?

Our problem is central in the ecumenical awakening of the present century, a problem at once practical and theoretical. Practically, it is our obligation to recognize, realize, and manifest the unity that is of the very being of the Church, in the midst of the diversity and division that veils and in some respects contradicts our unity. Theoretically, our task is to seek better understanding of our actual situation, of its roots and past developments, its vital forms and stresses, its real possibilities for amendment.

A first fundamental insight, shared by all of us, is that both our unity and our diversity—even our division—arise out of God's working with men in history. To try to separate divine initiative and human response in the life of the Church is to obscure the real nature of our problem. To assign diversity and division, for example, solely to human obliquity gives a false impression of the depth and subtlety of the task of seeking the unity that is vital to the Church's being. It is necessary to recognize that the unity we seek cannot exist at all without diversity, in which are disclosed the bounty of God and the manifold gifts of his Spirit, not less truly than the weaknesses of men. Even our divisions and dissensions, which we are in duty bound to overcome, bear witness—sometimes in tortured ways—to God's demand for devotion to truth, as well as to man's frequent confusion as to what is true. It may well be that more vivid realization of other dimensions of our problem than those we are accustomed to see and to stress can bring us an important step closer to the unity we need.

Past efforts to attain that goal through better mutual understanding of our differences have been fruitful but inconclusive. They have taught us much about ourselves and about one another, and have opened major lines of inquiry that call for continuing study. Moreover, engaging in common study of our differences has given us personal experience of community at one significant level, as individual members representing many traditions and organized communions within the Church, while it has made us the more sensitive to our need for much deeper and more inclusive unity. At the same time, study that focuses attention primarily upon ourselves and our differences has inherent limitations as a way to overcome division. For the unity we seek lies, in a vital sense, beyond us, as well as buried deep within us; and to attend too much to clarifying and understanding our differences can, in the absence of powerful correctives, have the effect of making divergent loyalties seem more compelling and exclusive than ever.

The present course of study, therefore, is deliberately centered on the unity we have not first of all in ourselves, but in God: in our Creator, Redeemer, sanctifying Life-Giver. It is meant to go forward on two levels. One is technically theological. We are directed to inquire as sharply and systematically as we can into the meaning our common faith discerns in the active presence of God, in Jesus Christ, in the Holy Spirit for the Church, and especially for her vital unity. The other level is existential. Together we seek such openness to the divine working and to one another that vital unity may in fact be more fully realized in and through us in ways beyond our understanding and conscious intent.

Especially since this paper is addressed to many who have not shared directly in the sessions of our theological study commission since 1953, and is meant to draw together various strands of thought expressed and implied in our prior discussions, it seems proper to speak first of our theological perspective, and then of the Church in that context.

I. OUR THEOLOGICAL PERSPECTIVE

Four main themes chiefly concern us here: faith in response to God; God for Christian faith; the centrality of Jesus Christ; the Holy Spirit. Of these, the last two are expressly included in our assignment for study; and it is hardly practicable to deal with them helpfully except in close relation with the first two.

A. *Faith in Response to God*

The appropriate response of man to the presence of God, at once revealed and hidden, transcendent and near at hand, is faith. In Christian history the word has various meanings. At the simplest, shallowest level it means merely cognitive assent, belief, *assensus*. When I say yes to a proposition, or judge that a thing or a person is before me, or that an event happened yesterday or will happen tomorrow, I exercise belief of this least profound sort. Even here some risk is involved, in as far as my assertion goes beyond the most patent facts, and all the more if I stand ready to act in line with my belief.

A second level or mode of faith is trust, confidence, *fiducia,* characteristically directed to persons or groups whom I judge dependable, and in whose keeping I am ready to place cherished possessions, my safety, my good name. It is thus that I may have faith in my friend, my comrades in arms, my country. Both involvement and risk are greater, and the import of this second sort of response for my personal existence is more profound than that of simple assent. "The devils also believe," but they do not trust and their belief leaves them essentially unchanged.

But even trust is not the full meaning of faith in God. When I trust my closest friend, my colleagues, my country, there is always one limitation that I cannot break without violating my deepest obligation as a morally responsible person. I cannot entrust to any fellow man nor to any beloved community my responsibility for moral decision. Trust in any fellow creature must properly be bound by the condition: "as far as conscience will permit." But when it is God who confronts me and evokes my belief and trust, this condition is meaningless. Faith in the God and Father of Jesus Christ is response to the One who gives existence, direction, and meaning to conscience itself—which is a shortened way of saying the One who gives existence, direction, and meaning to personal selfhood, without whom we could not be persons at all. In this context, faith in God (*credere in deum,* that goes beyond *credere deum* and *credere deo*) is commitment of my whole being—not simply of my mind, nor of mind and conscious will. It includes both of these (*assensus* and *fiducia*), but it involves also the very roots of my existence from which acts of thought and will arise. Faith in God is reorientation of my whole self. It is this sort of redirection of personal existence that the existence of the Church at once presupposes, exemplifies, and nurtures.

But if this is to be said without the most flagrant circularity, it must be said at once that such faith is first of all a gift of God. With him and not with us is the beginning. His urgent, gracious presence evokes response in me, once the way is clear, as surely as sunlight evokes in a seeing eye the response that gives the eye its proper fulfillment. Faith, like vision, is a gift. At the same time it is free commitment. For no mechanical, coerced reaction could bring fulfillment to persons, compact of mind, feeling, and will, created to acknowledge, love, and serve God as sons, not to be chattels and puppets. The response is evoked "once the way is clear," and that means, among other things, once I cease my refusal to acknowledge the light. This is not to say I must first let down the bars and *then* God will grant me life-giving faith. It is he who prompts and enables me to open my eyes, while at the same time it is I who must open them. The initiative is always with God, the response is mine. It is free response in the sense that in it I affirm God as the ground and goal of my own being, and thus, as in every act of love and loyalty, find fulfillment and liberation—precisely because in such a moment I can do no other. It is then that I become not less but more fully myself.

In this situation is exemplified in small compass the realization of a covenant relationship. It goes without saying that in the Bible, whether in Exodus or Isaiah or the letter to the Hebrews, covenant does not mean a contract entered into for advantage and terminated at will. The covenant is established by God as an indispensable condition of full personal life for man. It has in view man's essential nature as social being, and is itself constitutive, not to say creative, of social, moral, personal existence. It is established in love and faithfulness on God's side, and it demands faith and love from man, not as an arbitrary *quid pro quo* but as the only way of life in which man can become fully the person that God has created him to be. The covenant of law and grace (the two sides cannot really be separated) is God's gift—an exacting and costly gift, and at the same time an inescapable one. Whether men know it or not, they live as obligated members of a chosen, covenant-bound people—obedient or disobedient, but bound:— bound, as Paul says, "in hope," that in faith and love they may become free, covenanted heirs and not indentured slaves.

For faith is a way of sharing in the freedom and bounty of God's household. In faith man apprehends and participates in a realm of truth, right, life, and love that extends always far beyond his grasp. In faith he is enabled to transcend himself in a new way, and so to live with new horizons, in hope of a new homeland. Faith is not knowledge, though it brings new knowledge and vitalizes what is old. Faith is not attainment, but participation—both having and having-not, pressing on toward fulfillment that has been disclosed but not possessed.

B. *God for Christian Faith*

Perhaps the simplest way to identify the God in whom we believe is the most familiar. He is the living God known in the history of Israel, especially to the discerning eyes of prophets and seers, by his mighty acts of judgment and mercy; decisively revealed in Jesus Christ; and thus recognizable by faith as unceasingly and all-powerfully active in the life of the Church and of the entire world. To begin thus is to affirm once for all that the Bible—the whole Bible, and not some fraction of it—is indispensable as guide to Christian faith. Probing critical study that tries incessantly to press closer to what the biblical writers really say and mean, and candid, responsible use of the results of such study are presupposed. Otherwise we should find ourselves being guided not by acquaintance with the Bible as it is, but by notions of our own as to what it ought to be.

To take the Scriptures thus seriously does not mean that we are restricted to the biblical text for either our acquaintance with God, who confronts us daily, or the words and ideas by which we try to convey to ourselves and others something of what we mean when we say: "our God." Most notably the Church, in seeking to make clear what is meant when it affirms that "the God and Father of our Lord Jesus Christ" is *one*, has found it indispensable to declare that the oneness of God is not abstract, like the unity of a point or a proposition, but concrete, living, personal triunity. In so saying, Christian theology has gone beyond anything that is expressly affirmed in the Bible; and this (as Calvin and Barth, for example, have argued) because the Church has found that the God proclaimed in the Old and New Testaments can all too easily be obscured in theological discourse by oversimplification.

For Christians aware, whether reflectively or intuitively, of the force of this doctrinal decision, it has become "natural" though not always consciously reasoned to believe in God as triune: Father, Son, Holy Spirit, one Supreme Being self-related, self-reflective, indivisible in existence and in action. This means among other things that in relation to every created being—the Church and all else in nature and history—God acts always as *one*. Whether in creation, redemption, or sanctification, it is God who acts—never Father or Son or Holy Spirit alone, but all together in mutuality and harmony.

Trinitarian doctrine thus gives distinctive shape to another Christian affirmation: that God immeasurably transcends the whole created world, and that he is everywhere and always concomitant and immanent, actively present with and within it. This affirmation applies alike to Father, Son, and Holy Spirit, and not (in analogy with some non-Christian theologies) so as to present the Father alone as transcendent, the Holy Spirit as immanent, the Son as somewhere between.

Closely related to this declaration that God is at once transcendent and immanent is a similar one: that he is at once hidden and revealed. Again, the meaning is not that he is partly open to man's comprehension and in some other part closed away. The point is precisely that God as self-disclosed to us men remains mystery, not only in some secrets of his Being that remain undisclosed but also in his self-revelation itself. Like "the peace of God that passes all understanding," so too his justice and truth, his mercy and grace, his love, inescapably disclosed in Jesus Christ, baffle all our attempts at comprehension, at the same time that they flood our minds and hearts with light.

C. *The Centrality of Jesus Christ*

Decisive disclosure has come in Jesus Christ, known to us first of all through the Scriptures. For Christian faith man's history finds its center and its crux in him. Man's history on earth makes sense only as the living fabric of God's creative, redemptive, and sanctifying life with men. But this is a perspective that unfocused history by itself could not provide. In Jesus Christ, for the eyes of faith, God provides it in the only conceivable way: in a personal embodiment of God's life with man that does in fact give meaning to both past and future, and relate the whole grim struggle triumphantly to the reign of God.

For man, created to find his full manhood in covenanted communion with his Maker, in faith and in love toward God and neighbor, has a long, unpromising record of failure. Instead of trusting God, too often he has tried to win security for himself by violence and deceit. Instead of seeking the good of his neighbors as having equal claims, too often he has exploited or betrayed them for his own gain. Instead of fighting valiantly against the evils that threaten all men, too often he has been callous or cowardly unless he was directly threatened. This is, of course, not the whole story. Men and women in every time and culture have on occasion been brave and faithful, generous, kind, and humble. What is still more vital, even at their worst they have not been able to break away from God's care. The chief of sinners is still bound by the covenant of command and promise. God has never abandoned any man. But man in heedlessness, self-conceit, cruelty, and falsehood has turned against God, against fellow man, and against his own true self as God's servant and child. Moreover, through generations of corporate living in families, tribes, and peoples, he has become enwound in the web of sin and its consequences, beyond his power to free himself. His very nature as social and moral self is twisted and vitiated, until the springs of his thought and action are corrupted, though not destroyed. Only the love and power of God can make him whole.

The heart of the Christian Gospel is a word of hope for man thus enslaved to sin: "God was in Christ reconciling the world to himself."

In the New Testament we have a record, sketchy but varied and vivid, of the impact Jesus made on men of his own time and the two or three generations that followed. One thing they said about him in various ways is that he was a mediator between God and man. One possible reading of that statement the Church has long since rejected: he is not an intermediate being, a third party intervening between men and God. It is vital to Christian faith and understanding that God is his own mediator, "reconciling the world to himself." But it remains true that Jesus is mediator in many ways that are crucial for men's redemption from distrust of God and the ills that follow. He is the decisive revealer of man to himself, of the deadly power of sin, of the sovereign judgment and mercy of God, of the springs of new life in repentance, and the reality of eternal life in time. He is one who stirs in men revulsion against evil; disgust with self-centered, idolatrous, distorted selfhood; and radical conversion toward God. And all this because he is one who shares fully the plight of feeble men, caught in the tangled mass of original sin and plagued by the fears, deceits, and aggressions that spring from it, for our sake made "to be sin who knew no sin"; yet who by the power of God breaks those ancient bonds and opens the way to freedom.

In his ministry and on his cross, he is mediator of such unanswerable judgment as men never clearly knew before—the judgment of God's own self-sacrifice, that leaves man no place to hide. But in the same sacrificial life and death he is mediator, in these very same acts and sufferings, of God's unconditional mercy that seeks out man before man knows his own need. He is embodiment and mediator of the covenant—of law and grace, of commandment and promise, of judgment and mercy: the creative, ordaining word that embraces mankind and makes possible personal existence and community. He is mediator of the transforming spirit of holiness, of truth and love, that makes the covenant a word not of death but of life.

Following the judgments of the earliest Christians, the Church has affirmed that Jesus Christ as mediator of divine judgment and mercy is himself God-man, the Word incarnate. We make no pretense to understand how this can be. For us, as for the writer to the Colossians, Christ is still "God's mystery," unveiled but not explained. Yet there are affirmations concerning his existence as God-man that seem congruous with the Church's faith. We say he is at once truly man and truly God. As true man he is in all essential ways one of us. He is an *individual* human person, body, mind, and spirit, child of a particular place and time, a man of his people, involved as we are in the finite web of nature and culture. Our weaknesses, perils, and frustrations were his also, and he felt them more acutely and profoundly than we can do. He entered also into the accumulated mass of our sinfulness, in love identifying himself with us in all our misery, though in him the power of righteousness triumphed over our sin. To say that he was an individual human person is not to say that at any time he existed as a man apart from God. It is to say that he was truly man, individual and finite as every man must be.

Precisely this full sharing of our lot is indispensable to his being truly *universal* man, embodying God's purpose "as a plan for the fulness of time, to sum up all things in him." Irenaeus in his central and continual stress on "recapitulation" or "summation" (*anakephalaiosis,* from Eph. 1:10) as the key to both Christology and redemption doctrine had a clear and profound grasp of this truth: that in Jesus Christ, universality is grounded in individual being and inseparable from it. Against every antihistorical sort of gnosticism within and without the Church, this insistence is always vital, not to diminish but to strengthen the ascription of universal character and effect to Jesus' life and death.

In at least two ways his existence as man is of universal import: it illuminates all human existence, and it alters the entire human situation. This is to say, first, that in the presence of Jesus Christ, the nature and meaning of human existence in all its characteristic powers and limitations, its promise and its corruption, are made clear as they were not and could not be without him. It is to say, secondly, that by his coming, the actual conditions under which human life goes on are permanently changed, both for those who know him and for those who as yet do not. The world is a different place for men to live in because he has lived in it as a man among men. It is not enough to regard his individual existence simply as an instance or illustration of general principles already fully in force. The point is that his actual existence brings into being and effect a new historical situation that alters both the balance of forces at work in human life, and the meaning that such life can have. All this involves in another context the reality of *participation,* already noticed in what was said about faith. The universal impact of Jesus Christ as individual human person entails, on the one hand, unrestricted participation by him in the lot of mankind, and on the other hand participation by all other men, in varying ways and degrees, in the new mode of human life brought into being by his coming.

If we ask what is this new mode of human life, a full answer would have to attempt at the very least to portray in some detail the deep anxieties and the surface frivolities, the capricious brilliance, instability, and cruelty along with the stern heroism of the ancient pagan world; the moral insight and exalted vision along with the religious exclusiveness, the stress on legal rectitude, and the fierce theocratic nationalism of the Jewish community in Palestine; and the growing emancipation and redirection of human life, a liberation hampered and distorted but never annulled by failures of many sorts, as the Christian Gospel has become effective for one people after another. This obviously is a task for major historical works, not for a paragraph here. What can be said briefly is that in Jesus Christ a new living basis for hope, a new standard and stimulus for a shared life of faith and love, and a new focus of unity came into human existence.

This unity is not simple but enormously complex, precisely because it results not from the application of a formula but from the impact and indwelling of a person. It involves the unity of corporate remembrance: living memory among Christians of the first generation and for others remembrance guided by their written testimonies. Such reference to Jesus Christ as Pioneer affirms a unity of formative impulse that radiates from his life into the lives of other men, most evident in the Church at its best, but discernible whenever men take sides for or against his way. Moreover, this creative impulse is by no means confined to the past. As living Lord of the Church and the world of men he acts in every age as norm and motive for both individual and corporate life, who, since he is one in whom God acts with reconciling power, "breaking down the middle wall of division" wherever it exists, prompts and guides men toward unity. For he who is the source of the Church's life is also, as the one fully obedient, faithful Son of our universal Father, its proper goal, by whom all men are and will be judged. Thus to him, as to one in whom "all things" are summed up, we look as the embodiment, the source, guide and fulfillment of the living oneness, full of diversity reconciled but not annulled, that is vital to the Church and to mankind.

When Christian faith sees him as God-man, it has in view as one major factor this unprecedented impact of his life on all human existence. In declaring that this is a decisive act of God incarnate, there must be no weakening of the vital stress on his full manhood. "God was in Christ reconciling the world to himself" not so as to infringe but so as to fulfill his human existence. In him God is at once decisively revealed, and still hidden. Christ as God-man is both *logos* and *mysterion*, word and mystery. The word of truth, love, and life that shines in him with the pure brightness of God's own being confronts men with God's very presence, and makes God known as never before, and with finality that can never be repeated, altered, or supplanted. At the same time, the mystery of God's infinite being—of his power, omniscience, and unending omnipresence—is effectively symbolized and so disclosed, but not resolved. Even in the Incarnation God's *incognito* is not wholly laid aside.

In the new light of the resurrection also this remains true. He who is raised from the dead in glory and power, whom we acknowledge as Savior and Lord, is the same who suffered and died: not God simply, but God-man. At the same time, he who has died and risen has become the mediator of God's power over the lives of men, the Lord for each and every man, far beyond the range of his influence in the days of his earthly ministry. The Church of the apostolic age is born not simply of Jesus' preaching in Galilee but of his full impact as living, crucified, and risen—and of the work of the Holy Spirit. Without the Lord and the Spirit, the Church as we know it could not exist.

D. *The Holy Spirit*

When we speak of the Holy Spirit, we are speaking of God. For Christian faith, there can be no dividing of the triune Godhead, as though the Spirit were a subordinate force or agency, intermediate between God and earthly creatures. Moreover, the Holy Spirit and his activity has no beginning in time, as though at Pentecost or at Jesus' baptism or at the annunciation, or at least in the New Testament era, the Holy Spirit first begins to be, to act, or to be known among men. We cannot rightly understand the relation of the Christian Church and the Holy Spirit if we think of them as beginning together, still less if we should think of them as of the same order of existence—the Spirit as confined within the life of the Church, or the Church itself as in its essential being simply divine.

If we seek in the Bible for clear leads, we remember that the doctrine of the Trinity is a later clarification of Christian thought, not a part of the biblical text, and that what we may suitably look for are simpler affirmations about the Spirit that can when necessary be brought more directly into the context of trinitarian faith. On these terms we may well find our first lead in the creation stories at the very beginning of Genesis: the Spirit of God that blew across the dark waters, and the gift of breath that makes man a living self. Here is spirit as moving, life-giving power—in that simple sense *creator spiritus;* and it comes from God. But far more numerous in the Old Testament are instances in which the Spirit of God is distinguished from other spirits as the source of wisdom, judgment and righteousness, of revelation, and of prophecy. There can be little doubt that though the term Holy Spirit is not characteristic of the Old Testament, it would be appropriate for that Spirit of God that gives not only life but righteousness. Indeed what seems to be novel in the New Testament accounts is not that the Holy Spirit now for the first time appears, or is known as such, but that now the Spirit is "poured out" among men as never before, and that this outpouring at Pentecost and thereafter is now connected with Jesus Christ as never, in the Old Testament, with the expected Messiah.

As usual it is Paul who urges the most drastic rethinking of the familiar doctrine. For him it is not enough to connect the outpouring of the Spirit and the gifts of tongues, prophecy, and healing in some general way with the resurrection and ascension of the

Lord. It is necessary to identify the Spirit so closely with him that it seems natural to say, "the Spirit of Christ," or "the Spirit of the Lord," or even, "Now the Lord is the Spirit." To live "according to the Spirit" is the same as to live "in Christ," and this is the indispensable norm for every Christian and for the Church as Christian community. Not the more startling "gifts," though these in their proper place are well enough, but "the higher gifts" of Christlike living—above all faith, hope, and love—mark the presence of the Holy Spirit, that is at the same time "the Spirit of God," "the Spirit of him who raised Jesus from the dead."

For our present purpose, two continuing works of the Holy Spirit among men are of especial import. One is establishing, maintaining, and extending community, *koinonia,* living communication, sharing, spiritual oneness. We have spoken more than once of the vital importance of participation, for personal existence, for personal renewal, and the life of faith and love. In Christian thought, most of all in Pauline thought, it is the Spirit especially that "helps us in our weakness," enabling us to call God Father, to say, "Jesus is Lord!" and to have our place in the community of faith. There is no room here even to outline the immense scope of this insight; but it may be in place to suggest that what is involved is seeing in the Spirit the basis of human society itself, which in the community of faith is more clearly discernible than elsewhere, demanding that we seek ever more fully realized unity not merely for our sakes but for the sake of all mankind. "The Spirit helps us in our weakness."

The other distinctive work of the Spirit is sanctification: not only to make us one in community, but in some sense to make us holy. This is not the place for technical argument over the precise limits of sanctification in the Christian life: how it is related to justification, how far it can be achieved here, and in what terms it is to be judged. We know at least how it must begin: with repentance and acknowledgment of need. We know too the far-off goal: "to grow up in every way into him who is the head, into Christ." And we know that whatever mode and measure of growth becomes real for us is the work of the Spirit—which is to say of God, whose "love has been poured into our hearts through the Holy Spirit which has been given to us."

II. THE CHURCH

In what has been said of the Christian understanding of God and of human response, the Church has been noticed more than once. It might well have appeared much more often, as the community within which all Christian doctrine develops. That matrix, of course, that underlies our theological perspective is the Church as living reality, not a specific doctrine of the Church. Such a doctrine, to which we now turn, belongs within the perspective and is largely determined by it. In the precis that follows, we shall look at the Church in two aspects: as "new creation," and as growing community. These aspects are not separable, either in time or in essential meaning. We must not think that the Church is first, at some particular moment, a new creation, and only after that a growing community: it is both, at every moment of its earthly career. Similarly we must not suppose that these two terms refer exclusively, the one to what God does, the other to what man does, in the Church's life: both God and man are involved in all that the Church is and does. "New creation" and "growing community" specify two perspectives in which the single complex being of the Church may conveniently be examined, the one giving especial (but not exclusive) attention to what God has done, is doing, and will do, the other similarly to the doings of men, without any attempt to draw a boundary line between them.

A. As New Creation in History

The primary reality that brings the Christian Church into being is two-sided: God's act and man's response. The basic truth is set out briefly and clearly in the Johannine prologue: "The true light that enlightens every man was coming into the world . . . yet the world knew him not. . . . But to all who received him, who believed in his name, he gave power to become children of God; who were born, not of blood nor of the will of the flesh nor of the will of man, but of God." Here the initiative is unmistakably God's and not man's. "The light" that comes into the world is the eternal Son, the ever-active Word, God's wisdom and power, by whom the world is made and the mind of man filled with the gift of reason, yet all too often ignored or rejected by his own, even after he entered visibly into man's plight, incarnate in Jesus Christ. But to those in every age who responded in faith he granted another gift: to be not only rational creatures but "children of God," not by physical ancestry or natural inclination, nor by social contact, but by God's gracious act. Essentially the same view is spelled out with express reference to the Church in the late letter to the Ephesians. Here the central figure of Jesus Christ is explicitly backed by the purpose, power and grace of the Father, and the living presence of the Holy Spirit. God's initiative and man's response bring the community of believers into being, and for the Christian Church God's act centers in Jesus Christ and the work of the Holy Spirit.

We may regard this believing community strictly as the Christian body that began its earthly life after Jesus' death and resurrection. Or like Paul we may trace it back to the covenant with Abraham as man of faith; or like Augustine we may see it taking shape from the beginning of man's life on earth, under God's providence and the leading of Word and Spirit. It is no accident that in the Johannine prologue, those "who received him, who believed in his name," are spoken of before the incarnation; and that the author of Acts 10 has Peter, reluctant as he had been to visit Cornelius, the Gentile captain, acknowledge: "Truly I perceive that God shows no partiality, but in every nation any one who fears him and does what is right is acceptable to him." If the believing community be understood in this wider sense, it is not less truly a new creation: new in kind rather than simply in date, an earnest of God's creative purpose to "make all things new."

However broadly or narrowly the believing community be understood, it has by its very nature the ambivalence of all historical reality. God is faithful, but man is variable. Even in his best moments he is finite and fallible, and most of the time he is not at his best. In both individual and corporate response to God's holy presence, he betrays the imperfections of his spatially and temporally restricted, biologically and socially conditioned, insecure and sin-scarred existence. It is the grace of God, not the goodness of man, that keeps the Church, more than any other historical, institutional community, open toward heaven. This is another way of saying that the existence of the Church is eschatologically as well as historically determined. The Church of the Lord's purpose and of our hope, to be "presented before him in splendor, without spot or wrinkle," is most naturally to be understood as the Church fulfilled beyond the end of earthly history. To this issue we must return in due course.

Meanwhile, we shall do well to examine briefly the rich characterization of the Church in the New Testament. Both descriptive references and interpretative figures abound. We may begin with the primary name taken directly from the Greek Old Testament that served most early Christians as Scripture: *ekklesia,* an assembly summoned into being from among men and nations by the Word of God. In accord with the Johannine passage on the coming of the Light, this assembly differed from the ethnic churches bound together by blood-kinship, and from all simply cultural or voluntary religious associations. Its charter was a divine calling, decisively embodied in Jesus Christ. Moreover, it was not a loose aggregation of individuals, but an inwardly united community with the powerful sense of corporate identity and individual involvement that were so characteristic of Old Testament religion. The Church was but *one*, though its members were many and diverse. There are, of course, references to "churches" *(ekklesiai)*, but it seems generally agreed that these passages have essentially the same meaning as such phrases as "the church of the Thessalonians," or "the church of God which is at Corinth," or "to Nympha and the church in her house." The Church is one and the same, whether a congregation be assembled in Thessalonica or in Corinth or in a Laodicean home.

This one community is further characterized by a profusion of interpretative figures, which in spite of their variety help to build up a broadly coherent view.[1] We may notice five groups of such figures, and the facets they contribute to the total portrait.

(1) The Church is, first of all, a *chosen* community. It is God's people, over which he reigns, or his anointed one for him. It is a new Israel, "the twelve tribes in the dispersion," "Abraham's offspring," "like Isaac, children of promise," borne of a new covenant. It is God's flock, whose "chief shepherd" is Jesus Christ. It is an elect company of both Jews and Gentiles, whom God chose "in Christ . . . before the foundation of the world," "whose names are in the book of life." Each of these figures is elaborated, varied, and repeated in ways far too numerous to list. They are paralleled and strengthened by other figures that stress yet more powerfully the intimate personal relations into which the Church is drawn by God's choosing. It is "the household of God," and its members are "heirs of the kingdom," "children of God, and if children, then heirs, heirs of God and fellow heirs with Christ," his "brothers." Most daring of all these figures of election, reminiscent of the great prophetic images of Yahweh as the husband of Israel, is the image (tentative in Ephesians, climactic in the Apocalypse) of the Church as the bride of Christ, chosen, beloved, and sanctified at great cost. Basic to all of the figures just noticed is the concept of divine election: God has chosen us, not the other way about.

[1]Especial acknowledgment here is due to a widely used unpublished study prepared by Prof. Paul Minear in 1955, for the *Theological Commission on Christ and the Church*.

(2) Next comes a group of images representing the Church as a *holy* community. She is not only elect, called, chosen. She is the corporate assembly of "the saints," often called "they who are sanctified"; of "those that believe"; she is "the household of faith." Nay more, the Church is "the temple of God," in which God's Spirit dwells, a temple that is holy; and not only a temple but "a royal priesthood, a holy nation," "a spiritual house, . . . a holy priesthood." So elaborately is a variant of this theme worked out in the letter to the Hebrews that it forms, with the covenant motif, a large part of that sizeable epistle. The Church here is not temple or priesthood, but again a covenanted people and household whose "great high priest" by appointment of God is "Jesus, the Son of God," "the mediator of a new covenant." It is "a better covenant," under which there is only one sacrifice for sins: "when Christ had offered for all time a single sacrifice for sins, he sat down at the right hand of God," and by his sacrifice "we have been sanctified . . . once for all." So sternly is this insistence on sanctity maintained that any lapse into the apostasy of deliberate sin after baptism means no hope of further repentance, "but a fearful prospect of judgment, and a fury of fire." For this writer, and in somewhat milder terms for the author of 1 John, the holiness of the Church entails the sinlessness of all its members.

(3) A familiar group of images stress the *oneness* of the Church as a closely knit living whole. Here belongs the many passages, often descriptive rather than figurative, that center about the basic theme of *koinonia,* communion, participation—too often feebly translated "fellowship," which for present-day readers misses almost the whole meaning of such powerful phrases as "called into the *koinonia* of his Son, Jesus Christ our Lord," or "the *koinonia* of the Holy Spirit"; or "that you may have *koinonia* with us; and our *koinonia* is with the Father and with his Son Jesus Christ." Such expressions stress oneness, not mere togetherness; but not identity. With them belong the images of living vine and branches and the olive tree whose branches, natural or grafted, are "holy" because "the root is holy." Here too belongs the familiar and striking image of the body and its diverse members: the body that is one not despite but by reason of the ordered diversity of form and function of hand, foot, eye and ear. This figure is not uniformly but freely and variously used. Paul can say, "Now you are the body of Christ and individually members of

it," or, "so we, though many, are one body in Christ, and individually members one of another." In Colossians the cosmic Word in whom "all things were created," who "is before all things," and in whom "all things hold together"—"He is the head of the body, the church"; and then, "I rejoice in my sufferings . . . and in my flesh I complete what is lacking in Christ's afflictions for the sake of his body, that is, the church." So the writer to the Ephesians can say that Christ is the head from whom and into whom the whole body grows, or that Christ in glory is made "the head over all things for the church, which is his body, the fulness of him who fills all in all." It seems plain that this impressive figure, whose primary import in Romans and 1 Corinthians is clear enough, is used not with careful consistency as a technical doctrine, but as a powerful theme with free variations, some of them startling and not all of them easily harmonized.

(4) This figure of the body has its place also in a fourth group of images that present the Church as a *medium of divine action* in history. Here are the metaphors from the synoptic records, there applied to Jesus' disciples but presumably pertinent also to the growing Church: the salt of the earth, yeast in the lump, the torch in its holder giving light "to all in the house." Likewise, the Church as temple is not simply a dwelling but a place of intercession. The Church, moreover, with its worship and teaching, is a "way," and an entrance into the eternal sanctuary. Its members are slaves of God and of Christ, servants, stewards, ministers, ambassadors; they are disciples, witnesses, confessors. Through them God makes his appeal to the world of men. It seems right to include here also the figure of the body as instrument. Its members with their varied gifts, endowed and imbued with the Holy Spirit, do their part as prophets, deacons, teachers, preachers, givers, helpers, friends in need; so the work of God and of Jesus Christ goes on among men, and not least his sacrificial suffering, in a corporate community that is ready to suffer with him for mankind.

(5) Finally, the Church is an *eschatologically oriented* community. On earth it is a pilgrim people, a *diaspora,* a vast company of faithful "strangers and exiles on the earth . . . seeking a homeland" that is not here. On earth it is a rock-based fortress from which the gates of hell are being stormed. But in final truth it is "the new Jerusalem." Its members have "the Jerusalem above" as their mother, and they can endure suffering joyfully with a view to "the glory that is to be revealed." The writer to the

Hebrews by a superb *tour de force* of anticipation can write: "But you have come to Mount Zion and to the city of the living God, the heavenly Jerusalem, and to innumerable angels, in festal gathering, and to the assembly *(ekklesia)* of the first born who are enrolled in heaven, and to a judge who is God of all, and to the spirits of just men made perfect, and to Jesus, the mediator of a new covenant." Thus present and future and "a kingdom that cannot be shaken" blend in ecstatic vision.

The Church that understood its own existence in so richly and freely poetic, profound, and demanding ways naturally sought to acknowledge God's bounty and to reaffirm its faith worthily. The modes of acknowledgment and reaffirmation that developed are too familiar for detailed description. They can be summarized as word, sacrament, and ministry, shaped and implemented by order and discipline. In all these modes of church life, God's active presence and man's responses are everywhere involved.

The word, of preachers, prophets, and at length writers, presumably had two main bases: the living memory of the growing community, focused around the oft-repeated content of the *kerygma*, and the gradually accumulating results of "searching the scriptures" for support and illumination of the new teaching. The *kerygma*, the hard core of the preachers' message concerning the Messiah crucified and risen, evidently took a standardized form handed down from the eye witnesses and honored from a very early date (witness Paul's words) as "tradition," normative for proper reporting of the staggering events in which the Church's "gospel" centered. Like the *kerygma* and the more extensive and individually varied *evangelion* of the early preachers, the searching of the Scriptures—meaning almost always, it would seem, the Septuagint, that combined with the Old Testament an important handful of apocryphal books—kept the figure of Jesus Christ in the foreground. Its purpose was to seek out passages in the Pentateuch, the Prophets, the Psalms, the wisdom writings that seemed to substantiate the Church's teaching that the crucified one was in fact the Messiah, whose suffering had been foretold; that in him the very Wisdom of Yahweh, discernible in the reported theophanies of patriarchal times as well as in the explicit accounts in the wisdom literature, and variously called the hand, the arm, the power of Yahweh, was incarnate; that his resurrection as well as his suffering had been prophesied; that the supplanting of the synagogue by the Church could be learned from Isaiah; in a word, that the Old Testament closely studied and rightly understood gave authoritative support not to recalcitrant Judaism but to the new gospel. All these insights came under the guidance of the Holy Spirit—the same who enabled genuine believers to pronounce the earliest creedal statement we know: "Jesus is Lord!"

At the same time that "the word" was developing in several directions—oral tradition coming to be paralleled by written tradition within which at length a new canon of scripture came to be recognized, simple preaching and confession evolving into doctrine and creed—the Church in worship offered her thanks and affirmed her oneness and her faith and hope also in sacramental acts, *mysteria,* that served at once to express faith and to sustain it. In baptism each new convert, in Paul's understanding, could experience through the action of the Holy Spirit a sacramental participation in the Lord's death and resurrection: the ending of an old life and the beginning of a new one. In the Eucharist, an act of shared thanksgiving, believers at once commemorated the Lord's self-sacrifice for them, pledged anew their devotion to him and to one another, and reaffirmed their eager hope for the coming end and their reunion with him in heaven, all this again as sacramental participation in a shared life of body and spirit. In each of these sacraments the appropriate words—the traditional formula for baptism in the names of Father, Son, and Holy Ghost, the remembered words from the Last Supper and suitable eucharistic prayers—were an integral part. And the sacramental acts, in turn, had the force of enacted words. Of the Eucharist, Paul could say: "For as often as you eat this bread and drink the cup, you proclaim [*katangellete*] the Lord's death until he come."

The unhappy fact, attested by Paul's letters and the Book of Acts, that the oneness of the Church affirmed in both word and sacrament was too often violated in fact, even at the Lord's table, must not obscure the proper meaning and intent of these affirmations. The violations are characteristic evidence of that ambivalence of the life of the Church as historical community to which reference has already been made. They are the more shocking, perhaps, because of a long-standing tendency to idealize the first century community. Kept in due perspective, they may be salutary reminders that the unity we seek is to be found not by attempting to copy a past segment of history, but by opening the far more complex life of the Church in our day to the primary meanings of word and sacrament and to the onward movement of the Holy Spirit.

Not less basic than word and sacrament in the life of the Church is ministry to the world. Indeed, it would not be difficult to argue that in the recorded injunctions of Jesus to his disciples, ministry and mission have the primary place. "The Son of man came not to be served but to serve, and to give his life." "But I am among you as one who serves." "The harvest is plentiful, but the laborers are few. . . . Go your way; behold, I send you out. . . ." Add the words ascribed to the risen Lord: "As the Father has sent me, even so I send you." "Go therefore and make disciples of all nations." And in the tremendous vision of the final judgment: ". . . the King will answer them, 'Truly, I say to you, as you did it to one of the least of these my brethren, you did it to me.' " Included in these injunctions to ministry and mission, as the early Church came to understand them, are preaching of the Word, administration of baptism, and service to those who are in need. Ministry in the broadest sense embraces them all. The Church like the Master must serve, else its witness is empty and its sacraments falsified.

Partly for this reason, order and discipline in the New Testament Church were factors of growing importance, but now by no means easy to describe or appraise. Obviously the ecstatic freedom of a congregation in which prophesying and speaking with tongues could produce a new Babel, and disorder at the Lord's table a sheer sacrilege, could not go on unchecked, without affront to One who is "not a God of confusion but of peace." Similarly, the moral problems of new converts from paganism, to say nothing of the legalistic scruples of some converts from Judaism, required sober practical wisdom and firm leadership. That such leadership took form initially from a number of existential factors in combination seems likely: carry-over of Jewish tradition and practice in the earliest generations, prestige of the apostles and men like James, the Lord's brother, division of labor to suit the new conditions of life in a mistrusted, occasionally persecuted minority sect, and recognition of diverse individual "gifts." It may be that "bishops" (*episkopoi*, supervisors) and "deacons" (*diakonoi*, assistants) are first to emerge from the informal medley of God's "appointees" (1 Cor. 12:28; cf. 1 Tim. 3:1-13), but "presbyters" (*presbyteroi*, elders) "who rule well" seem to have similarly honorable mention, "especially those who labor in preaching and teaching." (1 Tim. 4:17.)

It is well known that the proliferation of irregular versions of Christian preaching, teaching, and living prompted closer control all along the line: adoption of an authoritative canon of New Testament scriptures, formulation and requirement of creedal "watchwords" *(symbola)*, elaborate catechetical preparation for baptism. In line with these other measures, exaltation of episcopal authority at least in the local congregation, and efforts to work out a practical Christian ethic for the changing life of the Church and its members, were appropriate developments of order and discipline.

B. *As Growing Community in History*

To speak of such developments, at once adaptive and indigenous to the Church, is to turn attention from its beginnings to its protracted struggle with the world and with itself. In this section it is obvious that not even an outline is feasible, but only some marginal comments.

We may well begin with a familiar evidence of the Church's increasingly reflective, critical self-consciousness and its need for clearer differentiation of itself not only from "the world" but also from the multitude of *haireseis*—"heretical" sects following arbitrary, erratic versions of the Christian teaching and way of life. By the end of the patristic period, four "notes" or distinguishing characters of the Church had come to be generally affirmed, though the precise meaning ascribed to each could vary with different interpreters. By common consent the true Church was declared to be one, holy, catholic, and apostolic.

Its *unity,* which in the earliest days could be directly and vividly felt, very early had to be spelled out and consciously urged: "There is one body and one Spirit, . . . one hope, . . . one Lord, one faith, one baptism, one God and Father of us all." As new congregations were established in many parts of the empire, separated by differences of region, language, and culture, direct awareness of unity became more difficult, at the same time that the challenge of multiplying heresies and schisms made a defensible claim to unity more imperative. The practical solution was to stress tests of unity more objective than immediate intuition: acceptance of the one "rule of faith" or "rule of truth," increasingly represented by formal creeds; acknowledgment of the one authoritative tradition taught since the days of the eyewitnesses, written down in the canonical Gospels, Epistles, and Apocalypse, and guaranteed by the testimony of Law, Prophets, and Writings of the Old Testament; and maintenance of formal communion with an increasingly hierarchical clergy. This practical working concept of unity was meant not to displace the more immediate experience of oneness "in the Spirit," expressed in unanimity of witness, but to implement and support it. Yet there is little doubt that under the pressure of apologetic and polemical needs, the direction of emphasis was being shifted.

Holiness like unity was, as we have seen, a basic character in the New Testament pictures of the Church. But its precise meaning was even less easy to agree upon than the meaning of unity. For one thing, holiness was a term of dual ancestry (though ultimately both strains had a common source, itself ambivalent). On the one hand, holiness meant apartness, sacredness, awesomeness, showing kinship with the powerful charismatic mysteries of *mana* and *tabu*. On the other hand, in prophetic Hebrew religion holiness had come especially to mean transcendent righteousness. When the Church of the first three centuries was called holy, both of these strains were included, with varying emphases and with very many complications in detail and shifts of direction, as the life of the Church and its forms of order have become more diverse.

The primary distinction springs from the original duality in meaning of the term *holy*.[2] Some have laid chief stress on the ethical sense of the term, and have understood the phrase "holy Church" to mean primarily a Church somehow distinguished by moral worthiness. To such a Church the powerful presence and the gifts of the Holy Spirit are granted. Others have put first the sacramental or charismatic sense of the term. For them the Church is holy primarily as recipient and custodian on earth of "the means of grace": the Word and especially the sacraments. They hold that the sanctifying power therein is God's power, whose acts are not conditioned upon the moral rectitude of men, but are truly acts of unmerited grace, that work to overcome evil with good.

Each of these major views has taken diverse special forms. Moral rigorists in the early Church and in various later sects have held that the entire membership of the Christian community must be free from sin, or at least from "mortal sins," and that grave offenders must be expelled. Others have held that at least a faithful nucleus must live as saints: the clergy or at least the higher clergy, monastic followers of a more exacting "way of perfection," an inner circle of "true believers" in distinction from nominal or indolent church members. Still others reject every claim to simple rectitude either for the whole community or for any of its mem-

---

[2] The pattern of these paragraphs results from a suggestion of Prof. E. R. Hardy.

bers, and hold that the only righteousness possible for men is the
God-given status of forgiven sinners. Common to all these views
is the conviction that the existence of the Church cannot be so
held apart from the lives of its members that the Church remains
essentially unaffected by what they are and do. At the same time,
all would agree that man's righteousness comes from God, that
the Holy Spirit works freely through means of his own choosing,
and that the Church's holiness is God's gift.

It is at this point that the closest approach is made to the second major view: that the holiness of the Church is most fitly
understood as primarily sacramental or charismatic, rather than
moral. Granted that the Spirit is free to act through many means
to save men, it remains true that the Word and the recognized
sacraments (two, or seven, or some other number) have been
especially appointed as "means of grace." These have been entrusted to the Church, whose holiness consists first of all in this
trust and the saving power it embodies. This view, like the former,
is held in various ways. Some hold that Word and sacraments have
been entrusted to the whole congregation of believers, who com-
pose the "holy Church." Others hold that not in practical expediency alone, but in reality, the means of grace are given into
the keeping of priests and bishops, or of ministers, "rightly ordained" who administer Word and sacraments not as representatives of the congregation but as consecrated appointees of the
Lord. To them especially and essentially the sacramental power
and holiness of the Church pertains. Still others affirm that the
holy Church is a real being distinct from its members, both clergy
and laity, and that its holiness is the true perfection of a living
body that is even now "without spot or wrinkle, . . . holy and
without blemish."

Next among the "notes of the Church" is *catholicity,* another
term of varied meaning. The primary and most obvious sense, of
course, is wholeness and universality, whether in geographic extent, inclusiveness of membership, or freedom from provincialism
in temper and interest. When Ignatius of Antioch first used the
phrase *ekklesia katholike,* it seems to have been in this first sense,
or in an even simpler sense: "The Church as a whole," in contrast
to the Church in Antioch, in Smyrna, in Rome. But before the
second century ended, the term was used at least as often to mean
the orthodox Church as against the sectarian heresies. Enthusiasts
like Tertullian and the Montanists used it scornfully to label the
majority Church as dull-spirited and unheroic, and the Donatists

later did the same. Against these would-be followers of Cyprian, Augustine proposed a modified combination of the first two meanings. For him the catholic Church is both orthodox and inclusive, though not all-embracing, having members in every nation and in every social class and walk of life. Finally, with the quick succession of changes and divisions in the sixteenth and seventeenth centuries, the term has been claimed especially by conservative defenders of ancient tradition, liturgy, and order, and of the primacy of the sacraments in the life of the Church; and, somewhat ironically, the same term (with a small c) is claimed by some ultra-liberals who are uneasy at being called Protestants. In short, this word that seems to promise room for all Christians has been made an instrument of partisanship.

The fourth "note" is *apostolicity*. Here the initial meaning was simple and clear: the Church *sent* by divine appointment, as apostles are sent, on mission to the world. But other meanings quickly overlaid this one. Apostolic churches in the first two centuries were congregations in particular cities that were known or believed to have been founded by apostles or their close companions. Again the polemic against heresies brought complication. For against the novelty and variety of heretical teachings, the Church's appeal was to the antiquity and unity of the apostolic tradition; and Irenaeus argued strongly that the simplest way for the Church to establish its title to the authentic teaching of the apostles was to show an unbroken line of known witnesses in churches of apostolic foundation. Here the primary stress was on the traditional teaching, and the line of successive bishops in an apostolic foundation was to guarantee that the teaching was truly that received from the eyewitnesses. But with the rivalries among the great sees for preferment, claims were pressed on the ground of apostolic inheritance not only to authentic teaching but to jurisdictional authority for successors to the apostles. Most of all at Rome, and perhaps most forcefully in patristic times by Leo I, this claim was carried a final step further. As Peter had been given jurisdiction even over his fellow apostles, so his successors in Rome (called in due course "the Apostolic See") had rightful jurisdiction over all other Christians, including their fellow bishops and patriarchs.

In face of these accumulated complications, is it possible so to characterize the Church in history that the cherishable values signalized by the traditional "notes" may be conserved? I suggest two sorts of characterization.

The first was proposed years ago by an Anglican friend who asked whether the current existence of the Church might be described as "sacramental existence": the phenomena of the Church's life on its human side being the outward visible sign of an inward spiritual grace. This seems to me right. It takes seriously both clauses in the creed: "the communion of saints, the forgiveness of sins" (*communionem sanctorum, remissionem peccatorum*), and treats them as not separable. It views the Church as living community at once of grace and of faith.

The Church thus is seen as genuinely historical reality, having its true being not simply within any moment or segment of time, yet not apart from time, since the grace of God, the decisive redemption in Jesus Christ, and the power of the Holy Spirit work within time and space and history, yet from beyond all these. The historical variations and deviations of the Church are then to be viewed as truly ingredients in its historical existence: not as irrelevancies or unrealities, but as real and visible signs of struggle, of gain and loss, to be transcended but not to be minimized.

A second characterization comes from the New Testament age, when indeed it was sometimes all too prominent, and disavows the habit many centuries old of treating the Church almost as a secular *fait accompli*. It affirms again that the Church is an eschatologically oriented community. Just as in the preceding view its source of life works from before and beyond, but not apart from the events of its earthly history, so in this view its goal and fulfillment is beyond the boundary toward which its history moves, yet already accessible to faith and hope, and inseparable from the Church's present existence—inseparable, but not simply continuation of it; for in this perspective fulfillment involves transformation so drastic that death and resurrection provide the terms in which we try to think of it.

In these two perspectives, the traditional "notes" can have vital meaning. Our unity is real now primarily in God and his gracious action in our history, not primarily in what we do. It is real in Jesus Christ as our head and quickener of our faith, and in the Holy Spirit tirelessly giving us life. But by participation it is real also in us, when we cease to claim it and instead open ourselves to it in penitence and common prayer. By insisting on making unity in our own image, we accentuate our differences. In seeking to see more clearly and steadily the springing of our many streams from one fountain, we find ourselves startled again and again by the realization that "the river of truth is one." Our unity is real also in the end toward which we all move. And again by participation that unity is effective and imperative in our existence now.

To speak thus is to speak the language of faith, concerning the life of faith as continuing gift of God. We cannot point to any moment or form or order of the Church's earthly life and say, "Here unity is perfectly achieved." We can trust God's purpose and power to maintain and to enhance living unity among us and within us. We can look in faith to Jesus Christ as Lord of the Church and of mankind and see in him—who is one Lord of us all—the power and wisdom of God making us one. We can discern, often in ways unexpected and sometimes disconcerting, the flooding and dissolving of old barriers, and the surging of new life in new interrelations, where the Holy Spirit is at work.

Such God-given unity is wholeness. But wholeness is health and holiness. And wholeness is catholicity. The unity we seek is all of these together: God's saving gift evoking our response.

So, too, holiness belongs to God, not to us. Yet again the Church and we its members are participants in it when "the mind that was in Christ Jesus" works in us as norm and motive. It is not possible to separate the Church from its members, and to ascribe perfect holiness now to the Church though not to its members. But neither is it possible to reduce the Church to a sum of individuals, and its holiness to their virtues. The Church as sacramental corporate community is in distinctive ways the meeting-place of God and man; and where God is—in bush or stable or "the place of a skull"—there is holy ground, but not holiness unclouded, even in the Church. And even at the end, we shall not become God and so achieve perfection. Our hope is, rather, that in the Church transformed and purged, we may see and rejoice in God's holiness, and in our ways reflect it and be lighted by it.

The catholicity of the Church, we have said, is wholeness— which is to say inseparable from the unity and holiness of God-given health. Because the Church for faith and hope is one and holy, she is in the most basic sense catholic. At the same time, she must be catholic also in two other historic senses of the word: inclusive and "orthodox," believing rightly.

The catholicity of the Church must be at least inclusiveness in intent and effort. As God wills that all men shall be saved, so must the Church will and give herself wholeheartedly to that end. Catholicity cannot mean indifference or unconcern for truth and right. Without these no one can be saved. But it must mean communion among all Christians and recognition among all Christian communions with trust that God can deal with our honest differences but cannot be served by a withholding of generous response to any neighbor who needs our understanding and brotherhood.

To see catholicity as inclusiveness in purpose and devotion is to see it as inseparable from apostolic mission. To see it as orthodoxy is at once to declare its involvement with the apostolic tradition that is our common heritage. The Church that is thus catholic must be apostolic, in outreach and in continuity of message.

But apostolicity goes much further in its meaning for the Church's life. Unity and holiness are likewise determined by it in essential ways. The unity we seek cannot be self-centered or self-seeking unity. It must be the unity of a devoted embassy from one beloved Sovereign, with one urgent message to a world in need. The holiness given to the Church is not a possession but a trust for others. Its measure of health is to be found, not in retirement and apartness, but in outgoing service: in the life that spends itself and only thus can find its own fulfillment. The one holy catholic Church must be, in this self-giving way, the apostolic Church, sent "not to be served but to serve."

The unity we seek is real now. But it is not our possession. It is our source of life and our goal in the mercy of God.

Our Common History as Christians

ADDRESS BY PROFESSOR ALBERT C. OUTLER
SEPTEMBER 4, 1957

It is a great honor and privilege for me to be able to speak to you tonight as chairman of the North American Section of the Commission on Tradition and Traditions. I have no official findings of our commission to report, for we have not yet reached that stage in our work. Nor do I pretend to represent the unanimous opinion of our group—for the commission was not chosen with a view to easy agreement and thus far our only real consensus centers on the importance and relevance of our problem rather than in any massive substantive conclusions. Instead, I shall try to interpret for you the basic issues with which we are wrestling—and something of the mood in which we are going about our work. I should also like to give you some notion of the urgent, practical bearing which our project has for all of the concerns which have brought us together here at Oberlin. But, most of all (and here I do speak for the whole commission), we want to enlist you and your churches in this tremendous undertaking of exploring the theological import of the historical experience of the Christian community. We are attempting nothing less than the reappraisal of the significance of the history of Christianity because we believe that, in such a reappraisal, we may recover a sense of our common Christian history as a vital force in all our present searchings for unity. Our project is not merely an affair for historians, however. It asks of every Christian, who is even dimly aware of the historical continuity of the Christian community from New Testament times down to our own, this question: What is the present meaning, to you and to your fellow Christians, of this vast and baffling heritage of nineteen centuries? This question arises, inevitably, in one form or another, at every turn in our ecumenical conversations, and a lack of well-founded answers contributes to the difficulty of most ecumenical discussion. We believe, therefore, that alongside the great issues of the other study commissions of Faith and Order, our commission has a theme that concerns all Christians. It follows from our Lord's imperative that those who bear his name shall share in his *koinonia*. Hence our hope that we may have your interest and your aid and that our project may become a general concern in all our churches.

Every ecumenical gathering—and Oberlin is as good an example as any—presents a strange and painful anomaly. We are here as Christians who recognize our oneness in Christ and our dividedness in the churches. We would not be here unless we already knew that the bonds that unite us are stronger than the bars that separate us. And yet we also would not be here unless we were aware that the unity we seek is something far richer and more vital than the unity we already have. We have uneasy consciences about our distance from each other; we feel *some* pain and frustration that we cannot enter directly into full communion with each other, and this is true even of those who withhold their communion from others. And yet most of us have good consciences about our divisions, too. For they represent concerns about the Christian Gospel to which we feel we must be faithful even at the cost of estrangement from some of our Christian brethren. We feel the scandal of disunity and we acknowledge the divine imperative to community. But we are also committed to the essentials of the Gospel truth, as we have received them. We cannot surrender any *essential* element in the Gospel as the price of unity, and we will resist the imposition of any nonessential as if it belonged to the essence of the Gospel and the Church. We are sincere in our ecumenical profession. But what price unity? And what assurance do we have that the unity *we* seek is the unity which *God* wills for his people? This conflict of convictions cannot be reduced by good will alone.

It is possible, if we speak in general enough terms, to describe the nature of the unity we are seeking. One can see its motifs in the papers produced by our pre-Oberlin study groups and in the ecumenical literature generally. What we are after is a *community* (a *koinonia*) of Christians who share, among themselves, one Lord, one faith, one baptism, one Eucharist and one mission—in which all who confess our Lord Jesus Christ as God and Savior have a responsible place and a true belonging. We are seeking a *community* of Christian faith and teaching, of hope and expectation, of worship and mission. Yet, for the life of us, we cannot frame the formulae by which this *koinonia* may be achieved. Some of us are rather impatient that this should be so. We are, we think, ready for union now, and we are offended by those who reject our own eager, openhearted advances on the ground that, in their eyes, our doctrines are not pure enough or our sacraments are defective or irregular. And some of us are very patient about the situation as it is, so patient, indeed, that one wonders if they are not a little pleased that God seems to move so slowly in such affairs that they are unlikely to suffer any drastic change in their traditions in their own lifetime.

I have a vivid memory of an incident at Lund when things had got very sticky in our section and we were all being very "confessional" and defensive. I felt impelled to complain of this deadlock in what I supposed was a tone of righteous indignation! It was the late, beloved Pierre Maury who replied to my outburst, and afterwards I knew what it was to have been dealt with by a saint. He spoke, with deep feeling of *la tristesse oecumenique,* the ecumenical sadness, that Christians feel who see their eager will to unity frustrated. But then he reminded us that progress in this cause is never gained by votes or victories in debate. Divided Christians are brought together by the inner, imperceptible changes wrought by the Holy Spirit in the hearts and minds of men who are centered on their common Lord and mindful of their common history in the Gospel. Once said, it seemed self-evident. But it is easily forgotten and bears repetition.

We have come to Oberlin to face this ecumenical anomaly *together,* for when we are apart, it is all too easy to pass it by as we press on to our more urgent business in our ecclesiastical Jerichos. We have come here to speak and to listen; to be led, to be changed, but only by the Spirit who testifies to the Lordship of Christ and our oneness in him. And if we *are* deeply changed (in the literal sense of *metanoesis*), we may then become agents of change in our churches. And if *this* happens, Oberlin will mark the breakthrough of the ecumenical cause into the broad midrange of North American Christianity, and a much-needed new frontier in our search for unity will have been opened up.

OUR PLURAL TRADITIONS

Some such perspective as this guides the work of the Theological Study Commissions, and it is in some such light as this that our several projects are properly to be understood and evaluated. In each instance, the common aim is to find a way toward the unity we seek by penetrating more deeply into the meaning of the unity we have, God-given in Christ Jesus.

The approach of our Commission on Tradition and Traditions can best be understood, I think, if we begin with this conference here at Oberlin as a sort of case-study in the problem of tradition and traditions. Here we are, representatives of and spokesmen for some forty different traditions, and we call them all "Christian," in *some* sense or other. But, in order to converse intelligibly with Christians of different backgrounds than our own, we must be able to stand both in and out of our own traditions and move at least a little way into the *other* traditions represented here. Our ability—and our disposition—to do this is one of the basic measures of our real catholicity. But how *can* we do this? What makes it possible? What do our plural traditions have in common that warrants our calling each one of them "Christian," in *some* sense or other? The right answers to these questions would go a long way to reducing the ecumenical anomaly, and it is just such answers that our commission is groping for.

Our problem can be defined, in yet another way, by asking a different sort of question about our conference: How did we all *get* to Oberlin anyhow? Would it interest you if it were possible to reverse the reel of church history and run it backwards, slowly enough so that we could trace the maze of pathways that now converge on this particular occasion, this unique *kairos?* What a panorama it would make—and what a jumble! Each of us could trace his own tradition's pathway back through time, but this still would not bring us all out at one spot and one time when there was only one, single, historical tradition to which *some* Christians have clung, without any change whatsoever, and from which the rest of us have fallen away into plural, schismatic traditions. Historical inquiry simply cannot discover such a single, unaltered empirical continuity, visible to the critical historian, in the whole historical experience of the Christian community. This is one reason why so much modern church history is so heavily partisan or so boldly relativistic.

We all know how it feels to live inside our own familiar, partisan traditions. I know my own Methodist tradition, after a fashion. But do I know much about yours, and yours? And do I really understand my own until I have also understood yours? And, vice versa, do you really understand yours until you have understood the rest of us well enough to recognize what we do, or what we could have in common with you and what we have only to ourselves? But even if we all sincerely tried to do this retracing of our plural histories backward, we would still have a problem. We cannot, on order, cancel our separate histories in favor of a common history which we have not actually experienced. These separate histories of ours have done their work of separating us, and they now constitute an unavoidable part of our present anomaly.

The Methodist history I can trace and the Anglican history my Anglican brethren can trace constitute both a bond and a bar between us. We cannot annul this, nor can they. Nor can either ask the other to repudiate his own history, for that particular history was the means by which the Gospel was mediated to him and to his people.

The tragic fact is, then, that our separate traditions have divided us and keep us still divided in spite of all our longings for unity. Moreover, their separate histories continue to separate Christians who have much else in common, as among the Lutherans despite Augustana; as between the Orthodox and the Romans despite their common dogmas; as between Lutherans and Calvinists despite their common appeal to *sola Scriptura;* as among the motley of the American "free churches" despite their common ethos. The fact is that there are so many Christian traditions and they are so divisive that the first and obvious conclusion of modern historical inquiry is that Christian history is incurably pluralistic and relativistic. It is no wonder, then, that modern Christians find it difficult to think of historical knowledge as an ecumenical resource or of our common history as Christians.

THE CHRISTIAN TRADITION

And yet here, as in many another realm, a little learning is a dangerous thing. We cannot re-enact the past or rewrite the script of history. And if this is what we are after, then historical understanding is useless, at least for the cause of Christian unity. It is even something of a handicap to know too many of the sordid details of our Christian past. *But there is something else that we can do.* We can, in the living present, re-enter the "dead past" and discover what made it alive when it was the living present! We can think and feel our way back into our own traditions and those of other Christians, with an open eye and heart to the presence and power of Jesus Christ in them, as *the* vital tradition common to them all. We can discover that our common Christian history is not so much a matter of *a* tradition superior to all the rest as it is the influence of *the* Christian tradition in them all, continuously informing and measuring all the *traditiones ecclesiarum.* This reliving, rethinking, refeeling the past does not change the past so much as it transforms our own situation in the present and the future! The bad essence of *traditionalism,* which some of us fear so much, is simply letting the past continue to dominate the oncoming future without its being relived and renewed in the living present. The good essence of historical insight is that it opens the way to our making a present decision toward the past and so to change our posture toward the future. If we could really renew our sense of history, we could begin to re-orient our plural and divisive traditions toward the future in such a way as to make us ready for the changes and challenges it will bring. The unity that we seek is not so much to be recovered from some past unity as it is *to be grown into,* under the guidance and power of the Holy Spirit who is still with us to lead us into the fullness of the truth in Christ Jesus. This is the truth that would make us free, indeed; free *from* the dead past, free in the living present, free for the oncoming future. But no man and no group can grow into this future unless their sense of history is clear and full enough to give them creative freedom toward their respective pasts. If we are to grow into the fullness of the unity we have, we must recover and fill out our Christian memories. For it is in this Christian past which now divides us that we shall also find a clue to the unity that we have and the unity that we seek.

The creative use of Christian history may be seen when Christians whose histories separate them can recognize in all their several histories the action of the Holy Spirit in *renewing* the Gospel as it was received in them from the preceding generations. The Gospel is transmitted from age to age, but it is stultified by simple repetition. It must be renewed every time it is "received," else it is not really received. The original Christian "traditio" (handing over) was God's gift of Jesus Christ for us men and our salvation, and the essential *church* tradition is the apostolic witnessing to this deed and its meaning for mankind (deed and witness). *The* Christian tradition is, to put it quite simply, God's deed and man's faithful witness to that deed. When this tradition is "traditioned" (handed over) to any oncoming generation by the Church (through the Word and the sacraments), it must still be *renewed* by an *actus tradendi*—an act of traditioning—which changes the *recital* of the apostolic history into a living encounter with the living Lord in the living present. And this *actus tradendi,* as we can plainly see in the New Testament and in the life of the Church, is the act and office of the Holy Spirit. This process of transforming the apostolic witness into living faith and fellowship is what we may recognize as *the* Christian tradition in all Christian history. The process has gone on in many different historical settings and in many different traditions, but it has never fallen prisoner to any one of them. *The* Christian tradition is the life's blood of all church traditions and their valid measure. When we can recognize the Spirit's act of traditioning in our own history and in the histories of other Christians, we thereby recognize our common history as Christians. From this recognition comes then an understanding of what is identical and continuous in our plural histories; what it is that makes us able to recognize each other as Christians; what it is that justifies the use of the adjective "Christian" as a valid modified.

THE UNIQUE HISTORICAL EVENT

Our common Christian history is not merely the sum of our separate histories and certainly not their lowest common denominator. Rather, it is the sense and insight which Christians have that God has been at work in our history and in the histories of others and that these histories have been the medium appointed or permitted through which his revelation has been transmitted through space and time. Such a conception implies that the history which separates us from the event of Christ (as *traditum*) is also the indispensable nexus which connects us with that event (in the *actus tradendi* of the Holy Spirit). The histories which separate us from each other contain the common history which still holds us together.

Christianity is a historical religion. This means more than that Christianity is a historical phenomenon, that it *has* a history. It means that everything in the Christian message roots in a unique historical event, which gathers up the old history of the people of Israel and creates the new history of the Christian community. The Christian Gospel inescapably has to do with events in time, in and through which God has revealed himself and in such a fashion that the revelation can never be abstracted from its historical context. We believe that God has chosen to reveal himself in genuinely human events and to appoint the procession of human events (history) as the bond between the revelatory events and all consequent events. The Christian community emerged as the effect of such a revelatory event, the event of Jesus Christ, God's unique act of self-revelation which sums up (and reveals) *all* his revelations. This community has continued to the present moment by means of the traditionary process of receiving, renewing and transmitting the essential witness of that first community and the encounter with Christ which this effects. We today, in our separated communions, are dependent upon the infinitely complex process of transmission by which the apostolic witness has reached us and on the integrity of this historical process which links us to the originative event of Christianity. History is thus an essential ingredient in the *whole* Gospel!

Every Christian has a Christian history. It is the sum of all the past events accessible to his memory and will, which have served to represent to him the apostolic witness to Jesus Christ. It is the impact of the Christian past which confronts him—and others— with the claim of Jesus Christ to be the living center of his existence. It was in some sort of Christian community that each of us heard the Gospel preached and at a time when we could not judge whether it was preached well or ill. Then, as we discovered the history of our own communion, and the histories of other and disparate communions, we began to have some fuller measure of the common meaning of what we have heard and believed and what other Christians have heard and believed. It is in some such way as this that the discovery of our *total* Christian past can become one of the most effective means of fuller initiation into the *whole* Christian community.

It is, then, this search for the identity and continuity of the Christian message as a whole, in the historical experience of the Christian community, that is the essential project of the Commission on Tradition and Traditions. It is obviously a formidable and baffling undertaking. We have chosen to approach it under a somewhat strange rubric. Many Protestants, on first hearing the phrase "Tradition and Traditions," leap to the conclusion that it contains a predetermined thesis which they are disposed to reject at the outset. It smacks of traditionalism, and we tend to forget that traditionalism can, and does, afflict even the least traditionary churches. Others fear that we may try to set up tradition as an equal and parallel authority to Holy Scripture. It is, they suspect, a large and needless concession to the Orthodox doctrine of Holy Tradition or even the Roman.

Actually, these baleful suspicions are unjust, as are most suspicions founded on fear and mistrust, for traditions are simply the residues or *deposita* of history. They are just that part of history that "sticks" and continues to function in a later age and situation. If we are to study the theological import of history, the most efficient way to do it, we think, is to explore the historical residues (i.e., traditions) that have developed in the Christian community, and to ask if, and wherein, they exhibit anything in common which can honestly be called the unitive or essential continuity of Christian history. We are not trying to decide which of the existing Christian traditions is *the* Christian tradition—we know where that would end! But we are eager to confirm the hypothesis first proposed by the Lund Report that in our ecumenical experience we have found a common history, which we share as Christians, which is longer, richer and more truly catholic than any of the separate histories of our divided churches. And we invite you to join us in this testing of the Lund hypothesis.

THE WORK OF THE COMMISSION

For the project, we have enlisted the services of two remarkable groups of Christian scholars, in a European and an American section. The chairman of the European section is Professor K. E. Skydsgaard of Copenhagen. The other members of the section are Professor Constantine Bonis of Athens, Daniel Jenkins of London, Dean Einar Molland of Oslo, Canon S. L. Greenslade of Durham, Professor Gerhard Ebeling of Zurich and Professor J. L. Leuba of Neuchatel. In our North American section, we have Father Georges Florovsky of Harvard, David W. Hay of Knox College, Toronto, Professor Eugene R. Fairweather of Trinity College, Toronto, Professor Wilhelm Pauck of Union, Professor Jaroslav Jan Pelikan of Chicago, and Professor William A. Clebsch of the Episcopal Seminary of the Southwest. The very personnel of these commissions furnishes us with a sort of laboratory situation for testing our theories. Almost every major tradition in Christendom (except the Roman Catholic) is represented in them and our plan is to enlarge both sections in order to make them even more fully representative. The groups exhibit a wide diversity of theological and historiographical positions. But there is one outstanding common trait in every member: an unswerving theological integrity (which includes, incidentally, a rugged individualism). You will readily understand that our heterogeneity adds to our difficulties in getting ahead with our work. Yet it also adds immensely to the value of the work we do get done.

The European section is focusing mainly on the problem of tradition in the New Testament and the early church. They are grappling with such issues as the Canon and the Church, the Holy Spirit and History, Tradition and Dogma. The North American section has chosen, for its part, a more synoptic and descriptive program. We hope eventually to provide historical surveys of the conception and function of tradition (in both its unitive and

pluralistic senses) in various crucial periods of the experience of
the Christian community: the ante-Nicene church; the Ecumenical Councils; the Reformation and the Protestant scholastics;
Anglicanism, from the sixteenth through the nineteenth centuries;
Nonconformity in England and Scotland, etc. . . . In addition,
we aim to survey the impact of modern historical knowledge on
the concept of tradition and the problem of "the essence of Christianity" in the nineteenth and twentieth centuries. We are also
in the process of formulating a project on the distinctive shifts in
the concept of tradition in American Christianity. Working papers
have been produced on most of these topics; they have come under
vigorous review and criticism. Two of our papers have been published and others will be. I have tried to develop my own understanding of how our theme bears on the whole cause of Christian
unity in a little book, *The Christian Tradition and the Unity We
Seek*. It is, however, in no sense an official publication of the commission.

There is some evidence that our work is helping to stimulate
interest in the reform of church history both as a theological discipline and as an ecumenical resource. The Ecumenical Institute
at Bossey has already sponsored one such consultation of historians
and is planning another. The American Church History Society
is sharing our concern and giving it a place in its programs. And
while we have been groping our way into our problem, which still
has an unfamiliar "feel" in Protestant hands, our Roman Catholic
brethren are also turning out a very impressive amount of work, in
review and reappraisal of their now "traditional" (i.e., Tridentine)
doctrine of tradition. You may be interested to see Father Tavard's
The Concept of Tradition Before and After Trent and Professor
Geiselmann's (Tubingen) monumental three-volume symposium
on tradition. From these studies we can all profit immensely.

It is a quite extraordinary privilege to be working with such
a group of men and in such an enterprise. We are firmly convinced, after three years of fumbling labor, that we are at grips
with a basic, unevadable issue, a real ecumenical problem which,
though vast and probably unmanageable, is nonetheless relevant
and urgent.

OUR BOND OF UNITY

What final form our work will—and should—take is beyond
our present knowing. What matters more than that is whether
the churches, now divided by their separate histories, will begin

to consider and share with us this inquiry into the significance of our Christian past for our Christian hope.

The very power that prompts us now to rejoice in our God-given unity in Christ and to recognize each other as Christians comes in part from this historical experience of the Christian community. For this is what links us through the ages with the apostolic age. This is what has brought to us the tradition to which the apostles are the primary witnesses. This tradition, received from the past and through historical time, is being renewed for us in the present by the *actus tradendi* of the Holy Spirit, and may be transmitted to the oncoming future by the Word and the sacraments in the churches. This is what keeps the Church from having to be *bound* to its past (traditionalism). This is what keeps us really open to the future and to the eschatological consummation of tradition when the Son shall reverse the traditionary process and *hand back* the kingdom to the Father, that God may be all in all.

God's spirit has never left the Church which he brought forth and which he has been sustaining through the long drama of its history and which he continues to upbuild and guide while time shall last. And all those who acknowledge the Spirit's gifts and fruits in other Christians of other traditions are thus enabled to recognize the common history which they share with them. Within and behind our plural traditions we become aware of a singular and per-durable tradition which is our bond of unity and the vital medium in which we may be led by the Spirit into the unity we seek, but which, of course, may be quite different from the unity we now expect. We are not asked to despise, but, alternatively, also not to absolutize, our own traditions. Rather, we must become really open to the traditions of other Christians; we must be willing to "grow together into a holy temple in the Lord."

I said, in the beginning, that this is not merely an affair for specialists. This is worth repeating now, at the end. For what your commission is trying to do is also a part of the proper business of *all* of us who have any care for the common life in the body of Christ. Only in such a *koinonia* (of common faith and common history) can we learn to speak and to do the truth in love. Only so can we grow up *together* into him who is our Head, into Christ, who was and is and shall be the Lord of life, of the Scriptures and of his Church!

Institutionalism in Relation to Unity and Disunity

ADDRESS BY DEAN WALTER G. MUELDER

SEPTEMBER 5, 1957

More than doctrine divides the churches. This fact, commonly recognized in the ecumenical movement, provides the background of the work of the Commission on Institutionalism. The study of institutionalism concentrates on but a small part of that large number of social, economic, political and cultural factors which beset the efforts at expressing the unity of the church. These factors—always operative, sometimes decisive—have been largely neglected by the Faith and Order program as a whole. This neglect points up the well-known self-sufficiency and introversion of much theologizing, both traditional and current. The neglect of a serious study by theologians of institutional factors may itself reflect their assumptions about the nature of Christianity and the interrelations of church and society. We may ask, "Is this neglect a symptom of the subtle docetism which remains such a pervasive and persuasive temptation in Christian thought?" The situation certainly reflects the incompatibility of temper and research methods still existing between theology and sociology; their blessed marriage is still part of the eschatological hope.

I. Historical Background of the Commission on Institutionalism

In our report to the Commission on Faith and Order in 1956 we traced briefly the repeated attempts made by the commission to focus attention on the indisputable ingredient of the social and cultural factors in all interchurch relations. In preparation for the Edinburgh Conference in 1937, an American group under Dean Sperry produced a pioneering report on "The Non-theological Factors in the Making and Unmaking of Church Union." It shared the not infrequent fate of preparatory reports in receiving hardly any attention at the conference, and even less afterwards. The reappraisal of the ecumenical situation after the Second World War —including reflections on the Amsterdam Assembly of 1948— made it evident that a new inquiry was called for. In June, 1949, Professor C. H. Dodd, in a now famous letter, strikingly highlighted the fact of unavowed motivations and unconscious assumptions in interchurch attitudes. This letter was followed up by an international consultation, and the ensuing report, "Social and Cultural Factors in Church Division," was presented to the Lund Conference on Faith and Order in 1952. Here the problem received considerable attention, and the conference recommended it for intensive study. Indeed, in the revised constitution of the commission it was given a firm place among the basic terms of reference for study by Faith and Order.

In 1953 the Faith and Order Secretary was instructed to circularize universities and theological seminaries "with a view to promoting research in concrete situations where social and cultural factors operated." One of the difficulties which presents itself is the wide range of these factors and the tendency to list or compile a score or more that in one way or another affect ecumenical negotiations. I refer to language, nationalism, race, class, power, establishment, polity, denominational size, geographical location and the like. The very large scope of these problems made for diffusion rather than for concentrated analysis.

At the Davos (Switzerland) meeting in 1955 the working committee felt that the time had come to focus on institutionalism as a fruitful point of attack. This subject was taken, not because institutionalism is always the most important, but because it is found in every situation to some significant degree. Accordingly, the terms of reference for this study were defined in 1955 as follows:

To make a study of institutionalism as it affects all churches and in particular:

1. The self-criticism of churches by which they may see their own structures sociologically as well as theologically;

2. The relations both positive and negative of the churches to each other in the ecumenical conversation;

3. The pattern of church relations which is finding expression in the World Council of Churches as an institution.

When churches of varying traditions engage each other in a dynamic conversation, they threaten each other institutionally. It is important to explore the points at which, in the development of the ecumenical movement, the greatest threat to institutional integrity takes place. When churches confront each other they are likely to have some projected image of what the desired form of unity will be. Many churches act as if the nature of the unity they seek were already given in their institutional self-images. We are therefore required to ask this question, "What goals or processes of mutual exploration will lift the quality of institutional participation in the World Council of Churches above the fixed images of their present existence?" The commission is only in the early stages of its enquiries.

Before leaving this historical orientation to the work of the Commission on Institutionalism, and before taking up a definition of such terms as *institution* and *institutionalism,* I should like to relate the general problem of social factors to two of the orientation papers from Minneapolis and Durham, N. C., prepared for this Conference. In the balance of this presentation I shall have occasion to refer to several others, since they make such significant contributions to this aspect of our common task. The reports from Minneapolis and Durham are important because of the relation of doctrinal to non-doctrinal problems.

The Minneapolis Discussion Group dealt with Doctrinal Consensus and Conflict. A wide variety of denominations was represented in this study group. Their work was focused on 5,000 responses to a check-list questionnaire, which indicated a broad homogeneity in expressions of theological faith. The group found that a kind of theological ecumenicity already exists within each of the denominations. There is considerable agreement on the nature of the church, the ground of salvation, the Person of Christ, and the sacraments of the Lord's Supper. On four of the theological areas surveyed all the respondents could be included in the Methodist Church without increasing the diversity which is already represented by the Methodist clergy. Ninety-four per cent could join the Lutheran or Presbyterian churches without increasing the diversity in the views of the Bible, which already exist in the clergy of these denominations. Approximately the same would be true with regard to the doctrine of Christ and the ground of salvation. Seventy-two per cent could be Episcopalian or Lutherans on the doctrine of the sacrament of baptism, and more than 95 per cent could be Presbyterians. Four or five possible positions on the Lord's Supper are taken by Episcopal clergy and these account for 96.38 per cent of the total responses. However, despite this statistical consensus, there is no institutional drive for organic unity.

These very interesting statistical data suggest that the differences that matter most are not theological. "It is clear," says the orientation paper, "that neither clergy nor laity feel any great urge toward organizational unity." Both clergy and laity reject an interpretation of Christian unity which means ". . . the gathering of all Christians into one visible church organization" (all except 7.87% of clergy and 11.67% of laity). Both reject also the other extreme, that of ". . . a spiritual oneness without interest in organizational co-operation" (all except 3.7% of clergy and 3.06% of the laity). However, 50.26 per cent of the laity and 36.57 per cent of the clergy chose ". . . a spiritual oneness indifferent to organizational forms but based on agreement as to the fundamentals of Christian faith." Almost a fourth of the laity chose ". . . the maintenance of various denominations, but each mutually respecting one another's validity as churches." Thirty per cent of the clergy checked ". . . a spiritual oneness manifested partially in organizational co-operation." It is significant, we may add, that only the Episcopal clergy gave preference to "one visible church organization," but their lay members distributed their choices according to the general pattern of all lay choices. From an institutional perspective it is interesting that the denominations not affiliated with the ecumenical movement do not differ significantly from the rest in their conception of the desirable form of Christian unity.

Now let us turn to a different but nonetheless significant pattern of institutional response in North Carolina. This has to do with the racial and economic stratification of the churches. Here, too, a variety of denominational doctrines and polities were represented in the study. The Durham Study Group says, "What has been striking about our own work on the problems of race and class in the local church . . . is that differences of a denominational sort have been of no significance at all. . . . Differences of the Faith and Order variety are artificial and of negligible moment in comparison to differences created by the cultural environment in which the churches are set." Issues of "race" and "class" turned out to be inseparable issues. The correlation between church stratification, based upon income level and the divisions arising from color, were so close and plain that both issues could be treated simultaneously. Whether a church were Episcopal or Baptist or Methodist made no difference whatever.

II. Meaning of Institution and Institutionalism

One of the issues requiring clarification resides in the very definition of *institution* and *institutionalism*. What is the meaning of these terms? The word *institution* is used both in the social sciences and in theology. The commission uses the concept as it appears in the social sciences with such further refinement as may be demanded by the data of church life. I shall presently indicate the importance of these data. Definitions of *institution* range widely from any persistent pattern of activity surrounding a human need,

on the one hand, to a precisely defined list of traits or characteristics such as the purpose of a group, the charter of an organization, the personnel, the relative stability of a pattern of activity,
and norms of social behavior, on the other hand. Furthermore,
the sociologist of religion is confronted by theology and its significance for the Church. This enters into the self-interpretation of
the churches, and thus affects their primary organization and
ways of work.

The positive values of organizational and other institutional
forms for the life, mission, and unity of the people of God are evident. These forms exist to manifest the being (*esse*) of the Church
or as instruments to be used in carrying out the essential tasks of
the Church. When the churches divert their institutions from their
true purposes or use them as ends in themselves, they manifest
what may be called *institutionalism.* This perversion of the use of
institutions, rather than the institutions themselves, is a major
hindrance to the life, mission, and unity of the Church.

The commission has initiated a series of case studies of church
schisms, church unions, efforts at union that have failed, and ecumenical institutions. These phenomena will be analysed in order
to shed light on the structures, functions, and dynamics of the behavior of churches and their agencies. Patterns of leadership appear to be of special importance. Studies already submitted to the
commission indicate that certain commonly used ideal-types, such
as the contrasting classifications of "church," "cult," and "sect,"
need revision. We need to help the churches understand themselves
institutionally in terms of self-analysis involving structure, functions,
dynamics, and leadership.

The relationship of institution to institutionalism is best understood through the sociological conception of institutionalization.
What is it that institutionalizes? This question may be answered
by posing two further questions: what function or role does the
institution expect to perform? To what expectations in the environment does it respond? Initiation and response are crucial and
closely inter-related. Denominations are institutionalized in terms
of their ideas of fellowship, mission, theology, tradition, and the
like. We may call this process self-institutionalization. Denominations are institutionalized also by their responses to the whole cultural environment or by a portion of it. Churches are not always
self-aware of the tension that ought to exist between faithful self-
institutionalizing and responses to the environment that mean
unfaithfulness to the Gospel. Dependence on the environment is

one of the chief sources of institutionalism. (See Berndt Gustafs-son, "Schisms and Types of Institutionalization of Religious In-stitutions," a paper prepared for Commission on Institutionalism.)

These two general sources of institutionalization affect the struc-tures, functions, dynamics and leadership of the Church. We may illustrate from some of the orientation papers. The Honolulu Study Group on "Local Church Unity and Its Ecumenical Im-plications" points out that the unity of a local church is a com-posite of group dynamics and Christian disciplines. There is, ac-cordingly, an inescapable tension between the growing unity of a local church and the desire for broader unity. The local church (and denomination) is subject to institutional introversion, which grows out of a protectiveness and a *self-perpetuating ethnocentrism* which is of the very nature of group life. Its fellowship exists on a basis of deeply personal and voluntary affiliation; and this quality of group life may work against the wider unity of the mission of the Church.

Other forms of self-absorption may be due to *social inertia,* to concentrating on immediate tasks, and to ecclesiastical pride. In a period of revival of interest in religion and of successful expan-sion of membership there may be an institutionalism which is really a form of ecclesiastical *imperialism* in a denomination. Insti-tutional prosperity is not always an ecumenical blessing.

When we turn from self-institutionalization to responses to the expectations of the environment, we may note also a variety of accommodations. Denominations which were established churches in Europe, enjoying an almost monopoly position in the state, may be small voluntary associations in the United States. Conversely major American denominations have practically a sect status when transplanted abroad. In one sense denominational diversity and disunity in the United States is a function of European Chris-tianity operating in a free society. American cultural pluralism is a result of the variety of national and ethnic groups transplanted here; but it is also an environmental pattern which has institu-tionalizing effects on church life.

The New York Study Group on Authority and Freedom in Church Government has noted the institutionalizing power of the idea of *freedom.*

"The American scene," says this report, "has historically emphasized freedom: Here many strong statements concerning religious freedom in its many facets have been framed; here the principle of the separation of Church and state has meant that all churches are in some sense 'free churches'; here denominations which have emphasized certain aspects of freedom have mushroomed into giant size. But this very stress on freedom has sometimes been magnified into an end in itself. Thus understood, it has been one of the contributing factors in the too-easy schism of communions and the rapid growth of new denominations along lines strongly sociological, ethnic, or sectional. In becoming an end in itself, it has helped to nourish an atmosphere in which Christians could understand the Gospel too much in the light of their cultural heritage, instead of seeing their cultural heritage in the light of the Gospel." (Orientation Paper: Section 7, p. 11)

This emphasis on freedom, since it undermines the idea of authority, has significance for the institutionalism of *power*. All social institutions generate power. "A one-sided stress on freedom tends to minimize the role of power, and thereby permits power to be wielded on congregations and denominations in authoritarian and unchristian ways." The desire for power itself may be an illicit response to the cult of power in great American institutions. Denominational expansion and even patterns of co-operative Christianity may follow *success-patterns* of the organizational revolution in the United States.

There are many other illustrations which could be cited of how the *self-images* of the churches affect their *roles* with respect to rural or urban constituencies, national language groups, racial minorities, economic class, sectional interests and the like. There are also many other illustrations of the way the social environment shapes the development of polity, worship, ethics and theology. We must turn our attention, however, to three institutional problems of a general character which influence the relations of the churches to each other, namely, the self-fulfilling prophecy, bureaucracy and polity.

1. We begin with the maxim of W. I. Thomas: "If men define situations as real, they are real in their consequences." Suppose a denomination has a partial, inadequate, or even false definition of another or of the situation regarding co-operation or of the goal of ecumenicity—that definition of the situation evokes the kind of behavior which makes the originally erroneous conception come true. Why is this? *Social beliefs father social realities*. Theological beliefs, creeds, confessions, worship practices are matters of *inclusion* and *exclusion*. The in-group defines the out-group and in part determines its reality. To overcome this institutional tendency requires a dynamic self-awareness which refuses to prejudge

the nature of the unity we seek and which accelerates the rate of interinstitutional communication.

2. Another group of problems have to do with bureaucracy, or as some prefer to say, the administrative top. The role of bureaucracy in churches is analogous to that in all institutions. Church bureaucrats dominate ecumenical discussions. Bureaucracy maximizes vocational security and promotes technical efficiency. Tenure, pensions, incremental salaries, regularized procedure for promotion are related to leadership control. Control, continuity, administrative discretion, and rational order make for institutional efficiency. However, bureaucracy tends to separate the average member, the so-called layman, from the expert who holds the position of legitimate administrative authority. This separation which obtains in any complex organization is increased when the ecclesiastical bureaucrat is also an ordained clergyman. Ecumenicity, the bureaucrat may forget, is a function of the whole church—not of its clerical and administrative top alone.

Though bureaucracy makes for rational efficiency and institutional security, it also tends to develop certain dysfunctions, such as: blindness to needed change; trained incapacity to sense new needs; inflexibility in applying skills and resources to changing conditions; occupational psychoses whereby personnel develop special preferences, antipathies, discriminations and emphases not adapted to social reality as a whole; fixation on goals and objectives however obsolescent; excessive conformity to prescribed patterns which have become routine; transference of sentiments and motivations from the aims of the organization to the particular details of behavior required by rules and rubrics, and transforming means into ends so that instrumental values become terminal values. These dysfunctions are no respecters of denominational polities and apply to boards and agencies as well as to fundamental church structure.

The consequence of these dysfunctions is that the discipline once designed to assist efficiency becomes an intrinsic value and loyalty to ultimate ideals on the part of subordinates is measured by obedience to superiors in the hierarchy of the institution. One becomes an "organization man." Bureaucracy thus breeds overconformity. This partial analysis suggests some leading questions which may be addressed to the denominations here represented: (1) To what extent is the behavior of your church characterized by institutional conformity—with formalized procedures and ritualistic regularity—continued at the expense of membership participation? (2) Has such formalism in your church ever encouraged deviant behavior or revolts in the form of sectarian protest or creative, but unaccepted, innovation? (3) To what extent does your denomination identify its own institutional practices, forms, conceptual formulations, ritual and even sacramental rubrics with ultimate norms? (4) To what extent do the goals and procedures of your local church and denomination encourage its members to seek new ways of achieving Christian values when the traditional ways seem dead or ineffective? (5) Is correct ritualistic performance given a high place in the life of your church? (6) Are the lofty goals of the Christian witness, service, and mission scaled down to the institutional norms of success? (7) Has the Christian way become an institutional rut?

3. These questions have a bearing not only on bureaucracy but on institutional questions of polity. Here we may profitably refer to the work of the Central Study Group of the Massachusetts Council of Churches. Organization and polity, they found, comprise a field in which the life of a denomination meshes most tangibly with the social and cultural realities of its environment. These matters are usually determined more by practical expediency than by religious principle. Some churches say explicitly that organization is not a confessional principle. Even those who affirm an unchangeable order of the Church recognize that it can be embodied in a variety of organizational forms. Some denominations place primary emphasis on the episcopal form of government, others on the presbyterial or congregational. But it is "a characteristic feature of the present situation that many denominations are moving toward a re-combination of the values of these three systems." (Boston: Central Study Group, p. 24) Both Lausanne in 1927 and Edinburgh in 1937 agreed that a reunited Church would recognize the appropriate place of the episcopal, presbyterial, and congregational systems of government. It is significant that in practice most denominations operate in structures and procedures that employ all these institutional forms.

III. ORDER AND ORGANIZATION

The Commission on Institutionalism emphasizes the theological as well as the sociological definition of institution. Thus far we have noted primarily some pervasive sociological traits in church life as they bear on unity and disunity. It is important to turn briefly to the relation of theological institution, or order, to organization. The Oberlin Conference has taken this dimension of its problem into account by asking the Study Group at Toronto to work on order and organization. It is beyond my province to make a theological judgment on their report, but I do express gratitude for the clarity with which they have defined the issues and the constructive proposals they have made. (See Toronto, Orientation Paper: Section 8)

The problem is one of distinguishing a "primary" organization or "order" and a secondary organization, that is, "between an ordered structure which at all times and in all places serves as the means by which God constitutes the Church as the Church and an organization which under particular circumstances gives effective expression to some aspect or other of the primary structure" (ibid., p. 4). This is the problem of looking for "the principles of discrimination between such a primary organization as is essential to the continuous existence and identity of the Church as a visible society and the variety of administrative structures through which this 'order' can be made operative" (loc. cit.). What is needed is the criterion for the "essential distinction between constant *function* and diversified *embodiment*." If the Commission on Institutionalism is to do its work well, it needs the assistance of a thorough theological discussion of this point. What is that "order" which distinguishes the church from every other "religious society"? One of the projects of the commission is a number of studies on the Church as a spiritual community and an institution. Aspects of this study include institution and institutionalism in the early church as well as statements from theologians in Europe, Asia and North America. The thesis of the Toronto Group that the distinguishing criterion is functional order plus apostolicity deserves extensive discussion.

IV. CONCLUDING OBSERVATIONS

On the basis of studies already prepared for the commission and a survey of the orientation papers written for this conference I should like to lift up some significant issues and problems in conclusion.

1. Institutionalism must be confronted at all levels of church life; from the local congregation to national denominational organization and international patterns; from local and state councils of churches to national councils and world ecumenical bodies.

2. The local church is crucial. The Nashville Study Group says pointedly:

"The loyalties that move us most profoundly are associated with concrete particular symbols, including objects and experiences. A building, a group of people among whom one finds acceptance and status, family associations, satisfying educational experiences that stretch our minds, enjoyment of the security of the familiar, music and hymnody . . . these are only a few."

But these are found mostly at the local level. If Christians are to be loyal to a universal Church, it cannot be an abstract Church; it must have concrete symbolization in recurrent experiences. The crucial character of the concrete local community of Christians is apparent also from the Durham report and the one from Honolulu. We cannot escape the question: "Do the sources of unity which are most effective in the life of the local congregation tend to project the local church's life outward toward a growing unity with other churches, or is the tendency in the opposite direction?"

3. Something more than the natural tendencies of group life are essential to a growing ecumenicity. To a greater degree than is true of a local church's unity, the unity between churches is dependent upon a conscious outreach, motivated and disciplined by distinctly Christian concerns. Ecumenicity rests on the *renewal* of the Church. "The ecumenical movement," says the Honolulu group, "ultimately rests on a foundation of religious necessity and hope rather than on practical considerations. . . . It is salvation rather than unity which we seek" (Orientation Paper: Section 5, p. 14). The Minneapolis Study Group says much the same:

"It would appear that the movement toward unity cannot rely heavily on the desire for unity in the contemporary churches. It must rest on an imperative that grows out of the Christian gospel and the very nature of the Christian faith, about which churches must become more aware than seems presently to be the case" (Orientation Paper: Section 2, p. 8).

4. Widespread doctrinal consensus among denominations may be combined with institutional complacency and accommodation of a most serious kind from the perspective of Christian faith. Since more than doctrine divides the churches, more than theological consensus is required for unity.

5. The various denominational polities—no matter how different in history and form—appear to screen power-structures which are strikingly similar in their foci of power and contemporary

operation (Orientation Paper: Section 7, p. 7). Diversity, flexibility, and freedom must be protected in any structural expression of Christian unity (Ibid., p. 12). There is a correlation between church polity and the dynamics of concern for church unity (Ibid., p. 8). The drive will tend in the direction consistent with the ecclesiology of a denomination. If there is no ecumenicity built into the self-image of the denomination, it will not tend toward ecumenical participation.

6. American denominations have developed a widespread pragmatic attitude toward polity. This tendency toward flexibility of institutional expression may be an important contribution to the world Christian community (Section 7, p. 9).

7. The significant problem of the relation of authority to freedom has been institutionalized in the United States in the direction of ultimate membership control. It is pointed out that "many who oppose organic union do so not on the basis that the proposed union will affect adversely the freedoms enjoyed by the church in its present form, but because they see such a union as furthering the process of centralization which has already materially threatened the freedoms supposedly enjoyed in a church based upon the autonomy of the congregation." The problem in this form becomes not one of union but of *institutional centralization*. Hence the problem of freedom which must be solved is not so much the union of one denomination with another, but of the relationship of the local congregation to the whole church (Section 7, p. 10). Americans may be tempted to meet this challenge by introducing more political democracy into the churches, but the solution may more adequately be found in the relationship of the Lordship of Christ to the free life of the congregation. Sociological and theological understanding must unite to achieve this result.

8. We have noted that one of the motives which has created councils of churches is that disunity should not stand in the way of mission and service. Yet all the denominations have compromised mission by various degrees of conformity to the American social environment. The New York Study Group on Authority and Freedom in Church Government concluded on the basis of American experience

"that no single polity, no matter how effectively it may be demonstrated in history or assured by authoritative canon law, is able to guard the Church against a diminishing of its force and a blurring of its vital witness" (Section 7, p. 10).

The implication of this finding is that the ecumenical process may well encourage, on the one hand, "greater freedom and flexibility in the form of polity and more conscious and committed loyalty to the source of all authority for the Church."

9. As powerful denominations confront each other they are tempted to measure their performance in relation to one another rather than by the Gospel. Two of the sinister forms of institutionalism are denominational imitation and competition. The unity we seek certainly lies beyond the cult of power and imperialism, beyond competition and monolithic control, and must be found in mutual service and responsibility enlivened by the unifying Spirit of God. (Section 7, p. 11, Boston Central Group, pp. 25-26)

10. The ecumenical encounter poses special problems for leadership, both for the leaders of small denominational units and for powerful bureaucrats. The leader of small units is often reluctant to contemplate the heightened competition implied in mergers which would inevitably demand superior standards of competence (Section 7, p. 8). The bureaucratically powerful person may develop into an ecumenical virtuoso, not realizing how this personality is shaped by the roles he is accustomed to play. Or again, leaders who have developed personal power and security in the context of a council of churches may resist the uncertainties of a fuller and more fundamental ecumenical unity. Even so, however, the professional denominational leaders usually act in a protective capacity in a council of churches both with respect to local church interests and those of their denominations.

11. Far greater tension between the faith of the Gospel and the institutional forms of the local church is required to achieve full ecumenical unity than has been required by the movement for cooperative Christianity.

12. Churches that are truly dedicated to full ecumenical unity must be prepared to institutionalize themselves as truly universal fellowships. Such ecumenical institutionalization requires a degree of Christian self-awareness that lies beyond the self-image and present insights of any denomination. The Commission on Institutionalism can serve only to aid in that growing self-awareness.

The Shape of the Church's Response in Worship

ADDRESS BY PROFESSOR JOSEPH SITTLER
SEPTEMBER 6, 1957

I. THE PROBLEM: A DESCRIPTION

Faith and Order created a Commission on Worship in acknowledgment of a fact. The fact is that the way Christian people worship is declarative of what they believe. This declaration as made in worship may well be at a depth and with a fulness seldom attained in creedal propositions.

Very early in Faith and Order enquiries it became apparent that formal comparative examination of the confessional and other utterances of the churches was not adequate for a responsible understanding either of what these churches affirmed in common or asserted in difference. There is a worship of the one God by his one people; that is why a Commission on Worship is possible and necessary. And there is a wild and bewildering variety in ways of worship of the one God by this one people: that is why the work of this commission is difficult.

It is not necessary to go into great detail concerning the present constitution of the commission as reorganized following the Second Assembly of the World Council of Churches at Evanston. It's enough to our present purpose to remember that three commissions in widely separated and quite different areas were established: one in Europe, one in East Asia, one in North America. While some preliminary correspondence has been carried on with the European commission, and while all of us in the area-commission are aware of and grateful for the vigorous and productive work of the East Asian group—this hour will be given to a discussion of matters which have arisen in the two meetings which have been held under my chairmanship here in North America. Insofar as what I say is reportorial I speak for our commission; the section of this paper which looks ahead is indeed under debt to my colleagues in the North American commission, but they are not in any way responsible for it.

One cannot get very far in constructive thought about a problem until the nature of the problem has been clearly exposed. Our work of exposure is by no means complete; but certain aspects are clear enough that I can point them out in the confidence that any concerned listener will recognize what I am talking about.

1. *The problem presented by the term worship.* At the second meeting of our commission Prof. Leonard Trinterud, with characteristic bluntness and clarity, excised this particular problem in these words.

"Our English word 'worship' mis-states the whole content and significance of that which in the New Testament is called 'the service of God,' i.e., *leiturgia, latria, diakonia,* and their respective related terms.   In the N.T. these terms refer normatively to 'serving God,' 'doing the will of God,' in a great variety of ways most of which are without cultic significance or form, and which refer principally to that which is done for and among men—not to something done to or for God in a sanctuary. The New Testament knows nothing of a *leiturgia, latria, diakonia* which is localized in an edifice, or to fixed times of occurrence.   These terms refer to the whole round of the Christians' ordinary life as a people."

Prof. Trinterud made his second point as follows.

"Acts such as prayer, thanksgiving, breaking of bread are regarded in the New Testament as but an aspect of the 'service of God,' and not necessarily the controlling or central aspect. That which in the New Testament *is* central and controlling in the 'service of God' is the presence of Christ, the Head of the Church, in the Holy Spirit given to the Church. The living Christ, thus present, directs, guides, builds up the Church, and thus it 'serves God.' Our ideas of worship are too often rooted in the situation of the people of God before the Resurrection and Pentecost. There, indeed, priests, strictly so-called, performed cultic acts, in properly consecrated sanctuaries, acts addressed to God on behalf of the people. But the new aeon comes when the promise of God has been fulfilled, when the redeeming work of God has been done in Christ, and when the Holy Spirit has been given to all believers. God's people are now related to Him in a new and living way previously only promised. So also, God is now present among His people, by the Holy Spirit, a manner of presence which previously was but a promise.

"We cannot discuss 'worship' as though we were still in the old aeon, on the other side of Pentecost and the Resurrection."

One can disagree with a great deal of what Prof. Trinterud says; but such disagreement has nothing to do with the size or importance of the problem thus explicated. Our commission has been sufficiently impressed to agree upon the following ways of approach:

a. A thoroughgoing biblical enquiry into the relation between the "service of God" and what we have come to call the "service of worship" by the congregation of believers assembled in a specific place, has got to be undertaken. The enormous exegetical ferment which has been engendered by recent decades of brilliant and notion-cracking biblical studies makes it quite impossible to derive schematically neat ideas about worship from the New Testament community. Some old certainties as to how worship was then practiced have been made untenable, and a confusing and exciting richness of life has been exposed.

b. The interdependence of the work of the Commission on Worship and the Commission on Christ and the Church is transparently clear. Just as the doctrine of the Church was at Lund shifted to a position under the doctrine of Christ, so also, we think, the enquiry into worship must be illuminated from the same center.

A corollary of these convictions has shaped our commission's understanding of its task—and it may be expressed here as a kind of an aside. If any of us came to this study as liturgiologists, or were under the impression that by becoming such we could best advance our work, we have long since laid such notions aside. There is a place and a useful function to be served by such enquiries, but none of us is disposed to interpret our directive in such terms. Descriptive and analytical enquiries into ways of worship must follow a clear understanding of the nature and scope and meaning of worship. If liturgical considerations precede such studies, the deeper question is either dismissed or too quickly set in doctrinaire terms.

c. Enquiry into the nature of Christian worship of God has, particularly in North America, got to operate in a sphere of discourse which is already occupied. The name of the occupant, in very many of our congregations, is the psychology of worship. This strange roomer got into and established himself in the living room of church practice in roughly the following way: that people do worship God is an observable fact; and every fact is permeable to psychological enquiry. Psychology does not operate from hand to mouth; it has either open or unavowed presuppositions about the structure and dynamics of the psyche. If, then, it is argued, in worship people are in some way or other in search of a relationship to the Ineffable, there must be ways which lubricate and ways which hinder this search. The human animal is influenced by setting, accompaniment, symbols, silence, the gravity of statement and response, the solidarity-producing impact of solemn music and so forth.

So it has happened that experts in worship have arisen among us. All assume that the purpose of public worship is to create a mood; and he is the most admirable as the leader of worship who has mastered finesse in the mood-setting devices made available by the application of psychological categories. Thence has flowed that considerable and melancholy river of counsel whereby one may learn how to organize an assault upon the cognitive and critical faculties of the mind, how to anesthetize into easy seduction the non-verbalized but dependable anxieties that roam about in the solitary and collective unconscious, and how to conduct a brain-washing under the presumed banner of the Holy Ghost.

That this is what worship means in thousands of congregations is certainly true; it is equally true that the Scriptures know nothing about such ideas. Where we are enjoined to be still and know that God is God, the presupposition is not that stillness is good and speech is bad—but rather that God is *prior* to man and all God-man relationships are out of joint if that is not acknowledged.

d. The third problem of which we have become acutely aware is a big and general problem; and I cannot advance toward a description of it until I shove out of the way an unhappy term which is well on the way to ecumenical canonization. It is *a non-theological factor,* which is saying not only an unintelligible thing, but a patently untrue thing. For there are no nontheological factors in human existence. To suppose that there are is to misunderstand both the scope and intention of Christian theology and the actualities of human thought and feeling.

This tough problem, then, can best be delineated by starting with a proposition: that language is the primary creation and carrier of culture, and it follows the career of man's culture with absolute seriousness. Language, that is to say, in the structure, scope, and content of it, is an obedient transcript of what a people understands itself and its world to be like. When that world-understanding is monodimensional, language loses its opulence. When that world-meaning becomes a plane without extension or depth, language becomes designative and thin.

It is not within the scope of this paper to investigate why language in our time has become flat, nonallusive, and impoverished, but simply to note that it *has* and ask what this means for our churches as they seek to recover ways of worship which shall be more adequate to the object of worship, and more fully reflective of the long history of the people of God in their life of worship.

It is strange that this problem, so widely acknowledged and so profoundly disturbing outside the churches, has, so far as I know, not been systematically discussed among us. This is the more strange, because the more deeply a concern is loaded with history, the past, things accomplished long ago, the more a church understands herself as a "pilgrim people of God"—that is, called, continuous, on the way, starting with a constitutive deed and living out her life in a hope which is both given and an awaited consummation—the more clearly the Church understands *that,* the more embarrassing her problem with a flat and impoverished language. Just as our Christology becomes richer, our ecclesiology more organic, our anthropology more deep, our common language, the cultural instrument that must do the work of acknowledgment, praise and interpretation, is shrinking in obedience to a diminished realm of meaning.

The gravity of rhythmic speech is the mark of a culture that carries its past livingly in its present experience. Rhythmic speech is the outward and visible sign of rootedness. Every society has had its rhetoric of remembrance. "Come now, let us bring our reasoning to a close, saith the Lord . . . Israel doth not know, my people doth not consider . . . I am the Lord thy God that brought thee out of that great and terrible wilderness . . . I have called thee by thy name, thou art mine."

In the Scriptures each moment is heavy with all past moments; for the God of the moment is the Creator of the continuity. The old prayers of the church understood this so well and felt it so deeply that every one of them jump into the moment's petitions after a running start in the eventful history of the people of God. "O God, who didst teach the hearts of Thy faithful people by sending to them the light of Thy Holy Spirit: Grant us by the same Spirit to have a right judgment in all things, and evermore to rejoice in His holy comfort. . . ." This is great rhetoric because it roots the life of the moment in the grace of the past; it evokes a response in depth because it is not only a report but also a reverberation. It is an expectant episode in a people's life because it is a note in ancient and continuing music. It is as big as the heart because it is as old as the people of God.

How many times, in reading the liturgy for the Holy Communion, I have felt both exultation and despair at the moment of the *Sanctus:* "Therefore with Angels and Archangels, and with all the company of heaven, we laud and magnify Thy glorious Name; evermore praising Thee, and saying: Holy, Holy, Holy,

Lord God of Sabaoth. . . ." One is exalted because in this language, this place and time the company of momentary lives are interpreted and blessed within the scope of an eternal action of God, released from the tyranny of death, and what Dylan Thomas has so movingly alluded to when he laments that

> . . . time in all its tuneless turning affords
> So few, and such morning, songs . . .[1]

But also in despair, for to the flattened speech of our time Angels and Archangels are rather ridiculous terms—material, so to speak, nonfissionable by contemporary definition of fact.

Strange things, nevertheless, are happening in the present practice of language. Just when one is sodden with despair over the possibility of making alive the massive biblical symbol of *fire,* for instance—

> Come Holy Ghost, our souls inspire
> And lighten with celestial fire;—

Just then man does such things with language as to reinvest this symbol with meanings, undreamed of meanings, of terrible force. The immediate referent of *fire* in 1957 is not the celestial fire of God's descending and re-creating ardor—but a monstrous shape like a death-dealing mushroom. And out of this unimaginable hell a man envisions again an unbelievable grace, and writes in language which wildly fuses destroying atom-bombs and the descending Holy Ghost:

> The dove descending breaks the air
> With flame of incandescent terror
> Of which the tongues declare
> The one discharge from sin and error.
> The only hope, or else despair
>   Lies in the choice of pyre or pyre—
>   To be redeemed from fire by fire.
>
> Who then devised the torment? Love.
> Love is the unfamiliar Name
> Behind the hands that wove
> The intolerable shirt of flame
> Which human power cannot remove.
>   We only live, only suspire
>   Consumed by either fire or fire.[2]

---

[1]Copyright 1952, 1953 by Dylan Thomas.   Reprinted by permission of New Directions.

[2]From *Four Quartets* by T. S. Eliot, copyright, 1943, by T. S. Eliot. Reprinted by permission of Harcourt, Brace and Company, Inc.

Such speech judges one's tepid unbelief in the power of the Holy Spirit of God, reminds us in the Commission on Worship that the aggressive and ingenious love that can make the stones cry out can penetrate positivistic language too, and betimes torment its flatness into a kind of "negative" praise.

It is therefore proper to our study of worship to enquire what this revolution in language means for the public worship of our churches, to ask whether perhaps it is not a task of contemporary obedience and praise to find fresh forms of statement whereby intelligibly to set forth ancient facts and praises and encounters. It may well be that we are entering upon a period in the church's life wherein men's minds must be shocked open to entertain the suspicion that there are realms of meaning, promise, and judgment which ensconce God's incarnated action for their vague disquietudes.

II. The Problem: A Constructive Analysis

There has never been a church which has not declared its faith and order to be continuous with the apostolic tradition. Some churches have affirmed this explicitly in their confessions or other basic writings; others have unfolded their life, eschewing confessional statements, but claiming to celebrate this tradition in teaching, order, and piety.

This fact opens up a double way to make an entrance into the constructive part of our task. One way is to mobilize all resources for an ever-fresh encounter with the actual content of the apostolic tradition and judge the public worship in our churches according to their congruity with its announcement, promise, and demand. This does not of course assume that there *are* in the apostolic tradition clear and commanding directives concerning the form and content of public worship; it only affirms that ways of worship which ignore or distort the liberating message of God's Christly action must be corrected from that central action.

The other way is to examine the phenomena of public worship as carried on by the various churches, peer behind the accents and selections which have actually modified all of them, get behind the cultural deposits in the form of language, music, and gesture which cling to all of them, and ask if there is a *morphology* of the response of the people of God.

In the pages to follow both approaches will be used, in a brief and tentative way. The hope is that there may emerge among us, as we enquire into these matters, a way of thinking about worship which may serve to liberate us from our placid captivity within our separate traditions. We are asking, in other words, if there is a unity in the entire worshiping career of the entire responding faithful people of God,—whence this unity comes, and what is its essential content.

The earliest Christian communities to whose life we have literary access apparently believed there was such a unity. This consensus concerning the apostolic tradition is the more remarkable in view of the broad and detailed New Testament studies which have elaborated the rich and sometimes confusing variety out of which the voice of this consensus speaks. Before the Gospels, in the form we now know them, existed, the Church was giving voice to the general shape and content of what it believed God had accomplished in Christ—which action brought it into being, sustained and enabled its life, and furnished it with both task and power. God, it was affirmed, had engaged himself in a personal, incarnate action with man's estranged and captive predicament, had recapitulated in Jesus Christ the entire life of Adam (his created but now estranged human family), had involved himself with every tragedy, limitation, desolation, and even the death of man. This God-initiated, ingressive penetration of human life is the substance of those records which are the four Gospels. Each, to be sure, has its own character, each has sources unknown to or unused by the others, and each is shaped in accent and use of materials by circumstances known to us only in part.

But the morphology of the action of God in Christ is alike in all. Its shape is an inverted parabola. The starting point is the appearance of One who asserted that he came to announce and inaugurate the kingly rule of God in such a way as to actualize the hopes of the ancient people of God, make effective the liberating promise and power of God, establish men, by his life and teaching and deeds, in a new relationship to God and to one another. This lived-out action had a shape which was that of a descending curve which went down, into, through, and under every broken God-relationship, until this action itself was apparently destroyed at the nadir of its career on Good Friday.

The Gospels, however, are resurrection documents. They declare that God, who is alive, is not stopped in his purpose by the assault of death, but rather has carried his action through. His Word, Jesus Christ, is victorious over death, lives, reigns, is the second Adam, the Head of a new body, the Church. The old creed of the Church follows episodically the precise pattern of this parabola of the grace of God—born, suffered, died, arose, ascended, reigns with the Father.

This declaration is the core of the apostolic tradition. We confront it repeatedly in the Acts of the Apostles, and in that body of correspondence known to us as the Letters of Paul. Especially clarifying and impressive is the way Paul, caught in a polemical situation, again and again appeals to this tradition. In such situations the apostle reaches, as it were, back of himself and back of his hearers, back of the particular situation, gets ahold of the given core of what commands him and them—and strides into the point at issue as from a secure beachhead. That these moments occur in the course of the rough and tumble of his pastoral career, and not, as a rule, as calculated links in a chain of argument, makes them the more startling. Paul did not, apparently, so schematize his words to the Philippians so as to lead up to the great words in Chapter 2, verses 5-11. He is simply appealing to this community which was in a fix to be "likeminded" in the "fellowship of the Spirit." This fellowship involves a "lowliness of mind." And whence is that? Where shall one behold it, whence receive it? Led on, then, by the questions his own counsel has generated the apostle cannot stop short of sinking the present life of the Philippian community in the entire deed of God in Jesus Christ. So almost accidentally does the all-shaping apostolic core reveal its massive shape behind the occasional pastoral message. This passage (Phil. 2:1-12) is not Christology in order to Christology; it is Christology in order to ethics—and the more persuasive for that reason.

In the letter to the Romans Paul is called upon to confront a flippant and almost blasphemous *nonsequitur*—a situation not unknown to any preacher or teacher today. If grace abounds more abundantly where sin abounds in force, then one is in the amazingly fine situation of eating and having his cake at the same time! Against such total incomprehension of his message Paul wheels up the heavy artillery of the apostolic tradition. The shape of the deed of God, he declares, engenders a *total* human life in organic congruity with itself; and to be a Christian is to have one's life in *its* shape determined by the scope of what God has done. Therefore, says Paul, what happened to Christ is the God-given, redemptive pattern of our lives. "Know ye not that so many of us as were baptized into Jesus Christ were baptized into His death? Therefore we are buried with Him by baptism into death: that like as Christ was raised up from the dead by the glory of the Father, even so we also should walk in newness of life."

As then, the morphology of grace in the life, death, resurrection and exaltation of Jesus Christ imparts to and creates the believer in its own shape—so worship is the name proper to the celebration of this new being in Christ by his Body, the Church. Such a celebration has a scope broad enough to include all the New Testament means by *leiturgia, latria, diakonia* (the service of God) and has a specific concreteness enough to be verbalized in the liturgical life of the Church where it is assembled in public worship. Any definition of worship less rich than this comes under the judgment of such an admonition as Paul's in the 12th chapter of Romans. "I appeal to you therefore, brethren, by the mercies of God, to present your bodies as a living sacrifice, holy and acceptable to God, which is your spiritual worship."

As then we perceive the bare elements of the apostolic message, and observe how this shape, re-enacted within the believer by the power of the Holy Spirit, constituted Christian life in solitude and in the fellowship of the community, do we not also, perhaps, find a transconfessional pattern for Christian worship? Is there not here a given substance and morphology of response which presses upon all of us, calls all of us to attend, acknowledge, and celebrate? If that is so, then we are given a starting place where, from within our various churches, we ask after what is constitutive of and proper to the content of truly catholic worship.

Every tradition in Christian worship acknowledges that it does indeed stand under this given substance of the Gospel. This is overtly so among the churches which cherish liturgical patterns centuries old; it is covertly so among churches whose public worship is improvised, *ad hoc,* and so free as to make the term tradition seem strange. The directive of the churches represented in Faith and Order that a study of worship be pursued over a number of years indicates a recognition that there is a *giveness* to Christian worship, and that the common degradation of worship into gimmicks for religious mood-engendering is a kind of impoverishment, a failure, a positive disobedience hiding behind the face of individualism, spontaneity, freedom.

Remembering then the apostolic tradition, and having in mind the huge spectrum of forms of public worship within the churches —from nonliturgical churches on one side to Eastern Orthodoxy on the other—there are none that do not acknowledge in public worship the following five elements: Recollection, Thanksgiving, Participation, Proclamation, Expectation.

Recollection. A congregation of believers assembled for the public worship of God knows that it did not come into existence at that moment, knows that it is not alone, knows that what is happening is happening because something *has* happened, and that from God's side. What is announced is continuous with what has been announced since the resurrection. And therefore all sequences of public worship include, whether in formal-liturgical or informal ways, powerful elements of recollection. Mighty deeds have been done, a huge liberation has taken place, an event called Jesus Christ was, is, and is here—and everything that takes place in this moment presupposes that. "In the name of the Father, and of the Son, and of the Holy Ghost. . . . In the beginning was the Word, and the Word was with God, and the Word was God. . . ." In many and various ways God spoke of old to our fathers by the prophets; but in these last days he has spoken to us by a Son. . . . In all these things we are more than conquerors through him who loved us. . . ."

Celebration begins with recollection.

Recollection engenders *Thanksgiving.* The content of what is recalled in worship is not a cluster of episodes spiritually elevated above, but essentially continuous with, the structures of human history; these remembered deeds of creation, care, deliverance, and renewal are rather the recital of faith in which is perceived within the structure of history, the ultimate redemption of man. Exodus is an occurrence, and a power-bearing symbol; incarnation is an occurrence, and the radical mercy of God whereby he did and does what needs doing in the sin and death determined house of man's existence. As then ". . . although they knew God they did not honor him as God or give thanks to him"—nevertheless, ". . . when the time had fully come God sent forth his Son, born of a woman, born under the law, to redeem those who were under the law, so that we might receive adoption as sons." *Therefore,* "Thanks be to God for his inexpressible gift!" "And all the angels stood round the throne . . . and they fell on their faces before the throne and worshiped God, saying, 'Amen! Blessing and glory and wisdom and thanksgiving and honor and power and might be to our God for ever and ever! Amen.' "

The Church's thankful recollection of God's deed of redemption is at the same time a *participation.* Hearing, repentance, acceptance of mercy, forgiveness of sins—these are all the work of God whereby man receives no less than a "new-being in Christ." Rich and various are the New Testament images in which this new-being is promised and, given in faith, celebrated. Men are *before* Christ, who beholds them; they are *under* Christ, who judges them; for or against Christ, who addresses them. But the thrust and destiny of this Holy Encounter is that they may be *in* Christ! The language of participation dominates the New Testament speech about the fullness of the Christ-relationship. "I am the vine; you are the branches." "If any one is in Christ, he is a new creation, the old has passed away." "It is no longer I who live, but Christ who lives in me; and the life I now live in the flesh I live by faith in the Son, God, who loved me." "For you have died, and your life is hid with Christ in God."

Christian worship is *proclamation*. The substance of what is proclaimed is the same as what is recollected, the same as is now acknowledged by the congregation in thanksgiving as God's salvatory and present power, the same as is offered and received in participation of the members in the Head of the Church. Worship not only includes proclamation of the Gospel of salvation; it *is* proclamation. Every service of public worship is a banner of life flying among the banners of mortality. Every assembly of believers in the name of Christ is a proclamation of the *Regnum Dei* by subjects or sons who have been liberated and now live in the *Regnum Christi*. The celebration of the Supper of the Lord is indeed recollection, Eucharist, the seal of forgiveness of sins, and the gift and nurturing of life in the Lord of the feast. But it is something more; something immediate and poignant in the history of all the embattled "little flocks" of the first century, known again in our day by millions in shattered and cut-off lives in cells, rubble, behind wire, and behind curtains. It is the proclamation of engrafted membership in a kingdom not born of history, and therefore, not at the mercy of history's demonic tyrannies. The somber chalice of the table of the Lord has in our day again become a defiant sign uplifted, the believer's toast of terrible joy. "As often as you eat this bread and drink this cup, you proclaim the Lord's death until he comes."

But all of this, recollection, thanksgiving, participation, and proclamation is the worship, or true service of God, in the Body, within the theatre of this world, a response by the *pilgrim* people of God. And for that reason Christian worship is always *Expectation*. This expectation is not an element in a richer context; it is rather the pervading mood of the whole of Christian worship. If I had not been *given* an immeasurable gift I could not expect at all; if this gift were consummated within the conditions of human existence I could not expect, either.

The last word of the New Testament is a dramatic condensation of this "not yet—yet even now," which is the mood of all Christian worship. The Apocalypse of St. John concludes "Amen. Come, Lord Jesus!" The *Amen* leans backward toward the mighty salvatory deeds of God, affirms that the Church, the Body of Christ is held in God's hand against the powers of hell. The "Come, Lord Jesus" leans forward toward the consummation of "the fullness of him who fills all in all."

The Christian life is a life drawn taut between the *Amen* and the *Come*. This tautness has the suffering, the waiting, and the peculiar service of the Christian man in the world. And inasmuch as Christian worship has been the strange music of these taut and joyous lives in history, a deep study of worship points a steady finger to the nature of the unity we seek.

Worship: A Report from Asia
The East Asian Theological Commission on Worship

BY PRINCIPAL J. RUSSELL CHANDRAN
SEPTEMBER 6, 1957

Let me first express my sincere gratitude for the privilege of participating in this important ecumenical conference and for this opportunity of sharing with you some of the experiences of the East Asian Theological Commission on Worship.

The East Asian Theological Commission on Worship enjoys the uniqueness of being the only theological commission set up under the auspices of the World Council with direct reference to Asia. The commission was appointed in 1954, at the same time as the Commissions on Worship for Europe and America. The work of the commission had to be carried on under certain handicaps. The geographic area covered by the terms of reference of the commission is so vast, including the many countries from West Pakistan to Japan. The membership of the commission is distributed among these many countries and it has not been possible so far to have even one single meeting of the whole commission, the obvious obstacle being the vast distances and the consequent expenses involved. Even the officers of the commission could not meet together. The Chairman is from India, the Secretary from Ceylon and the two Vice-Chairmen from Burma and Japan, respectively. It was also thought wise not to plan a full meeting of the commission until some study had been made in each of the major countries in the region on the problems of worship. The diversities in the social, cultural and religious backgrounds of the different countries suggested that their problems of worship would not be identical. It was, therefore, decided to hold national conferences or consultations on worship in the different countries, and what I have to report here is mainly the result of such national conferences.

Before I mention the discussions at conferences I must point out that during the last few years there has been a considerable awakening of interest in worship in most churches in Asia. Even apart from any direct relation to the work of the commission, many churches have been engaged in the task of reviewing and improving their worship, wrestling with the problem of "how to worship God" in spirit and in truth. I may mention here the experiments at indigenisation of worship in the Christian Ashrams of India and Ceylon, the liturgical developments which have been going on for some years in the Anglican Church of India, Pakistan, Burma and Ceylon, the Church of South India, the Lutheran Churches in India, and the Anglican Church and the United Church of Christ in Japan. Christian periodicals have carried many articles relating to worship, particularly on the subject of indigenisation of forms of worship, church music, church architecture and the like. The *Japan Christian Quarterly* devoted two entire numbers last year (July and October, 1956) to the subject of worship. Some of the articles were reports of statistical studies, made on different aspects of Christian worship in Japan, and reflect a characteristically American approach to the study of any problem! In Indonesia, one of the younger ministers chose the subject of Christian Worship in Indonesia for his doctoral dissertation, and his observations are being studied by the churches there. The National Christian Council of Burma had "Christian Worship" as the main theme for its annual meeting in 1956.

During the last three years several national conferences have been held under the auspices of the commission. A conference was held in Ceylon in April, 1954, and two conferences were held in India, one in March, 1955, and the other in April, 1957. Similar conferences were organized in Indonesia, the Philippines and Japan when I visited these countries in May and June this year. As a result of these conferences, national continuation committees for the study of worship have been set up in these countries, and these committees function in close co-operation with the respective National Christian Councils.

One encouraging point to be noted about these conferences on worship is that they have not been limited to churches in the fellowship of the World Council of Churches. The Indian conferences had delegates from the Jacobite Church which is not a member of either the National Christian Council in India or the World Council of Churches. In the Philippines, the Philippine Independent Church and the Seventh Day Adventists were among the participants of the conference on worship, though neither of them is, at present, a member of the Philippine Federation of Churches or the World Council. The regional conferences on worship have thus been a means of advancing the cause of the ecumenical movement beyond the membership of the World Council of Churches.

The Asian conferences have been primarily concerned with the practical problems of making the worship of the churches more real and relevant. They did not reach the high level of theological discussions indicated in the program of study adopted by the European and North American Commissions on Worship. But this does not in any way mean indifference on the part of the Asian churches to theological issues. The main concern in all the conferences was to express the distinctive and universal elements of Christian worship in a manner meaningful and relevant for the worshiping community.

One common subject considered by all the conferences was indigenisation of Christian worship. This subject, however, has been discussed with greater seriousness in India, Ceylon and Indonesia than in the other countries. In the Philippines, it is difficult to determine what precisely is indigenous to them because Spanish imperialism had destroyed all indigenous culture. Moreover, as the dominant indigenous culture in the Philippines today is that of primitive Roman Catholicism, indigenisation cannot have the same meaning and urgency as in the other Asian countries. Japan has a dominant non-Christian culture. But for fear of syncretism, many of the leaders of the Japanese church are shy of considering indigenisation. A few of them are, however, of the opinion that the failure of the church in that country to penetrate among the rural people is to be attributed to the absence of indigenisation!

It was in the Indian conferences on worship that the subject of indigenisation received the most systematic consideration. Their discussions may be summed up under five points.

1. *Uncontroversial and Obvious Elements of Indigenisation.*

The most obvious thing under this category is music. For public worship most Protestant churches have preferred the use of hymns, translated from the Western hymns and set to Western music. But we have also collections of lyrics, composed by Indian Christian poets like H. A. Krishna Pillay and N. Vaman Tilak which are sung to Indian tunes. Some progress has already been made in the use of Indian music for Christian worship. Experiments are also being made for rendering a whole order of service like the C.S.I. liturgy or the order of Morning Worship in the Arcot Lutheran Church into Indian lyrical form with very encouraging results. The conferences asked for an increasing use of Indian music in Christian worship. It was emphasized that all that is precious in any culture should be dedicated to the worship of God in Christ.

2. Controversial Elements in Indigenisation.

The question was raised as to the wisdom of adopting certain meaningful national festivals like *Deepavali*, the festival of lights, for proclaiming Christian affirmation. It was pointed out that Christmas and Easter were originally pagan festivals. No conclusions have been reached on this question. A warning has been recorded that adoption of festivals with Hindu mythological associations may leave room for dangerous syncretism. But bold experiments in faith and courage may be the only way of overcoming false myths and proclaiming the Lordship of Christ.

3. Norms of Indigenisation.

It was clearly stated that all experiments of indigenisation should be subject to the judgment of the Word of God. All Christian worship should be the worship of the Triune God as revealed in the Bible.

4. Theology of Indigenisation.

Even though no systematic theology of indigenisation has emerged yet, the Indian discussions have suggested that the biblical doctrines of creation, incarnation and redemption throw light on the significance of indigenisation. The different cultures are part of the created order. Though they belong to an order which is fallen, God's answer to fallen creation is not rejection or damnation but redemption. In order to redeem the world, the Word became flesh, identifying himself with humanity in its particularity. The Church, therefore, has the task of identifying itself with the particular cultures, adopting their music and other forms of art, their techniques of religious life and the like, thereby redeeming them from their bondage and restoring their essential function of glorifying God. It was also recognized that indigenisation does not apply only to traditional ancient cultures. One essential principle of Christian indigenisation is that of relevancy. This principle should be borne in mind while considering the worship of people who are getting urbanized and uprooted from their traditional cultures.

5. Indigenisation and Unity.

Both in India and in Indonesia the question was asked whether indigenisation would not accentuate the diversities in the life of the Church and thereby create a new danger to the unity of the Church. While no final answer was given, it was pointed out that

the basis of Christian unity is neither uniformity nor even the re-
duction of diversities but our oneness in Christ. It is in Christ that
all diversities of God's gifts in creation can be held together without causing division or disunity. In the world without Christ the
diversities cause tension and are tragic. Indigenisation of Christian
worship is therefore one way of witnessing to the reconciling power
of Christ.

I must add that we have only begun to understand the meaning,
the dangers and the possibilities of indigenisation. But in further
study we see possibilities for the churches of enriching their worship and drawing closer to Christ and to one another.

Besides indigenisation, the Asian conferences have also discussed
issues like the significance of set forms and free forms of worship;
the place of the lectionary in worship; the place of the sacraments
in Christian worship; the relation between worship and the social
life of the community. In discussing these subjects, the Asian conferences have adopted both the pre-Lund and the post-Lund
methods of approach. The churches at the regional level also find
it necessary to interpret to one another their traditions and to ask
questions on one another's traditions before they go to discover
together the common heritage, rooted in the Bible and unfolded
in the history of the Church. But the fact that there are so many
United Churches in Asia, the progress made by the Church Union
Movement and the urgency of union in Asia, make it easy for
churches to listen to one another, to be enriched by one another
and to receive fresh guidance from the Word of God.

But the Asian churches cannot worship in isolation. They have
to learn from the rich traditions of churches all over the world.
They should be enriched by the traditions of devotion, discipline
and prayer of saints all over the world. It should also be said that
the East Asian Theological Commission cannot fulfill its task without the help of the commissions in Europe and America.

The Ground of Our Unity

SERMON BY THE REVEREND W. A. VISSER 'T HOOFT
FIRST CHURCH IN OBERLIN
SUNDAY, SEPTEMBER 8, 1957

Therefore, holy brethren, who share in a heavenly call, consider Jesus, the apostle and high priest of our confession. (Hebrews 3:1, RSV)

We are assembled in order to confront our lives with the Word of God and to receive his gifts of grace. But on this particular Sunday morning which comes in the midst of a conference of the churches on the unity of the Church of God, we are not together as mere individuals, but as responsible churchmen. Our Sunday worship is to throw light on our weekday struggle for truth. So let us ask what this passage of the Epistle to the Hebrews means for our task.

Our theme is: the unity we seek. But is it so certain that "we," that is the members of all the churches here represented, really seek unity?

There are a number of Christians who do not seem to be too dissatisfied with the present situation of the Christian churches. They see no reason for radical changes and do not suffer from our divisions. We hear it said that the great diversity of denominations is really an asset in that every type of person can somewhere find something which will suit his special need. The underlying assumption is, of course, that the Church exists in order to satisfy one of the many desires of men, and that the Church is therefore, in the last analysis, an instrument which belongs to men and which they have a right to fashion according to their own will and insight.

As long as that conception of the Church is so widely held, there is little hope for any true advance in unity. Considerations of efficiency, of the need for a common witness and a common strategy may limit our ecclesiastical anarchy to some extent, but unity will never be achieved as long as we remain imprisoned in a human, all-too-human view of the nature of the Church. Ecumenical education may widen our horizons, but it will fail in its basic purpose as long as the ecumenical seed is sown in the barren soil of man-centered church life. The ecumenical movement itself is in danger as long as its deepest intentions are not understood by the great mass of churchmen. There is therefore nothing more urgent than to ask what God's Word has to say about the nature of the

Church and of its unity. We read again Hebrews 3:1, and note that the literal translation is: *partners* or *partakers* in a heavenly call.

In the Bible the point of departure is a call. It is a person-to-person call from God who is a living, speaking God to individual men and women. To hear that call, to discover that there is not only the silence of loneliness, the music of voices which we love and the noise of the crowd, but that we are addressed by one who as Creator and Redeemer is the true sovereign of our lives, is the first step on the road toward Christian faith.

The Epistle speaks of a *heavenly* call. That does not mean a call which concerns our future existence alone, but a call which comes from beyond our world, a transcendent call, a call which is characterized by ultimate, fully sovereign authority and which reminds us that our true citizenship is citizenship in that kingdom of God, the full manifestation of which we expect and for the coming of which we pray. The call comes to all those who have ears to hear. They are in the language of St. Paul the "called saints." As soon as we are called we find ourselves in the company of other men and women who have heard the same voice and have decided to respond to its invitation.

And this company is not a collection of individuals; it is a body of fellow pilgrims. Our text defines the holy brethren as those who share in a heavenly call, literally as those who are partners in the call; that is, who participate in what is in the last analysis one and the same call.

With our deep-rooted modern individualism we tend to think of calling or vocation first of all in terms of the specific mandate which God addresses to each particular person. Now the New Testament speaks very clearly about such specific callings. In fact the variety of ministries and gifts of grace which we find in the life of the early church has practically never been equalled in the life of the church in later periods. But these particular calls are never considered as private affairs. They are part of the overall call to the people of God. The cohesion and oneness of God's work among men is constantly brought out. We are partners in that we have heard one and the same comprehensive call. What you have heard and what I have heard comes from one and the same God who speaks to us in one and the same man, Jesus Christ. We have one and the same hope of our calling—the hope for one and the same kingdom. If God's call to us is one call, that must mean that God sees us as one people, one family. We may draw

as many dividing lines as we can, we may organize specific confessions and denominations; in God's sight there is just the one
body of those who have heard his call and respond to it. God's
Church cannot be divided because its unity belongs to its very
essence. It has been remarked that in the impressive, monotonous
enumeration in Ephesians 4: one body, one Spirit, one hope, one
faith, one baptism, one Lord—we do not find the expression: one
Church. The reason is surely that the oneness of the Church is so
obvious to the New Testament generation that it need not be explicitly stated.

This, then, is the true ground of our unity. This is the reason
why we are not called to construct laboriously our unity out of a
great many fragments which do not seem to fit together. This is
why our search for unity is not in vain. What we are called to do
is to manifest what is inherent in our common call, to liberate the
Church of God from the man-made prisons in which we have
sought to capture it, to make visible to ourselves and to the world
that we are partners in one heavenly calling. This then is the first
consequence which we must draw from our text: our unity is
given in the will of God and in his plan. In that sense our unity
is *real,* for what can be more real than that which exists in God?
In another sense it is terribly unreal for we have obscured it by our
divisions. Even though by the grace of God we are no longer as
isolated from each other as we were and we have the World Council of Churches through which we can give expression to our sense
of belonging together, we are far from showing the world that
unique unity in faith, in life, in worship and order which is inherent
in the Christian Gospel. Such unity does not exclude a great and
rich variety, but it would exclude contradictions in essential affirmations of faith, separation at the Lord's table, competition except in
the form of spiritual emulation.

It is a dangerous misunderstanding to think that the only alternative to disunity is a monolithic, centralized and imperialistic
super-church, a sort of ecclesiastical leviathan. We are precisely
called to manifest that wonderful combination of authority and
freedom, of unity and diversity, of partnership in the call of God
and variety in the gifts of grace which is described in 1 Cor., chapter 12. It would be a sorry defeatism to believe that that is merely
an ecclesiastical castle in the air.

If we are really partners in one and the same call. Unity—visible,
convincing unity—is not a matter that Christians can be for or
against. It does not admit of neutrality. This is part of our Chris-

tian commitment. There is no place for neutrality. The pioneers of the ecumenical movement, men like Brent, Gardiner, Mott, Ainslie in this country were not the victims of some wild utopianism. They had rediscovered a basic biblical insight. "Dieu le veut." He who does not gather with the Lord—that is, he who does not work for the unity of the Church—scatters; that is, he is not on the side of the God who gathers his children together.

There will be no true advance in the ecumenical movement until this constraint, this pressure of our common calling, is felt by the whole membership of our churches. The finest systems of ecumenical education will be of no avail, unless it is preached and understood in our congregations that the Church is the Church of God and that he wills its unity. How can the very imperfect unity which we already have become the unity which we should have?

But how can we arrive at this unity? The answer is contained in our text. We are told to consider Jesus and to consider him as apostle and high priest. Is it strange that Jesus is called an apostle? Not if we remember that the verb *apostellein* is so often used by Jesus himself. In John 17 we read that Jesus prays: "As thou didst send me into the world, so I have sent them (the disciples) into the world." The apostle is God's special servant entrusted with a mission. And Jesus is in a very real sense the original apostle, as Hebrews 12 puts it: "the pioneer" whose life and death and resurrection are at the same time the beginning and the foundation of the mission to which God calls his people.

The fact that we are asked to consider Jesus as the one sent by God to perform a specific mission shows that the call we have heard is not simply a call to a new status. God did not call us to give us a claim to specific spiritual privileges. His call is a call to action, a mandate, an invitation to participate in the great mission entrusted to his people in the whole world. There is only one mission as there is one call and one Church. The mission consists in the ministry of reconciliation through which men are reconciled to God and with each other. It includes, of course, the witness to the ends of the earth among all who have not yet heard the call. For the very *raison d'être* of the Church lies in God's desire that his offer of reconciliation in Christ may be carried by his ambassadors to all nations, to all men. But mission refers to the total task of the Church and includes therefore the life which it exemplifies in its fellowship as it reconciles nations, races and classes, the disinterested service it renders to all in need, the witness through which it proclaims the Lordship of Christ over all realms of life and pronounces God's judgment on injustice, greed, lust for power. Since the mission is the response to the one call, it must be carried out in togetherness and fellowship. It is not simply that we waste our energies by failing to cooperate or to develop a common strategy. This goes deeper. We do not accomplish the full purpose of God unless we witness in unity, unless our whole approach to the world manifests the marvelous cohesion and harmony of God's plan, unless we demonstrate how God reconciles his own people among themselves. In the great encounter with the other religions which have found new vitality, in the conflict with totalitarianism, in the struggle against cheap caricatures of the Christian Gospel, our cause lacks convincing power as long as we do not prove that we live under the authority of the same Word of God and have received the same marching orders.

Unity grows as we realize that we share in one call and begin to fulfill our mission together. This means far more than co-operation between the churches—as-they-are. Churches can co-operate without being changed. They cannot participate in the total mission of the Church without their life being transformed. Once the common mission takes precedence over everything else, the whole center of attention is shifted, and the Church receives a new sense of proportion. Self-centered institutionalism is replaced by faithfulness to the divine plan, and the wonderful traffic of sharing of the gifts of grace begins to flow. Has that not been the most precious thing in the life of the ecumenical movement already, how the renewed obedience of some churches has helped other churches to rediscover the great common mission? How shallow, how poor would the ecumenical movement be today if it had not received the testimony of those churches which have found new life in the very moment of their greatest peril. We need unity in order that each of us, each of our churches, may be really surrounded by the great cloud of witnesses.

We have got to give attention to one further aspect of our text. We are not only to consider Jesus, the Apostle, but also Jesus, the High Priest. The ultimate reason why we are indestructibly linked together is the act by which Jesus performed once and for all the supreme sacrifice. The call which has come to us is an offer of reconciliation—not a possible reconciliation or a theory about reconciliation, but an effective, factual reconciliation. Our unity has its irremovable center in the cross. As we come nearer to that cross, we come nearer to each other. As we consider the High Priest who has shared our condition, tempted in every respect as we are, yet without sinning, we realize more deeply that our lack of unity is a denial of his work of salvation. At the Lord's table to which we are invited we will meet him as he shares with us his body, broken for us, and his blood, shed for us. We come as men and women who know only too well that they are not worthy to gather the crumbs under that table. We hear embarrassing questions. If this sacrament is the sacrament of unity *par excellence,* how can it be that we meet at this table and still remain separate in other ways? And have we the right to deny access to the Lord's table to any who believe sincerely that they will meet the Lord himself in this sacrament? But, thank God, at his table the Lord himself speaks the first and the last word. As he gives himself once again to us, he will convince us that he holds the initiative in our lives and that of our churches, that he continues to gather his disciples and that he will complete what he began.

The Significance of the Ecumenical Movement

SERMON BY BISHOP JOHANNES LILJE
SUNDAY, SEPTEMBER 8, 1957

When the great German philosopher Hegel, shortly before his death, heard about Christian world missions, he exclaimed: "This is the most significant event of our time." A hundred years later, one of the greatest Christian leaders of modern Church history, William Temple, at his consecration as Archbishop of Canterbury, made a similar statement in his inaugural address: "The rise of the ecumenical movement is the greatest event in modern Church history." This statement is doubtless true. There is scarcely another movement within the Christian Church which could compare with the ecumenical movement in vigor and comprehensiveness. A burning desire for greater Christian unity has spread and is spreading throughout Christendom like an irresistible, all-consuming prairie fire.

More than thirty years of prayer and labor, study and organization, have gone into the ecumenical movement. Christian leaders whom we shall never forget paved the way. Christian people of other lands joined the procession. Ancient churches, like those of Southern India, seemed to emerge out of the past into new life. New churches in Asia and Africa came into existence. Both helped to give new dimensions to the horizon of Christianity. A rich and wonderful heritage has been transmitted to us out of these thirty years.

But today is a new day, different and challenging. What is true of the Church, is true of the ecumenical movement also: no church, old and rich though her tradition may be, can afford today to live upon her past history or accomplishments alone; she has to face the present. Even so the ecumenical movement, though only a few decades old, dare not, must not become static. Our world has changed rapidly and radically in these thirty years. The first half of this present century was filled with bloodshed, cruel wars and human tragedies which far exceeded the experience of previous generations. We face a totally new situation.

We must rethink our ecumenical activities. If there ever was a time in which the unity of the Christian Church, unity in thought and action, was urgently needed, it is today. This means that we have to rethink our whole Christian status, our Christian message and our Christian way of living, in the light of greater Christian unity.

I. THE UNITY WE HAVE ACHIEVED

This would not be a true and faithful account if we did not start with the unity that actually has been achieved. At the outset we categorically repudiate the charge that the ecumenical movement is something fine and artificial, something imposed upon our congregations from without but not really known by them. I would rather assert that within the last generation, especially since World War II, there has been a steady growth of what I should like to call ecumenical consciousness. In particular this is true of the Christian churches of Europe, especially in the countries most afflicted by the war. The people in those countries—I mean the plain ordinary Christians—have realized as never before what the world-wide community of Christians can mean in this troubled world. They did not need intricate theological explanations concerning ecclesiology and ecumenicity but spontaneously, immediately grasped that reality of the Church Universal which exists in and by faith and which acts through love.

It is impossible to retreat behind this line. One cannot erase the memory of unforgettable experiences. We dare not ignore the ardent desire of so many plain Christians for a greater, more visible and more effective union of Christians and the Christian churches.

I should like to add one remark about our relationship to the Church of Rome. Where does she stand in relation to the ecumenical movement? We know that for centuries this church has said over and over again: "The only possible way to unity is for all the other churches to return to the bosom of the Church of Rome." We know, of course, that many Roman Catholics individually possess strong ecumenical sentiments and exercise friendliness and even Christian love toward non-Catholics; we know this spirit, so nobly represented in Abbe Couturier's phrase: "Unity at the time which God sets and with the means He gives." But it is perfectly obvious that this is not the ultimate attitude of Rome herself. Over against Protestantism with its manifold divisions Rome maintains with monotonous repetition that real and visible unity can be achieved only under the Pope. There seems to be no doubt that the ecumenical movement compares favorably with this rigidly inflexible attitude. It may not be amiss to call to mind that Protestantism, which is so frequently blamed for having sown the seed of disunity within Christendom, was neither the first nor the greatest schism which Rome had to suffer; the great schism of 1054—900 years before Evanston!—separated the large and important body of the Eastern Church from its Latin lord. And it is equally important to note that Protestantism, so often criticized for its tendency toward divisiveness, has in the ecumenical movement shown a noteworthy amount of flexibility, vitality and cohesiveness; moreover, while steadily advancing all along the line, the ecumenical movement has exercised a theological and doctrinal vigilance which is one of its most attractive and fruitful features.

Ecumenical consciousness is closely related to ecumenical action. The spontaneous desire of Christians to help each other not only affects the receiving partner, but it has far-reaching effects also upon those who are asked to give, act and sacrifice. Especially those churches which, under God, had the good fortune to change from the status of receiving churches to that of giving ones, experienced with unambiguous clarity that it is part of the full stature of Christianity to learn, to think, to plan, to decide and, most of all, to act in terms of Christian love. This, too, is part of the ecumenical reality within the churches. For love transcends all boundaries, including those of confessions and denominations.

I want to underscore once again the importance of the common process of theological thinking which has been going on for thirty years. In some respects this is the most tangible result of the ecumenical encounter of our generation. The number of outstanding publications is excellent proof of the fruitfulness of this worldwide exchange of theological thoughts.

It is necessary to mention a fourth element of the unity already achieved. Christianity throughout the world has regained a new sense of responsibility in public life. This is especially true in the sphere of politics, domestic as well as international. In a manner nearly unknown in the last two centuries, Christianity has learned anew to raise its prophetic voice with reference to the burning issues of political and social life. In facing some of the major crises of the political developments of recent years Christianity has learned soberly and realistically to weigh the facts involved and yet vigorously and fearlessly to proclaim the will of God and Christian standards. Experience has grown in this realm, and the Commission of the Churches on International Affairs, CCIA, has developed into an excellent instrument for handling those problems which arise continually in this turbulent world of ours.

II. THE UNITY WE SEEK

Christianity has developed a distinctive sense of ecumenicity. But still we face the question how to go on. Can we go on in the same way as the last twenty years? Would we want to do so? Or do we have to rethink radically our whole ecumenical approach? Have we gone in the wrong direction? Must we retrace our steps?

These questions are not rhetorical. There is, for instance, one fundamental presupposition which everybody seems to take for granted. That is the question whether we should have ecumenicity in the form of an organization. Do we have to organize at all? Is the One Holy Apostolic and Catholic Church a matter of organization? Is the Church that we confess in our Creed something which, even in part, can organize at all? Even in a more limited way this problem exists. Is it necessary for us to try to achieve uniformity in worship, doctrinal expression, church administration and the like? Is there any fundamental reason, based on Scripture or common Christian experience, which makes this indispensable?

If we take these questions seriously, then one thing is certain: the fundamental unity of the Church is something very different from formal uniformity. There must be a unity which goes far beyond our attempts to organize. The real unity of the Church must not be organized, but exercised.

This has to do with the very nature of the Church. All Christians agree that the One Holy Catholic Church of our Creed is not a human institution. She is God's creation within history. She is his chosen people. This Church exists and by her very nature she can only be one, whatever human diversities may have developed in the course of her earthly history. This statement, if true, has a number of consequences.

(a) The ultimate aim of the ecumenical movement cannot be confined to any achievement in the sphere of organization. It must be the rediscovery of the Church, her fullness and her real essence. The Church *is* one. No human effort is required to make her one or capable of doing so. All we have to do is to recognize and understand anew this basic fact.

Now this is just the sore point in all our deliberations: the Church certainly does not have the appearance of being one. This precisely is the predicament which has brought us together, that countless divisions and subdivisions seem to have split the body of the Church asunder. It is very doubtful whether we can escape this depressing reality by merely pointing to beautiful theological theories. We will have to deal with this problem in a minute.

(b) Before we do so, however, I must point out a few consequences which naturally result from the statement that the unity of the Church exists now. If this be true the solution of the problem of greater Christian unity cannot be found in a simple return to Rome. This would, indeed, be far too simple. In spite of the fact that modern historical research, also on the part of Protestant scholars, has revealed that there is a great deal to be said for the unique position which in the New Testament Peter holds among the apostles, this certainly does not include the total justification of the claims made by Peter's successors on the Papal throne. Moreover, I reject the notion that the Church needs that sort of historic guarantee of her continuity which is supposed to be given in the apostolic succession of bishops. Even while admitting that to some churches and to some Christians this idea has a rather traditional value, I could not agree to the claim that historical episcopacy is an essential and indispensable element of the order of salvation.

But, while a return to Rome would not solve the problem, neither would the mere rejection of Roman-Catholic dogma be sufficient for a real rediscovery of the Church. The true nature of the Church cannot be discovered by the method of theological limitation or negation.

(c) There is still another important aspect which must be mentioned. If we try to rediscover the Church in the midst of all our denominational differences we need an acute sense of self-criticism. We must be able with the utmost objectivity to consider the weaknesses, shortcomings and failures of our own particular Church. One of the most sinister impediments on the road to greater unity is theological *securitas,* that is, the assumption that all is well in one's own theological camp, the smug conceit that one's own denomination is superior to others, in short, confessionalistic pride. Where the sense of critical self-appraisal is underdeveloped, there the spiritual capacity for ecumenical encounters is correspondingly weak. Here is where the nontheological factors of the lower type creep into ecumenical relations and devastate them—e.g., the idea of a socially superior Church, a scientifically advanced Church and whatever other un-Christian standards of evaluation we may think of.

This, however, is one of the outstanding results of the ecumenical discussion of the past few years: no rediscovery of the Church is possible unless we place the main emphasis upon her Christocentricity. This is what we must stress, indeed: unless Christ is in the center, we have no valid point of orientation. All of us, of course, are quite willing to say so. There seems to be no disagreement at all concerning this point. Two remarks are necessary in order to save this statement from being misunderstood as a meaningless generality. The first is that our differing interpretations of Christ's person and work are precisely the sources of many of our diversities. The second point is a constructive one: no real and lasting renewal of the Church has ever taken place which was not based upon a new and comprehensive experience of Christ as the Living One.

In saying so we declare and affirm that this experience is still a possibility. If we really believe in the continuity of the revelation of God in Jesus Christ, then we believe too that his Church on earth can be given a new vision of his glory.

III. THE WAY TO UNITY

It is the merit of the ecumenical movement that it has developed throughout its history a number of remarkable methods for dealing with its main problems. It is in the nature of things that most of these methods are of a theological character. Though they have covered a wide field and proved to be very successful they have sometimes, on the other hand, constituted a particular danger. Still, no movement within the Church can be of any lasting effect if it is not based upon, and corrected by theology.

There have been other approaches, too. We have compared our ways of worship and discovered how much we have to learn and may actually learn from the attitude in which each individual church stands before God in adoration and confession. Finally, we have given a great deal of thought to dealing with the problems of Christian action in public and social life.

All this is not new. Still, we have to face time and again the question how we should seek unity and whether we do it in the right way. It is one of the peculiarities of relatively young movements that they stagnate more quickly than many of the old traditional forms of church organization. Radical rethinking of our methods is needed. At least four important points must be considered.

(a) The work of theological research must go on in an untiring, relentless way. We dare not stop investigating the history of the Christian churches. For we must seek to understand, as clearly as we can, our common heritage and at the same time the origins of our various divisions. We cannot be satisfied with mere statements of facts. We have to explore the background and hidden motives of these divisions. We must be very precise in our differentiation between those schisms which are the result of heretical movements and those separations which have arisen out of obedience to the truth. We must learn to discern between the origin of denominations which have been produced by human error and even sin, and those which have attempted to restore a corrupted Church to the purity of the New Testament. Here is where we come face to face with the basic problem of all ecumenical endeavors, and it will not be easy for the scholar to make an authentic and justifiable distinction between the two.

Christian dogma, its history and its present form, will be an indispensable part of such studies. In this field, the ecumenical movement faces no particularly new task. It has to do what the Church has to do at all times, i.e., to try to present the Christian message in terms of our generation. Here the best contribution to the ecumenical task of the Church is good and sound and solid theological work done by any conscientious theologian at the desk or in his study at home. Needless to say, no theological work can be genuinely true and fruitful unless it bears fruit in the life of the congregation.

(b) The second main requirement in all ecumenical tasks is what I should like to call Christlike simplicity. I do not mean naiveté. Christian doctrine is not simple. Even the New Testament records of our Lord are not simple. Out of the simple lines of the Gospel rises the image of the Lord, of the eschatological Jesus, who is not to be grasped by human categories. The same is true of all the great doctrines of the Christian Church. For they have their origin not in the human mind but in the revelation of that God who is the inscrutable one, and who reveals himself only where and when it pleases him—*ubi et quando visum est Deo.* Nevertheless, what we need is a Christlike simplicity. It is our Christian duty to do such thorough thinking that we are able to state in crystal-clear terms what we mean. If we cannot say simply what we believe, we either do not really understand or we do not really believe what we say. In a scientific age which is accustomed to precise statements this lucid and clear simplicity is of the utmost importance. This is a paramount task of the Church under any circumstances; but it is of the utmost importance if different Christian churches wish to cope with their disagreements in such a way that they can deliver a common witness to the world.

We use the term Christlike simplicity because Christ is the same yesterday, today, and for ever (Heb. 13:8). Truth is the same in Catholicism, Lutheranism or Congregationalism—or it is not truth. Revelation is the same in the sixteenth century as in the twentieth. Christ is the same throughout the ages. Humanly speaking, we will never be able to achieve absolute precision in our witness; but we are bound to speak as precisely as we can. We will never be able to deliver a common Christian witness to the world unless we reach out continually for this Christlike simplicity.

(c) A third requirement is what I would like to call courage of thought. This is a specific quality of the mind without which the ecumenical movement never will succeed. We need courageous thinking if we want freedom from prejudice. Every student of human nature knows the horrifying power of prejudice in human relationships. Prejudice is particularly poisonous in the life and witness of the Church. Without this type of courage which, of course, is a gift of God's Spirit, we will never get far in our endeavors to achieve greater unity.

But there are other weaknesses of the human mind we have to face. There is a peculiar type of intellectual laziness without which human prejudices would never be able to do as much damage as they actually do. In spite of everything the philosophers and psychologists tell us, man just does not like to think for himself. Intellectual independence seems to be one of those rare gifts which we receive only by an act of God's grace. The Christian churches will get nowhere unless they learn to act and think in this independence of mind. It is of particular importance that they do so in dealing with each other. Christian prejudices are the worst among all types of prejudices. But how vigorous they are! The subtle pride which seems to be inherent in all denominational self-assurance is one of the most serious obstacles to real Christian unity.

(d) The most important of all the requirements is the revitalization of Christian life. This goes for the individual as well as for the churches, for the preachers and teachers as well as for each congregation. If we do not even want to be renewed in our Christian life, we had better give up all ecumenical efforts at once. If we are not capable of taking seriously all those who honestly and sincerely strive for a new vigorous life of obedience, if we lose the sense of repentance, if we cease to pray for a new outpouring of God's Spirit, all our theological and organizational efforts will be in vain. The ultimate standard by which we have to measure the ecumenical movement of our day is certainly not its theological and administrative efficiency but only the power to help towards the renewal of the Church and of the individual Christian. Let us not strive to be better Lutherans, Episcopalians or Congregationalists, not even better members of the ecumenical movement—but let us strive to be better Christians.

The Basis of Christian Fellowship

ADDRESS AT CLOSING PLENARY SESSION BY
THE REVEREND EUGENE CARSON BLAKE

Luke 11:23. "He who is not with me is against me, and he who does not gather with me scatters."
Luke 9:50. "He that is not against you is for you."

Jesus was and is a controversial character. We see him one day casting out a demon. This was marvelous to the crowd. Here was a sick man in the grip of a power so great and evil that he could not speak; a man reduced to less than humanity by some evil chance and demonic purpose.

Jesus healed him. The demon's power was broken. The man became a full man again and spoke. As I said, the people marveled at the wonder.

But in the crowd were some who were so much opposed to Jesus that they said, "He casts out demons." All right—we cannot deny it, but he does it "by Beelzebul, the prince of demons."

And there were others in the crowd who didn't care how he did it, so long as they could see a marvel. So these said in effect, "Do it again! Prove to us that you are on the side of heaven." Jesus then said to the enemies who charged him with being in league with essential evil, even though he did apparent good, "The prince of demons, Beelzebul, is no fool to give anyone power to destroy him. His kingdom is not divided. If good is done by me, beware of charging me of using demonic power. Do not reject God and his kingdom by your prejudice against me." "He who is not with me is against me, and he who does not gather *with me,* scatters." And Matthew adds here that warning of an ultimate and unforgivable sin, the blasphemy against the Holy Spirit by calling him satanic. This is the ultimate and the only unforgivable evil, to let our own evil blind us to God when he acts.

On another occasion, and note how different the occasion was, Jesus and his disciples were alone together. Among the disciples there arose an argument. They were disputing as to which was the greatest of them. Jesus then set a child in their midst to rebuke them, and said two things. In effect he said "anyone who does good to this child (or to any least important member of humanity) 'in my name'—because of me, by the grace I have given

him—that man is mine, he receives me and God who sent me."
And, then in effect, he added, "A discussion of greatness is out of
place in the kingdom of God. Here the least is greatest. The servant to the smallest and least important child is greatest."

But John, most perspicacious of the twelve, asked a question,
"Master, we saw a man casting out demons in your name and we
forbade him, because he does not follow with us." But Jesus said
to him, "Do not forbid him, for he that is not against you is for
you."

FACING A PARADOX

Here then in their differing contexts are two sayings of our
Lord, which are in apparent contradiction: "He who is not with
me is against me," and "He that is not against you is for you."

How can these two sayings be reconciled? One apparently sup-
ports us in our most sectarian moods and attitudes. "He who is
not with me is against me." The other appears to encourage the
widest conceivable cooperation. "He that is not against you is for
you." How do we reconcile this paradox?

First of all, I think we may reject outright the simple solution
offered by some New Testament scholars who suggest that we
have here a single incident that in the hearing and transcribing
mixed up what Jesus said. These suggest that there was only one
saying of Jesus and one incident, but that we cannot tell now for
sure what Jesus really said. Here is New Testament scholarship at
its worst—trying to flatten out the contradictions of the Scriptures, instead of listening to what God would say to us in the apparent paradox.

But, if Jesus did on different occasions say such completely opposite sayings, how do we reconcile them? And, more important,
what then should our attitude be towards those with whom we
are in controversy about the Christian faith and life?

In such a week as this one here together, I suppose all of us
have felt on one occasion or another the urge to read certain others
out of the Christian fellowship entirely. But aside from irritated
moods, all of us have been asking ourselves, have we not, how can
we be and work in fellowship with all this variety of deviation
from truth as I see it, even heresy, here so blatantly revealed? Are
not the Missouri Synod Lutherans right in keeping their fellowship
radically separate from the ecumenical movement? Are not the
fundamentalists right when they charge us with being in favor of
Christian unity at the cost of Christian truth? On the other hand,

during this same week all of us, I am sure, have rejoiced in this fellowship and this unity. Struggling together to see through the problems of organizational structure and of theological belief, we have in exultation thanked our God for the unity he has given us in Jesus Christ. In common worship and in discussion, friend with friend, we have come again to the universal and ecumenical conviction that the unity we seek is here—the gift of Jesus Christ to his Church—torn and divided though we be. This paradox of typical ecumenical experience matches the paradox of the two sayings of Jesus, which are my texts. Let us see whether a closer examination of them may indicate to us the way our Lord would have us walk as we strive to continue as his disciples after Oberlin. Let us look at the second text first.

Note first of all that as Luke and Mark report the incident, it is in the context of a discussion among the disciples themselves. And they are in dispute as to which of them is greatest. It is almost a description of an ecumenical conference at its worst, isn't it? Oh, we are all subtle about it. We aren't quite so naive as John's mother when she asked our Lord for the places closest to Jesus on his right and left for her sons in his kingdom. We are polite in our disputes as to which church is nearest to our Lord.

THE BOUNDS OF FELLOWSHIP

It is when we have allowed ourselves to fall into this sin of ambition and pretension—and who is entirely free of it? Even the twelve stumbled here as we do—it is against this background that Jesus warns us that the first place in the kingdom is reserved for the disciple who serves, who will deny himself and sacrifice himself for others, for even the least of the little ones. Furthermore, the standard that John here proposes is whether the lone exorcist is in their company. The man is casting out demons in *your* name, but he does not follow with *us*. John is proposing that the practices and understanding of the disciples themselves should be used as the boundary of Christ's Church. But this is clearly wrong, not only by the authority of Jesus' clear word, "He that is not against you is for you," but by the sad proofs of all our Christian history. How conveniently we forget his word, "Judge not that you be not judged. For with the judgment you pronounce you will be judged, and the measure you give will be the measure you get." Which one of us dares pose as guiltless here? Whether we are considering one another's faith or polity, Billy Graham, or the Southern Baptists, or the Roman Church, it is so easy to judge them and to judge them by us and our standard. To us in this mood and in this context, our Lord clearly says, "Stop. Do not make your company so exclusive. He serves in my name, too. Do not forbid him. He that is not against you is for you."

Even Edwin Markham's poem, judged, I suppose, by most of us as shallow and sentimental, has its authentic Christian sentiment in this context.

> He drew a circle that shut me out—
> Heretic, rebel, a thing to flout.
> But Love and I had the wit to win
> And we drew a circle that took him in![1]

Our real trouble with Markham is that we know he oversimplifies the problem. Conviction is important. Creeds have fruits. Truth is in order to goodness. Opposing conviction about central matters makes co-operation questionable and unity impossible.

Look then at the other saying of Jesus—my companion text. Here the scene and stage is different even though the general background is again the casting out of a demon. Here it is Jesus who heals the man. And here the controversy is not among disciples, but with the world which, in the persons of the Pharisees and Rulers, are about to reject our Lord and at last to crucify him.

No one challenges the fact of the healing. The man who was dumb now speaks. So today, the world does not seriously challenge the social values of a Christian culture. But then and now the crucial and decisive question is whether we and the world will confess Jesus to be the Christ and the Son of the living God. The world would not. The world does not. What is more, there is in this rejection of Jesus Christ, combined with ordinary human sin, a negative and blasphemous confession. Jesus is too impelling to be ignored. Those who do not confess him Lord and God proceed to charge him with casting out demons by the power of the prince of demons. Prejudice against Jesus, hatred of Jesus, drive some to the ultimate sin of calling good evil, and of charging the Son of God with being in league with Beelzebul, the prince of evil. Here is the boundary. Here is the definition. Here is the decisive yes or no.

THE DECISIVE ISSUE

The basis of the World Council of Churches—those churches which accept Jesus Christ as God and Savior—has been challenged by some critics as inadequate theologically. It has been

---

[1]Reprinted by permission of Virgil Markham.

asked how the ecumenical movement dares choose one of the cardinal Christian doctrines, the incarnation, ignoring the rest, the
atonement, the resurrection, and the parousia in its Christian
definition. And even within our fellowship some have worried
about the theological inadequacy of the basis, wishing to make it
more specifically trinitarian and to tie it explicitly to the Scriptures. In a recent article, one conservative critic quotes Jesus himself as a warning to us, "Not every one who says to me, 'Lord, Lord,'
shall enter the kingdom of heaven." His implication was that the
World Council of Churches includes all who cry, "Lord, Lord."

But such a use of a New Testament verse entirely out of context is a misuse of the Scriptures. Jesus was here clearly warning
us of the dangers of profession without obedience. He was not sug-
gesting that some who confessed him Lord would not enter the
kingdom because they were otherwise heretical.

I remind you, as we have often been reminded, that the foundation of the ecumenical movement is the confession of Jesus Christ
as Lord. The New Testament again and again justifies the basis
of our ecumenical movement and warns that no other issue is
equally crucial. Not only this text, which makes it clear that what
is decisive is the relationship to the living Christ, "He who is not
with me is against me," but verse after verse makes the confession
of Jesus as the Son of God the decisive measure. "Blessed are you,
Simon Bar-Jona! For flesh and blood has not revealed this to you,
but my Father who is in heaven. And I tell you, you are Peter,
and on this rock I will build my church." And in 1 John, "By
this you know the Spirit of God: every spirit which confesses that
Jesus Christ has come in the flesh is of God." "Whoever confesses
that Jesus is the Son of God, God abides in him, and he in God."
"Everyone who believes that Jesus is the Christ is a child of God."

LESSONS FOR THE FUTURE

So in conclusion, I venture to remind you of three clear lessons
that you and I need to ponder and to learn from the two para-
doxical texts which I have discussed at the close of this ecumenical
conference.

1. First remember that the context of both texts is the healing
of a man by the power of Jesus Christ. Let us, therefore, whatever
else we do, never forget that Jesus himself has said, "By their fruits
ye shall know them." Whatever else we do, let us devote ourselves
in Christ's spirit to the sacrificial service of all sorts and conditions
of men. Let us remember that if we would be in the company of

Jesus Christ, we will be giving ourselves as he did to the healing of the sick, to the feeding of the hungry, to the visiting of the rejected, and to the casting out of demons.

2. Let us take to ourselves a warning. Beware of judging other followers of Christ by our own standards. Let others be warned too of their danger of so judging the ecumenical movement. But let us all be warned that the kingdom of evil is not divided and that no one is beyond the circle of our communion, except those who are antichrist, who call good evil and who reject him who is our Lord. Let us be warned of how easy it is to allow our prejudices to be decisive and to make our ways rather than Jesus Christ the decisive standard.

3. Finally, let us be encouraged despite all our problems of cooperation, communion and unity, to press on, in the way our fathers began, to seek more perfectly to exhibit to the world the unity which Christ has given to us that the world too may believe that Jesus Christ is the Son of God and its only Savior.

So dedicated, we may have faith that the Spirit of God will lead us through all our perplexities into the joy of Christ's kingdom and into unbroken communion with him and with one another.

THE DAILY
SCHEDULE OF THE CONFERENCE

Tuesday, September 3

3:00- 5:00 Opening Plenary Session
Chairman: Dr. Eugene Carson Blake
SERVICE OF WORSHIP
ADDRESS: The Rt. Rev. Angus Dun
WELCOME TO THE CONFERENCE:
President William E. Stevenson of Oberlin College

7:45- 9:30 Plenary Session
Chairman: The Rt. Rev. Angus Dun
REPORT: Dr. J. Robert Nelson
ADDRESS: "Christ and the Church"—Dr. Robert L. Calhoun
EVENING PRAYERS: The Rt. Rev. Georges L. Florovsky

Wednesday, September 4

8:40- 9:00 Morning Prayers: Dr. Wilfred C. Lockhart
9:00- 9:30 Bible Study: Dr. W. A. Visser 't Hooft
9:45-10:45 Section Meetings
11:00-12:00 Division Meetings
2:30- 5:30 Section Meetings
7:45- 9:30 Plenary Session
Chairman: Dr. Emlyn Davies
ADDRESS: "Our Common History as Christians"—
Dr. Albert C. Outler
EVENING PRAYERS: Dr. Eugene R. Fairweather

Thursday, September 5

8:40- 9:00 Morning Prayers: The Very Rev. Fr. F. M. Galdau
9:00- 9:30 Bible Study: Dr. Walter J. Harrelson
9:45-11:45 Section Meetings
2:00- 5:30 Section Meetings
7:45- 9:30 Plenary Session
Chairman: The Rt. Rev. Angus Dun
ADDRESS: "Institutions in Relation to Unity and Disunity"—
Dr. Walter G. Muelder
EVENING PRAYERS: Dr. Nils Ehrenstrom

Friday, September 6

8:40- 9:00 Morning Prayers: Dr. Cornelius Wierenga
9:00- 9:30 Bible Study: Dr. Walter J. Harrelson
9:45-11:45 Section Meetings
2:00- 4:00 Division Meetings
7:45- 9:30 Plenary Session
Chairman: Dr. Emlyn Davies

REPORT FROM ASIA: Dr. J. Russell Chandran
ADDRESS: "The Shape of the Church's Response
in Worship"—Dr. Joseph Sittler
EVENING PRAYERS: Dr. Winthrop Hudson

Saturday, September 7

8:40- 9:00   Morning Prayers: The Rev. W. O. Carrington
9:00- 9:30   Bible Study: Dr. Walter J. Harrelson
9:45-11:45   Section Meetings
2:30- 4:30   Plenary Session
Chairman: Dr. Eugene Carson Blake
Conference Business
Preliminary Reports from the Divisions
9:00-10:00   Organ Concert: Dr. Grigg Fountain

Sunday, September 8

11:00   Service of Morning Worship and Holy Communion by
invitation of First Church in Oberlin
Dr. Joseph King
Dr. Douglas Horton
Dr. W. A. Visser 't Hooft
3:30- 5:30   Reception: President and Mrs. William E. Stevenson
7:45- 9:30   Service of Ecumenical Worship
Presiding: The Rt. Rev. Angus Dun,
Assisted by overseas guests
SERMON: Bishop Johannes Lilje

Monday, September 9

8:40- 9:00   Morning Prayers: Dr. Carlyle Marney
9:00- 9:30   Bible Study: Dr. Walter J. Harrelson
9:45-11:45   Final Section and Division Meetings
2:00- 5:00   Plenary Session
Chairman: Dr. Eugene Carson Blake
Presentation and Discussion of Report from Division III
7:45- 9:30   Plenary Session
Chairman: Dr. Eugene Carson Blake
Presentation and Discussion of Report from Division II
EVENING PRAYERS: Dr. Franklin Clark Fry

Tuesday, September 10

8:40- 9:00   Morning Prayers: Dr. Robert S. Bilheimer
9:00- 9:30   Bible Study: Dr. Walter J. Harrelson
9:45-11:45   Plenary Session
Chairman: The Rt. Rev. Angus Dun
Presentation and Discussion of Report from Division I
2:00- 3:00   Closing Service of Worship
Chairman: The Rt. Rev. Angus Dun,
Assisted by Dr. Samuel McCrea Cavert
SERMON: Dr. Eugene Carson Blake

THE PROCEEDINGS OF THE CONFERENCE

The conference opened on Tuesday afternoon, September 3, with a service of worship and praise, led by Dr. Eugene Carson Blake and Professor Paul S. Minear. The hymns were "Blessing and Honor and Glory and Power," "All People that on Earth Do Dwell" and "The Church's One Foundation." The Scripture lesson was St. John 10:1-10. The prayers sought God's blessing on the Church and his guidance of the conference in seeking God's will for the Church. An address by Bishop Angus Dun interpreted the background of the conference, its objective and its spirit (see pages 31-43).

BUSINESS SESSION

Following the service of worship a cordial address of welcome to Oberlin College was given by its president, Dr. William E. Stevenson. He expressed his personal interest in the conference by recalling that his father, Dr. J. Ross Stevenson, had attended the World Missionary Conference at Edinburgh in 1910, which marked the organizational beginning of the ecumenical movement, the first World Conference on Faith and Order held in Lausanne in 1927, the Edinburgh Conference on Faith and Order in 1937, and the Utrecht Conference at which the constitution of the World Council of Churches was drafted. He then gave an interpretation of Oberlin College in terms of its historical background and present life.

In behalf of the Committee on Arrangements, representing the U.S. Conference for the World Council of Churches, the Canadian Council of Churches and the National Council of the Churches of Christ in the U.S.A., Dr. Samuel McCrea Cavert presented three recommendations, which were unanimously adopted:

(1) That the presiding officers of the conference be as follows:

Chairman	Bishop Angus Dun
Vice-Chairmen	Dr. Eugene Carson Blake
	Dr. Emlyn Davies

(2) That Dr. J. Robert Nelson be requested to serve as recording secretary of the plenary sessions.

(3) That a Steering Committee be appointed consisting of the three presiding officers (Dun, Blake and Davies), the chairmen of the three divisions (Dr. Gerald R. Cragg, Professor Robert Tobias and Dean Merrimon Cuninggim), together with Miss Leila W. Anderson, Chancellor John M. Ellison, Father William S. Schneirla and Professor Joseph A. Sittler, with Professor Paul S. Minear as secretary.

Dr. Minear, as secretary for study and program, explained the organization of the conference in three divisions, each with four sections, and introduced the leaders of the divisions and sections as follows:

General Theme: *The Nature of the Unity We Seek*

Division I—*In Faithfulness to the Eternal Gospel*
>   Dr. Gerald R. Cragg, Chairman
>   Prof. Hugh T. Kerr, Jr., Secretary

Section 1. *Imperatives and Motivations*
>   Bishop F. Gerald Ensley, Chairman
>   Prof. William O. Fennell, Secretary

Section 2. *Doctrinal Consensus and Conflict*
>   Pres. Edgar M. Carlson, Chairman
>   Pres. Walter N. Roberts, Secretary

Section 3. *Baptism into Christ*
>   Rt. Rev. Stephen F. Bayne, Chairman
>   Rev. George L. Hunt, Secretary

Section 4. *The Table of the Lord*
>   Dean James I. McCord, Chairman
>   Dr. Howard G. Hageman, Secretary

Division II—*In Terms of Organizational Structures*
>   Prof. Robert Tobias, Chairman
>   Prof. Georgia Harkness, Secretary

Section 5. *The Life of the Congregation*
>   Dr. Emlyn Davies, Chairman
>   Rev. Richard D. Isler, Secretary

Section 6. *The Work of State and Local Councils*
>   Prof. Elmer J. F. Arndt, Chairman
>   Dean William B. Blakemore, Secretary

Section 7. *Authority and Freedom in Church Government*
>   Dr. Truman B. Douglass, Chairman
>   Prof. Robert T. Handy, Secretary

Section   8.   *The Variations in Denominational Polities*
    Prof. David W. Hay, Chairman
    Rt. Rev. Robert T. Gibson, Secretary

Division III—*In View of Cultural Pressures*
    Dean Merrimon Cuninggim, Chairman
    Dean John B. Coburn, Secretary

Section   9.   *The Mobility of the Population*
    Rev. Walter Kloetzli, Chairman
    Dean Rembert Stokes, Secretary

Section 10.   *Governmental Policies and Programs*
    Dr. Roswell P. Barnes, Chairman
    Dr. Alford Carleton, Secretary

Section 11.   *Forces at Work on the College Campus*
    Rev. Henry Horn, Chairman
    Prof. Preston T. Roberts, Jr., Secretary

Section 12.   *Racial and Economic Stratification*
    Dr. J. Oscar Lee, Chairman
    Miss Isabel W. Rogers, Secretary

EVENING SESSIONS

The plenary sessions on four successive evenings were devoted to the subjects which are being studied over a period of several years by four theological commissions of the World Council's Commission on Faith and Order, as follows:

Christ and the Church
Tradition and the Traditions
Institutionalism
Worship

On Tuesday evening, September 3, Dean J. Robert Nelson, for the last four years secretary of the World Council's Commission on Faith and Order, spoke of the significance of the movement as a whole in the light of its development over thirty years and its present program (see pages 44-51). Professor Robert L. Calhoun of Yale Divinity School, chairman of the North American Commission on "Christ and the Church," then addressed the conference on that theme (see pages 52-78).

On Wednesday evening, September 4, Professor Albert C. Outler of Perkins School of Theology, chairman of the North American Commission on Tradition and the Traditions, spoke on the theme "Our Common History as Christians" (see pages 79-89).

On Thursday evening, September 5, Dean Walter G. Muelder of the Boston University School of Theology, chairman of the Faith and Order Commission on Institutionalism, gave an address on "Institutions in Relation to Unity and Disunity" (see pages 90-102).

On Friday evening, September 6, Professor Joseph A. Sittler of the Federated Theological Faculty of the University of Chicago, chairman of the North American Commission on Worship, spoke on the theme "The Shape of the Church's Response in Worship" (see pages 103-115). Principal J. Russell Chandran, of the United Theological College at Bangalore, India, also gave a report on the work of the Asian Commission on Worship, of which he is chairman (see pages 116-120).

The addresses interpreting the work of the four theological commissions were received with grateful enthusiasm. One seasoned veteran-attendant at both denominational and interdenominational gatherings remarked that he had never heard a series of addresses by four different speakers which maintained so high a level of stimulating thought.

PLENARY DISCUSSIONS

The basic work of the conference was done by the twelve sections. Beginning on Wednesday, September 4, and continuing until Saturday noon, September 7, all of the mornings and afternoons were set aside for their meetings—six times in their separate groupings and three times in their divisional formations. In the smaller intimate sessions there was a frank give-and-take of discussion, a creative sharing of insights—and sometimes an unexpected measure of agreement. Each section at the beginning of its work had one or more orientation papers before it, growing out of the work of the sixteen regional study groups in the U.S.A. and Canada during the preceding two years.

Before the reports of any of the divisions were drafted, there was a plenary session, held on Saturday afternoon, September 7, at which the officers of the divisions gave informal oral reports on the course of the discussions of the preceding days and the conclusions which seemed to be emerging. This afforded an opportunity for all delegates to express their reactions to any aspect of the whole theme. After a respite for reflection on Sunday the sections met again on Monday morning, either separately or within the divisional groupings, for putting reports into final shape.

At the beginning of the plenary session on Saturday afternoon, September 7, greetings were acknowledged from many friends interested in the conference, including Metropolitan Leonty, of the Russian Orthodox Greek Catholic Church of America; Bishop Kenneth G. Hamilton, of the General Synod of the Moravian Church; and Dr. Hendrikus Berkhof, director of the Driebergen Seminary of the Reformed Church of the Netherlands.

A recommendation of the Steering Committee that a committee be appointed to prepare a message from the conference to the churches was adopted and the following persons were named as members of the committee:

Dr. Truman B. Douglass, Convener

Dr. Hampton Adams	Dr. Ernest E. Long
Bishop Athenagoras	Mrs. Eugene R. McCarthy
Dean John B. Coburn	Dean Alexander Purdy
Judge John A. Fulton	President James H. L. Puxley
Bishop Nolan B. Harmon	Prof. Warren Quanbeck
Dr. Wilber G. Katz	Prof. Roger L. Shinn

Dr. Gerald R. Cragg made an oral summary of the work of Division I, "The Nature of the Unity We Seek in Faithfulness to the Eternal Gospel," and invited comment and criticism from the floor as a guide to the division in preparing the draft of its report.

Dean Walter G. Muelder inquired why "the insights which come to us from biblical theology" are the only "common resource" mentioned in the report. Dr. Cragg replied that the commission was concerned to emphasize the fact that there is today a widespread recognition of the Bible as common court of appeal.

Father Florovsky took exception to the reference to the mode of baptism as "insignificant" in comparison with the understanding of the essential meaning of baptism and suggested that it would be better to describe the mode as "not of decisive importance." He commented that the Orthodox and the Baptists agree that immersion was the biblical practice.

Professor Robert Tobias, as chairman, and Professor Georgia Harkness, as secretary, of Division II, "The Nature of the Unity We Seek in Terms of Organizational Structures," gave a preview of the contents of the division's report and invited comment and criticism.

Professor William O. Fennell felt that it was important to make a clearer distinction between "order" and "organization" and pointed out that the tentative outline of the report apparently ignores the importance of a common understanding of "order." Dean Douglas Horton called attention to the fact that Section 8 intimates that "order" never appears naked but always in the clothing of "organization."

Mr. Peter Day thought that the report ought not to make any reference to federated and community churches unless they are sponsored by councils of churches. Dr. Thomas B. McDormand suggested that community churches often submerged denominational heritages in a way which is non-ecumenical.

Rev. Stuart B. Coles suggested a treatment of unity in worship along the line indicated in Professor Sittler's address.

Dean William R. Cannon urged that more attention be given to the basic importance of freedom of conscience.

Rev. Kenneth E. Smith dissented from the judgment that "doing things together" by congregations can be counted upon to enlarge the vision of unity. Rev. Emlyn Davies expressed the desire that the report should make a Christian critique of society, which he felt to be an urgent need.

Dr. Louis H. Fowler asked that the report clarify its idea of the kind of organization which is requisite as an expression of unity.

Dean Merrimon Cuninggim presented an interpretation of the tentative conclusions of Division III, "The Nature of the Unity We Seek in View of Cultural Pressures" and invited comments and criticism.

Professor Fennell felt that the report might fall into a "basic dichotomy" in its approach to the relation of the Church to culture since the earlier part indicated that they should not be set against each other while a later part seemed to consider cultural factors from a wholly pragmatic standpoint while considering the Church from the theological standpoint. He urged the importance of approaching the problems of both Church and culture theologically and of judging them both in the light of the Lordship of Christ. Dr. Coles supported this viewpoint and suggested that the interest with which Division III is dealing may give new life to the interests of Faith and Order.

Judge John A. Fulton cautioned against overstressing the principle that "only God can give unity" lest it create the impression that men do not need to work at the problem.

Dean Stephanou called attention to the distinctive position of the Orthodox Church with reference to the relation of Church and culture, reminding the conference that Orthodoxy has always been closely identified with the culture of its people. He felt that in the West the disruption of religious unity had had a real connection with the disruption of cultural unity.

SUNDAY INTERLUDE

On Sunday morning and afternoon there were no sessions of the conference. At eleven o'clock the First Church of Oberlin (Congregational), which in many ways served as host to the conference, held a service of Holy Communion to which all were invited. The Rev. Joseph King, minister of the church, and Dean Douglas Horton conducted the service and Rev. W. A. Visser 't Hooft preached the sermon (see pages 121-126). At the same hour the Divine Liturgy of Saint John Chrysostom was celebrated in the Church of St. Nicholas at Lorain.

On Sunday afternoon the members of the conference were guests at a reception given by President and Mrs. William E. Stevenson of Oberlin College.

On Sunday evening there was a public meeting in Finney Chapel at which Bishop Johannes Lilje of Hanover, Germany, spoke on "The Significance of the Ecumenical Movement." Sharing in the worship of the occasion were Right Rev. Angus Dun, Right Rev. Athenagoras, Bishop Sante U. Barbieri (Argentina), Rev. Francis E. O'B. Geldenhuys (South Africa), Rev. V. E. Devadutt (India) and Rev. W. A. Visser 't Hooft (Netherlands). The order of worship, as also the orders for the opening and closing sessions of the conference, had been prepared by a committee under the chairmanship of Dr. George F. Harkins.

DISCUSSION OF REPORTS

At the beginning of the plenary session on Monday afternoon, September 9, the presiding officer, Dr. Blake, reminded the conference of two principles which prevail in Faith and Order conferences: (1) that complete freedom is given to all members to express the views they hold; (2) that the conference in no way approves or adopts the views of any individual that may be contrary to the conviction of any of the member churches. He referred, by way of illustration, to a paragraph in the address of the preceding evening. He then explained that the Eastern Orthodox delegation desired to make a statement concerning its position and setting forth its conviction that unity has been historically embodied and is realized today in the Orthodox Church. Bishop Athenagoras then presented the statement, the full text of which is given on pages 159-163.

A first tentative draft of a proposed Message to the Churches was submitted by Dr. Douglass. Father Georges Florovsky felt that the "depth of disagreement" in faith is underestimated in the Message and that its phraseology is too western and Protestant to reflect the views characteristic of Eastern Orthodoxy. Further discussion of the Message was deferred.

In behalf of Division III Dean Cuninggim then presented its report, which had been distributed to the delegates, and moved that it "be received by the conference and transmitted to the churches for information and study." After the motion had been duly seconded the discussion of the report was begun by Dr. Joseph A. Sittler, who expressed appreciation for the broadening of theological methodology involved in the effort to examine the relation of the eternal Gospel to contemporary culture. He felt, however, that one cannot arrive at a true and adequate statement of a social situation if he keeps the sociological description and the theological insight as separate as they are in the report. He further suggested that although the idea of unity as "local and operable" is important there is need to guard against the impression that the local church is identical with the Church of Christ.

Canon Douglas P. Watney felt that the situation in the university is more hopeful than the report implies.

Dr. Paul S. Wright expressed the desire for a clearer recognition that God is at work in cultural processes and is not confined within the boundaries of the Church.

Prof. John W. Grant hoped for a more definite statement of the connection between our need for unity and the fulfilment of the Christian mission in society.

Dr. Coles did not feel satisfied with the conception of the Church, reflected in the report, as being so separate from the world.

Mrs. J. Fount Tillman and Judge Fulton agreed that the report tends to underestimate the involvement of the clergy in society and the involvement of the laity in the churches.

Dr. Emlyn Davies asked whether the report should not affirm the duty of the Church to build a society which will represent a truly Christian pattern by being an expression of the Gospel in social, economic and political terms.

Dr. Francis E. Kearns urged that the reference to God as working through man should not be merely a parenthetical statement.

Dr. Graham Cotter felt it is wrong to connect "divisiveness" with differing doctrines and polities of denominations.

Objection was voiced to the reference to local churches as often being "social clubs." Miss Isabel Rogers, however, and Prof. Waldo Beach defended the language of the report. Dr. McDormand thought that the report unfortunately fails to recognize that many churches, especially in rural areas and small towns, are virtual cross-sections of the community. Prof. Gordon E. Jackson urged that the churches ought to challenge the middle-class culture of suburban communities instead of complacently reflecting it. Dr. James E. Wagner objected to the phrase "admit representatives"—which might seem to imply something like a quota system for membership in the church.

Dr. Gerald O. McCulloh questioned whether the "correlation" between the churches' manifestation of unity and the effectiveness of their witness is as "simple" as the report intimates.

Prof. Otto W. Heick, reverting to Dr. Sittler's concern over a divorce between sociological concern and theological concern, felt that the two realms cannot be merged. Prof. Fennell, on the other hand, expressed the view that the new exploration of culture in relation to the Church is a right direction for the Faith and Order Movement to take. He held that while the Church is not to "accommodate" itself to culture, "Church" and "World" should not be pictured as sharply over against each other. The right relation, he suggested, is a "dialectical conversation" in which the Church, appraising the culture, says yes to some things and no to others.

At the end of the discussion the motion to receive the Report of Division III and to transmit it to the churches for their information and study was unanimously adopted—with the understanding that in the editing of the report minor modifications might be made in the light of the discussion. (For final text of the report see pages 239-246.)

MONDAY EVENING, SEPTEMBER 9

At the beginning of the session discussion of the proposed Message to the Churches was resumed. Prof. Eugene R. Fairweather found that too little recognition was given to the depth of divisions due to conscientious convictions in matters of faith. President John A. Mackay urged a stronger emphasis on the obedient fulfilment of the Church's mission, including a reference to the biblical image of the Servant. Dean Blakemore suggested that the Message commend the reports of the Divisions and the presentations made by the chairmen of the Faith and Order theological commissions. Mr. Day suggested that the word "commend" might imply more than the conference wished to say. Dr. Murdo Nicolson did not feel satisfied with an unqualified statement that our Lord's prayer for unity (John 17:21) is unfulfilled. Prof. Bela Vassady preferred to have the Message addressed to the churches generally instead of to those churches represented at Oberlin. Dr. William J. Villaume urged a briefer message, but Prof. Edward T. Ramsdell thought the proposed draft is as brief as can do justice to the occasion.

Dr. Hiel D. Bollinger moved that the conference issue a Message embodying the points made in the first draft and of approximately the same length, with the understanding that in the light of the discussion the committee would present a revised draft later. The motion was carried without dissent.

Dr. Tobias presented the report of Division II, including three specific recommendations for action by the conference. He then moved the adoption of the first recommendation:

"that the U.S. Conference for the World Council of Churches, in consultation with the National Councils of Churches in Canada and the U.S.A., be requested to make provision for an ongoing deliberative theological study in the area of 'order and organization,' and suggests that the Toronto paper be included among papers to be studied."

The recommendation was adopted without dissenting vote.

In behalf of Division II Dr. Tobias then moved the adoption of its second recommendation:

"that the U.S. Conference for the World Council of Churches, in consultation with the National Councils of Churches in Canada and the U.S.A., be requested to make provision for an ongoing study of the ecclesiological significance of local, state and national councils of churches. The Division further suggests that in such a study attention be given to the ecclesiological significance of other organizational developments in the total life of the Church, such as community and federated churches."

Dr. Roswell P. Barnes felt it is unwise to include the reference to community and federated churches in a recommendation which has to do with councils of churches, since the community church does not have the same ecclesiological significance. Prof. Come asked whether councils of churches do, in practice, aid in establishing community churches. Ensuing comments indicated that at least a few councils do so. Dean Douglas Horton moved to amend the recommendation by omitting the sentence which refers to community and federated churches. Dean Blakemore, Dr. Hay, and Rev. Stanley E. Skinner believed that the issues raised by the community church need careful study and that a reference to them in the recommendation should be retained. Dean Horton's amendment was adopted by a majority vote and the recommendation as thus amended was then adopted.

In behalf of Division II Dr. Tobias then moved the adoption of its third resolution, as follows:

"that the U.S. Conference for the World Council of Churches and the National Council of Churches consider the creation of appropriate agencies (staff, committees, offices, etc.) as may best serve the churches in the U.S.A. in their common concerns for aspects of Faith and Order peculiar to the American scene and as may enhance their participation, separately and together, in the concerns for Faith and Order of the whole ecumenical movement."

Prof. Winthrop S. Hudson urged the importance of a close cooperation between the churches of the U.S.A. and of Canada and therefore moved that the recommendation be amended by adding the words, "it being understood that any general conference on Faith and Order that may normally be convened shall be held on a North American rather than a national basis." The amendment was unanimously approved.

Dr. J. Robert Nelson, in response to a question, strongly endorsed the recommendation, which was unanimously adopted as amended. The full text of the three recommendations, as adopted by the conference, is given on pages 210-212.

Dr. Tobias then moved that the Report of Division II be received by the conference and transmitted to the churches for information and study.

In the ensuing discussion Canon Watney asked whether the report does not overstress the importance of a visible unity expressed in organizational structure.

Dr. Franklin Clark Fry questioned whether the reference to councils of churches as fostering "community" churches should be retained since he felt that for a council to create a congregation would be to usurp the powers of the churches themselves. He also suggested that in the list of steps requisite to moving toward organizational unity an understanding of the *Gospel,* as well as of the nature of the Church and of the ministry, be included.

Mrs. S. Emlen Stokes felt that the report did not take adequate account of the position of the Friends in its references to the sacraments. Rev. David E. Witheridge felt that a rewriting of the paragraph referring to the distinction between "order" and "organization" is needed.

The motion to receive the report and transmit it to the churches for information and study, with the understanding that modifications might be made by the drafting committee in the light of the discussion, was adopted.

TUESDAY, SEPTEMBER 10

The Committee on Message to the Churches, through its chairman, Dr. Douglass, presented a revised draft to the conference, taking advantage of suggestions made during the discussion of the previous day.

Dr. Hay felt the need for a clear reference in the message to the eschatological aspect of unity and was supported by Dr. Coles. Dr. Davidson McDowell desired to see "the unity we have found" described as "unity in Christ." Dr. Coles suggested the insertion of the following statement at the beginning of the description of the nature of the unity we seek:

"a unity in Christ, who died for us, is risen, regnant, and will come again to gather together all things in His judgment and grace."

The suggestion was accepted by the conference.

Dr. Henry E. Horn felt that the reference to our sorrow over "our visible separation" ought to be revised so as to read "our visible and invisible separation." Dr. Blake suggested "our separations" as a substitute, which was favored by a majority.

Dr. Charles C. Merrill suggested that the sentence "This we have not done"—following the reference to giving Christ preeminence over our most cherished traditions—be changed to read, "This the Church as a whole has not done." Dr. R. H. Edwin Espy felt that the original statement is ambiguous. Dr. McDormand proposed the deletion of the sentence. A show of hands showed the majority as favoring the retention of the original wording.

Mr. Day thought that the sentence which introduces the description of the unity we seek ("This unity, we believe, is") needs modification and President Puxley suggested "This unity, we believe, is to be," which was favored by a majority. Dr. Hay desired to have some reference to the unity of the Church as derived from the unity of the Holy Trinity, but this was not supported by a majority.

Dr. McCulloh wondered whether it would not be better to omit the reference to "the productiveness of our labors."

Prof. V. E. Devadutt felt it would be helpful to add to the reference to the ministry as a ministry of and for all members the following phrase, "recovering thereby the wholeness of Christ's Church."

Dr. Edgar M. Carlson proposed that the reference to bringing the life of all churches "under the judgment of the whole Church" be changed so as to read "under the judgment of the Lord of the whole Church." The proposal was approved.

Father Florovsky said that from the Eastern Orthodox viewpoint the language of the Message is inadequate and might be misleading and offend the conscience of believers in the Orthodox position. He therefore asked that the Orthodox delegates be recorded as abstaining from voting on the Message. He added that this did not imply that the Orthodox Churches want to be dissociated from the conference or the process of ecumenical study.

The Message as revised in the course of the discussion was adopted.

In behalf of Division I Dr. Cragg then presented its report and moved that the conference receive the report and transmit it to the churches for information and study.

In opening the discussion Prof. Waldo Beach felt that one of the most significant values of the report is in reinforcing the principle that unity will always be unity in diversity. He suggested that instead of the word "unity," which implies an over-simplification, it might be well in future discussions to use the word "community." He questioned the use of the term "theology of comprehension" as being too cryptic to be helpful. He felt that in the treatment of doctrine and sacraments the report does not do full justice to the social-cultural context of the Church's life. Prof. Walter M. Horton supported the criticism of the phrase, "theology of comprehension."

Prof. Arthur A. Vogel favored a rephrasing of the reference in the second paragraph to the Savior of the world so that it would read: "who bore the punishment and consequences of the sin of mankind as the means of founding a new unity." Dr. Cragg commented that the original language was that of one of the sections.

Dr. Hampton Adams suggested that in the reference to those who insist on baptism by immersion it would be gracious to give the explanation of their reason by adding such a clause as: "because of testimony to it in the New Testament and its rich symbolism of the death of the old man and the resurrection of the new in redemption." Dr. Harkness thought that the reference to all churches as regarding baptism as "the means of entry into the Universal Church" should be changed to "*a* means," in order not to overlook the Friends. Prof. Purdy suggested that from the standpoint of the Friends the clause which is applied to baptism—viz., that "the spiritual event is the decisive factor"—should also be applied to the interpretation of the Eucharist.

Dean Bernhard Anderson stated that the reference to the methods of biblical theology as "one among a large number of useful tools" might be misunderstood. Dr. Murdo Nicolson suggested omitting from the same paragraph the sentence which refers to biblical theology as an "exciting development" and a revision of the reference to "uncritical bibliolatry." Prof. Sittler proposed an alternative treatment.

Prof. T. Canby Jones desired a more explicit reference to the Trinity in the paragraph which refers to "central affirmations."

Dean Blakemore commented on the two descriptions of the significance of baptism and wondered whether a third should not be added—a conception of baptism in its relation to conversion. Prof. Come wished to insert, after the reference to practicing infant baptism the words: "or the placing of an individual in the context of Christ's grace where his faith may be born, grow, and come to life."

The motion to receive the report and transmit it to the churches for information and study was then adopted, with the understanding that the drafting committee might edit it in the light of the discussion.

Bishop Dun, as chairman, then voiced the appreciation of the conference for those who had contributed much to the success of the conference. He first mentioned officers of the Faith and Order Commission, including Dean Douglas Horton as chairman and Dr. Keith Bridston as secretary; also Prof. Calhoun, Prof. Outler, Dean Muelder and Prof. Sittler, who had reported for the theological commissions. Bishop Dun then thanked the people of Oberlin College and the Oberlin community for their most generous cooperation: President and Mrs. William E. Stevenson and the staff of the college; Dean Leonard Stidley and the staff of the School of Theology; Dr. Joseph King, the minister of First Church, Mrs. Folk, the church secretary, the officers and congregation; the ministers of other Oberlin churches; Prof. Grigg Fountain of the Conservatory of Music for his organ concert on Saturday evening; Dean Walter J. Harrelson for his leadership in the daily Bible study; Dr. Henry S. Leiper for serving as organist; the leaders of the morning and evening services of worship; the officers and drafting committees of the divisions and the sections; the stewards and the messengers; the sixteen regional groups that helped in the preparatory studies; the consultants from foreign lands; the members of the staff of the U.S. Conference for the World Council, headed by Miss Eleanor K. Browne and Miss Frances Maeda. Finally, he paid tribute to Dr. Samuel McCrea Cavert and to Dr. Paul S. Minear, saying that if the conference "belongs" to anyone "it is Dr. Minear's."

The final session was a service of worship and thanksgiving held on Tuesday afternoon, September 10, in the First Church of Oberlin. The hymns were "Praise to the Lord, the Almighty, the King of Creation," "All Hail the Power of Jesus' Name," and "One Sole Baptismal Sign, One Lord, Below, Above." The Scripture lesson was St. Luke 11:14-23 and 9:46-50. The prayers centered in adoration, confession, thanksgiving and supplication for the Church and its unity. The leaders in worship were Bishop Dun and Dr. Cavert. The sermon was preached by Dr. Blake and the final benediction pronounced by Bishop Dun.

CHRISTIAN UNITY AS VIEWED BY THE EASTERN ORTHODOX CHURCH

*Statement of the Representatives of the Eastern
Orthodox Churches in the U.S.A. at the North American
Faith and Order Study Conference*

We are glad to take part in a study conference devoted to such a basic need of the Christian world as unity. All Christians should seek unity. On the other hand, we feel that the whole program of the forthcoming discussion has been framed from a point of view which we cannot conscientiously admit. "The unity we seek" is for us a *given* unity which has never been lost, and, as a Divine gift and an essential mark of Christian existence, could not have been lost. This unity in the Church of Christ is for us a unity in the historical Church, in the fulness of faith, in the fulness of continuous sacramental life. For us, this unity is embodied in the Orthodox Church, which kept, *catholikos* and *anelleipos,* both the integrity of the apostolic faith and the integrity of the apostolic order.

Our share in the study of Christian unity is determined by our firm conviction that this unity can be found only in the fellowship of the historical Church, preserving faithfully the catholic tradition, both in doctrine and in order. We cannot commit ourselves to any discussion of these basic assumptions, as if they were but hypothetical or problematic. We begin with a clear conception of the Church's unity, which we believe has been embodied and realized in the age-long history of the Orthodox Church, without any change or break since the times when the visible unity of Christendom was an obvious fact and was attested and witnessed to by an ecumenical unanimity, in the age of the Ecumenical Councils.

We admit, of course, that the unity of Christendom has been disrupted, that the unity of faith and the integrity of order have been sorely broken. But we do not admit that the unity of the Church, and precisely of the "visible" and historical Church, has ever been broken or lost, so as to now be a problem of search and discovery. The problem of unity is for us, therefore, the problem of the return to the fulness of faith and order, in full faithfulness to the message of Scripture and Tradition and in the obedience to the will of God: *"that all may be one."*

Long before the breakup of the unity of Western Christendom, the Orthodox Church has had a keen sense of the essential importance of the oneness of Christian believers and from her very inception she has deplored divisions within the Christian world. As in the past, so in the present, she laments disunity among those who claim to be followers of Jesus Christ whose purpose in the world was to unite all believers into one Body. The Orthodox Church feels that, since she has been unassociated with the events related to the breakdown of religious unity in the West, she bears a special responsibility to contribute toward the restoration of the Christian unity which alone can render the message of the Gospel effective in a world troubled by threats of world conflict and general uncertainty over the future.

It is with humility that we voice the conviction that the Orthodox Church can make a special contribution to the cause of Christian unity, because since Pentecost she has possessed the true unity intended by Christ. It is with this conviction that the Orthodox Church is always prepared to meet with Christians of other communions in interconfessional deliberations. She rejoices over the fact that she is able to join those of other denominations in ecumenical conversations that aim at removing the barriers to Christian unity. However, we feel compelled in all honesty, as representatives of the Orthodox Church, to confess that we must qualify our participation, as necessitated by the historic faith and practice of our Church, and also state the general position that must be taken at this interdenominational conference.

In considering firstly "the nature of the unity we seek," we wish to begin by making clear that our approach is at variance with that usually advocated and ordinarily expected by participating representatives. The Orthodox Church teaches that the unity of the Church has not been lost, because she is the Body of Christ, and, as such, can never be divided. It is Christ as her head and the indwelling of the Holy Spirit that secure the unity of the Church throughout the ages.

The presence of human imperfection among her members is powerless to obliterate the unity, for Christ himself promised that the "gates of hell shall not prevail against the Church." Satan has always sown tares in the field of the Lord and the forces of disunity have often threatened but have never actually succeeded in dividing the Church. No power can be mightier than the omnipotent will of Christ who founded one Church only in order to bring men into unity with God. Oneness is an essential mark of the Church.

If it be true that Christ founded the Church as a means of unifying men divided by sin, then it must naturally follow that the unity of the Church was preserved by his divine omnipotence. Unity, therefore, is not just a promise, or a potentiality, but belongs to the very nature of the Church. It is not something which has been lost and which should be recovered, but rather it is a permanent character of the structure of the Church.

Christian love impels us to speak candidly of our conviction that the Orthodox Church has not lost the unity of the Church intended by Christ, for she represents the oneness which in Western Christendom has only been a potentiality. The Orthodox Church teaches that she has no need to search for a "lost unity," because her historic consciousness dictates that she is the *Una Sancta* and that all Christian groups outside the Orthodox Church can recover their unity only by entering into the bosom of that Church which preserved its identity with early Christianity.

These are claims that arise not from presumptuousness, but from an inner historical awareness of the Orthodox Church. Indeed, this is the special message of Eastern Orthodoxy to a divided Western Christendom.

The Orthodox Church, true to her historical consciousness, declares that she has maintained an unbroken continuity with the church of Pentecost by preserving the apostolic faith and polity unadulterated. She has kept the "faith once delivered unto the saints" free from the distortions of human innovations. Man-made doctrines have never found their way into the Orthodox Church, since she has no necessary association in history with the name of one single father or theologian. She owes the fulness and the guarantee of unity and infallibility to the operation of the Holy Spirit and not to the service of one individual. It is for this reason that she has never felt the need for what is known as "a return to the purity of the apostolic faith." She maintains the necessary balance between freedom and authority and thus avoids the extremes of absolutism and individualism both of which have done violence to Christian unity.

We reassert that which was declared at Evanston and which has been made known in the past at all interdenominational conferences attended by delegates of the Orthodox Church. It is not due to our personal merit, but to divine condescension that we represent the Orthodox Church and are able to give expression to her claims. We are bound in conscience to state explicitly what is logically inferred; that all other bodies have been directly or indirectly separated from the Orthodox Church. Unity from the Orthodox standpoint means a return of the separated bodies to the historical Orthodox, One Holy Catholic and Apostolic Church.

The unity which Orthodoxy represents rests on identity of faith, order, and worship. All three aspects of the life of the Church are outwardly safeguarded by the reality of the unbroken succession of bishops which is the assurance of the Church's uninterrupted continuity with apostolic origins. This means that the uncompromised fulness of the Church requires the preservation of both its episcopal structure and sacramental life. Adhering tenaciously to her apostolic heritage, the Orthodox Church holds that no true unity is possible where episcopacy and sacraments are absent, and grieves over the fact that both institutions have either been discarded or distorted in certain quarters of Christendom. Any agreement on faith must rest on the authority of the enactments of the seven Ecumenical Councils which represent the mind of the one undivided Church of antiquity and the subsequent tradition as safeguarded in the life of the Orthodox Church.

We regret that the most vital problem of ministry and that of the apostolic succession, without which to our mind there is neither unity, nor Church, were not included in the program of the conference. All problems of order seem to be missing in the program. These, in our opinion, are basic for any study of unity.

Visible unity expressed in organizational union does not destroy the centrality of the Spirit among believers, but rather testifies to the reality of the oneness of the Spirit. Where there is the fulness of the Spirit, there too will outward unity be found. From apostolic times the unity of Christian believers was manifested by a visible, organizational structure. It is the unity in the Holy Spirit that is expressed in a unified visible organization.

The Holy Eucharist, as the chief act of worship, is the outward affirmation of the inner relation rising from unity in the Holy Spirit. But this unity involves a consensus of faith among those participating. Intercommunion, therefore, is possible only when there is agreement of faith. Common worship in every case must presuppose a common faith. The Orthodox Church maintains that worship of any nature cannot be sincere unless there is oneness of faith among those participating. It is with this belief that the Orthodox hesitate to share in joint prayer services and strictly refrain from attending interdenominational Communion services.

A common faith and a common worship are inseparable in the historical continuity of the Orthodox Church. However, in isolation neither can be preserved integral and intact. Both must be kept in organic and inner relationship with each other. It is for this reason that Christian unity cannot be realized merely by determining what articles of faith or what creed should be regarded as constituting the basis of unity. In addition to subscribing to certain doctrines of faith, it is necessary to achieve the experience of a common tradition or *communis sensus fidelium* preserved through common worship within the historic framework of the Orthodox Church. There can be no true unanimity of faith unless that faith remains within the life and sacred tradition of the Church which is identical throughout the ages. It is in the experience of worship that we affirm the true faith, and conversely, it is in the recognition of a common faith that we secure the reality of worship in spirit and in truth.

Thus the Orthodox Church in each locality insists on agreement of faith and worship before it will consider sharing in any interdenominational activity. Doctrinal differences constitute an obstacle in the way of unrestricted participation in such activities. In order to safeguard the purity of the faith and the integrity of the liturgical and spiritual life of the Orthodox Church, abstinence from interdenominational activities is encouraged on a local level. There is no phase of the Church's life unrelated to her faith. Intercommunion with another church must be grounded on a consensus of faith and a common understanding of the sacramental life. The Holy Eucharist especially must be the liturgical demonstration of the unity of faith.

We are fully aware of deep divergences which separate Christian denominations from each other, in all fields of Christian life and existence, in the understanding of faith, in the shaping of life, in the habits of worship. We are seeking, accordingly, a unanimity in faith, an identity of order, a fellowship in prayer. But for us all the three are organically linked together. Communion in worship is only possible in the unity of faith. Communion presupposes unity. Therefore, the term "intercommunion" seems to us an epitome of that conception which we are compelled to reject. An "intercommunion" presupposes the existence of several separate and separated denominations, which join occasionally in certain common acts or actions. In the true unity of Christ's Church there is no room for several "denominations." There is, therefore, no room for "intercommunion." When all are truly united in the apostolic faith and order, there will be all-inclusive communion and fellowship in all things.

It has been stated by the Orthodox delegates already in Edinburgh, in 1937, that many problems are presented at Faith and Order conferences in a manner and in a setting which are utterly uncongenial to the Orthodox. We again must repeat the same statement now. But again, as years ago at Edinburgh, we want to testify our readiness and willingness to participate in study, in order that the truth of the Gospel and the fulness of the apostolic tradition may be brought to the knowledge of all who truly, unselfishly, and devotedly seek unity in Our Blessed Lord and His Holy Church, One, Catholic, and Apostolic.

PART TWO

The Sections at Work

The reports from Divisions I, II, and III were received by the Conference in plenary sessions and transmitted to the churches for information and study. The section reports were prepared to go directly to the churches without discussion by the Conference as a whole. As a preface to each section report, we have reprinted the statement of situation and objectives which the Conference Program had provided for each section.

REPORT OF DIVISION I

The Nature of the Unity We Seek
In Faithfulness to the Eternal Gospel

CHAIRMAN: DR. GERALD R. CRAGG
SECRETARY: DR. HUGH T. KERR, JR.

The subject assigned to Division I is "The Nature of the Unity We Seek In Faithfulness to the Eternal Gospel." It covers what Bishop Angus Dun, in the opening address of this Conference, termed "certain of the more specially theological approaches to our problem." In an area where differences are both ancient and stubborn, quick or easy answers would be superficial if not wrong. And it is scarcely surprising that some sections found themselves baffled by difficulties which, in the past, have often proved their power to keep Christians apart. But results, though not spectacular, have been by no means negligible. And at certain points they surprised those taking part. The "ecumenical encounter" is always an educational process and the participants in this Division acknowledge that they have benefited from it, in achieving a more sympathetic understanding of unfamiliar convictions and a deeper charity towards those who hold views different from their own. In addition, genuine progress has been made in certain directions; old problems have appeared in a new light, and fruitful avenues of future advance have been indicated.

When discussing theological positions it is natural that areas of common conviction should be balanced by areas of disagreement. We would expect—and we have discovered—a grateful emphasis in all the sections on the meaning of our participation in the central beliefs of the faith: "Jesus Christ, the Word of God, the Gospel, the Church." Christ stands at the center of his people's faith; he is "the incarnate Word of God and the sacrificial Savior of the world in whom God bore the sin of mankind and founded a new humanity." Nor does this cardinal affirmation stand alone. The recognition of our area of agreement has steadily enlarged as new insights and the pressures of our times have shown the interrelation of various aspects of belief; but in the process the sovereign claims of Christ our Lord have acquired a heightened constraint. At the same time there is no disposition to ignore the areas of conscientious difference. These disagreements have not always appeared in the places or in the forms we might expect, and a study of the reports of sections 3 and 4 reveals some novel areas of conflict and of consent.

THE UNITY WE POSSESS

For the consideration of the churches it is important to note certain emphases which have clearly established a central place in ecumenical discussions. With significant reiteration the sectional reports, no less than the preparatory papers and the speeches to the plenary sessions, have recurred to the unity which the Church already possesses. This unity has brought us here; it gives us our imperatives and establishes our final goal. It confers immediate and profound satisfaction, and it promises us blessings which as yet we have not claimed. Our unity is a divine gift, not a human achievement. So far as unity is God's endowment of his Church it is ours already; so far as it is our response in obedience to his will we sadly lack it.

THE RESOURCES FOR OUR TASK

Similarly, the reports of the sections indicate the rewarding insights which we owe to recent study of the Scriptures. The emergence of biblical theology is one of the exciting developments of our time. As we acknowledge in common the authority and constraint of the Word of God we are brought into a new measure of agreement one with another. As an example of the way biblical theology has engaged our attention, we can cite the repeated emphasis at this conference on the significance of the servant image.

THE MEANING OF UNITY

The main theme of the conference naturally demanded, in one form or another, the attention of each of our sections. We want unity—otherwise we would not be here; but "we are not unified in our understanding of the unity we seek." We reassert (for it is an obvious fact which nevertheless needs constant repetition) that unity cannot be equated with uniformity. There is a widespread fear that we shall find ourselves committed to a "monolithic" structure which will smother variety, vitality, freedom and spontaneity. Yet we are familiar in our own denominations with a considerable degree of diversity in doctrines as well as in worship and organization. "The unity we seek is not to be found in enforced conformity to a detailed, complete, unchangeable system of doctrine. . . . Freedom to interpret Christian truth in varied ways . . . is part of Christian liberty." The doctrinal basis of unity is profound; its statement must be simple if it is to achieve the requisite response. It points to our interdependence as God's children, and to the common life we share in the household of faith. But a family presupposes a home; in that home it is intolerable that anyone should be ignored in his time of need or should be excluded from any fundamental aspect of family fellowship. This unity will not be fully achieved at once. And as we strive to express it more completely we shall discover that it is operative in varying degrees and different levels. It may begin with the elementary (but obligatory) discipline of greater interconfessional courtesy; it will express itself in various types of co-operation, and in certain cases it will lead to organic union. The level at which we endeavor to express our unity will determine the kind of doctrinal consensus we must achieve. It is obvious that civility imposes more elementary demands than reunion. And it is apparent that, while unity presupposes consensus, in its turn it also creates it. We may recapitulate much of what has been said in our sections in three propositions: (a) unity belongs to the essential nature of the Church; (b) that unity must be made visible to the world in a measure greater than that in which the corporate life of our churches currently manifest it; (c) it must provide freedom for an extensive measure of diversity.

IMPERATIVES

Concern for unity is not an option open to those who happen to be interested in ecumenical affairs. The God who has made us one calls us to be so in ever greater measure. Our motives are, therefore, rooted in his will; they derive from the record of his redemptive activity in Jesus Christ. The imperatives of the Gospel lay upon us their constraint and in pattern they correspond to the central affirmations of the faith—God in creation, Christ's work in salvation, the Holy Spirit's activity in equipping us for and sustaining us in our task. Unity is for mission. The acceptance of mission increases our unity, and as we come to understand the bearing of our faith, we also come to grasp its meaning. "We have found ourselves bound together in a common faith that impels us to a common witness. . . . The faith we share is a common commitment to the high calling of God in Christ Jesus, and a common mission to bring to mankind the message of the great salvation he offers." It is this awareness of our unfinished task that relates the biblical imperatives to the contemporary scene, and gives them a relevance which might otherwise escape our attention. In our divided state we are not meeting the demands of our age; our ineffectiveness in mission compels us to heed more closely the biblical demands for unity. We recognize, of course, the ambiguous character of many of the motives which effect our conduct. Sin is subtle as well as strong; valid reasons become corrupted, and wholly illegitimate ones are insinuated into our common life. Only in humble obedience can we discern the true from the false and discipline ourselves to admit only those motives which are in conformity with the Word rather than merely acceptable to our sinful and secular minds.

The Dialectic of Ecumenical Debate

In all the sections we note the emergence of a familiar pattern of agreement and disagreement. Each of the reports contains statements carefully qualified to allow for divergencies of view. We have already noted certain of the fundamental convictions which have come to expression in the documents of the sections, and it is notable that the agreement on our given unity in faith has been both wide and deep. Even our differences, which usually form so dreary a catalogue, have been redefined in novel and stimulating ways, and we are not left with the impasse of two lists of irreconcilable doctrines. Points of disagreement are nowhere ignored. A wide range of points of view has been accepted as a challenge as well as an obstacle. A useful distinction is drawn between "desirable diversity, *creative* conflict which helps to get truth stated and *destructive* conflict which obscures the truth." It is here that the suggested "theology of comprehension" opens a new and promising perspective. "When the seemingly conflicting doctrines of different churches are carefully defined in face-to-face conference, they are first found to be less contradictory than they appeared to be, and then found to be divergent aspects of a comprehensive truth which all need to consider in order to deepen and correct their views." This process was exemplified in discussion before it was codified as advice.

The Continuing Task

At this point we must note certain specific theological tasks which we wish to bequeath to the churches as a continuing responsibility.

1. The place of creeds and confessions requires further consideration. A superficial judgment might regard the use to which they are often put as barriers created against one another. But a study of the significance of this use might reveal much common ground and provide material for a common witness to our age. Perhaps the time has come not merely to repeat but to heed the call of the Lausanne Conference (1927) to re-examine the content, the historical significance and the meaning for us of the great ecumenical definitions of the early church councils.

2. The kind of theological exchange which has marked this conference, as well as the studies which provided the preparatory material for it, represents a process which should be continued and extended, and the bodies which are responsible for convening this conference are asked to give every encouragement to an appropriate program of study.

Sections 3 and 4 have been dealing with the two ordinances or sacraments: "Baptism into Christ" and "The Table of the Lord." The wording of these topics indicates that these sections, as is the case also for sections 1 and 2, emphasized the centrality of Christ. For example, section 3 observes that baptism "involves the re-affirmation by the Church of its faith in the Crucified and Risen Lord." And section 4 professes to "see in the Eucharist primarily what God in Christ is doing for our redemption as we look in faith to what he has done and forward in hope to what he shall do." This Christocentric accent in both sections, emphasizing what God has done for sinful mankind in Jesus Christ, represents an overarching unity of both thought and devotion which promises much for the ongoing discussion of our theological problems, our church divisions, and our conversations together on these subjects.

Under "Affirmations of Agreement," section 3 noted that baptism has been "almost universally practiced in some form in Christendom throughout the centuries"; the theological consensus that in baptism "God comes to man with a gracious and redemptive purpose, offering him forgiveness of sins and the new life in Christ and enabling him to grow by his grace and the gift of the Spirit into the fullness of his stature that we may be conformed to the image of his Son"; that although some churches insist upon immersion, all agree that "the spiritual event is the decisive factor" in baptism; and that "all churches regard baptism as the means of entry into the universal Church, and not only into membership of a particular denomination." These, we believe, are substantial agreements. We thank God for them as we rejoice in the given unity which they suggest and provide even now for our divided Christendom.

One further agreement, which can only be experienced as a rebuke to us all, is that our practice so often belies our profession in these matters. We note in all our churches "a widespread carelessness or apparent slackness in regard both to the practice of and the teaching concerning baptism." Thus, "despite its widespread observance, the significance and unifying effect of this ordinance or sacrament has been obscured."

Beyond this, however, we observe differences among us which cannot and must not be concealed. We differ, for example, on the relation of faith to baptism, and this divides us into those who practice only believer's baptism, and those who also practice infant baptism. We differ on the significance of the act of baptism itself, as, on the one hand, the vehicle of God's regenerative activity, or as, on the other hand, the symbol of a spiritual change which may already have taken place in an individual.

Our differences, in the final analysis, appear, however, to be related to our differing views of the Church. Here theology and tradition frequently determine our views and practices regarding baptism. If we must say, therefore, that a study of baptism by itself will scarcely offer any ultimate guidance in our search for unity, we wish also to say that "the question of the Church looks differently to us now that we have become more aware of our deep unity in baptism."

We would consequently address our concern on baptism to the churches for further and continuing study in the form of the following three searching questions: "(1) Of the churches which practice infant baptism, we ask—'How far is it true to say that among you the obedient use of every gift and resource of the Church is made in order that the infant may reach that point of personal faith and response which would be the proper fulfillment of baptismal vows? What is the responsibility of the Church to the baptized person who does not become a believer?' (2) Of the churches which practice only believer's baptism, we ask—'Is sufficient justice done among you to the fact that God's grace is active in and through the Christian community from the very beginning of a person's life, preparing him for the full confession and experience of the faith? What is the responsibility of the Church to the unbaptized child?" (3) Finally, we ask all Christians—'Do we in our lives bear witness to our baptism into the death and resurrection of Christ? In what ways do we show that we are not our own but disciples of our sovereign Lord?' "

Section 4 states bluntly that "it is at the table of the Lord, given to us as the continuing sacrament of unity, that Christians in history have been divided from each other and continue to be separated." Yet it has been possible to hold Christian conversation on this subject, and such current movements as the renewed interest in liturgy and the revival of biblical theology have considerably increased our readiness to listen and learn from one another. Thus we are able to report a broad base of mutually agreed affirmations. We agree, for example, that "at the Table of the Lord, the Church remembers in thanksgiving and gratitude the life, death and resurrection of Jesus Christ." This commemoration, however, is more than recollection, for it implies Christ's present mediation to us and our hope for the consummation of his redemptive purpose.

For these reasons we may say that "the Eucharist is therefore in the center of the response of the worshipping Church to God's gracious activity in Christ. That which is offered and received in the Eucharist is central to the Christian life. . . . Liturgy in the narrow sense is not enough; the service of God by his people in their witness in the world and in winning others to Christ is inextricably bound up with their eucharistic life. The preached Word of God is not to be set over against the Supper of the Lord. Both are commanded by Christ; both are involved in his work of redemption."

All agree that "by personal participation in the body and blood of the One Lord Jesus Christ, we are strengthened for life in the corporate community of the new covenant and enabled to discern our oneness with each other. The blessings we receive at the table of the Lord empower us for our witness and work in the world into which we are sent."

In discussing the table of the Lord, the section was acutely aware at all times of the difficult problems of order and the ministry as these relate to the administration and reception of the Eucharist. Yet the group found it possible to express their "common understanding and fellowship apart from and prior to agreement on all matters of order. It may be that the time is not yet ripe for a really fruitful exploration of these long-standing disagreements. But the time for that *is* coming and will be hastened as Christians in all the churches engage in some such enterprise as this one in which we have received so rich a blessing and such a sure token of our community in Christ's self-giving love."

The section was fully aware that it could not solve for the churches all the problems which cluster around this topic, but they summed up their own ecumenical experience together by directing a strong appeal to the churches. This appeal is to "the larger task which still confronts" us all. "This task, put in its simplest terms, is the heightening or, in some cases, a recovery of an utter seriousness for the Eucharist as the sacrament of communion between Christ and his Body and the sacrament of unity in the Body. We are convinced that this task can be greatly aided by the process of ecumenical study, the process, that is, of surveying our respective traditions, of facing seriously the crucial problem of intercommunion, of taking upon ourselves the pain of our division at the Table of the Lord, of searching and finding new agreements in our understanding of the gracious mystery of Christ's act and promise in Holy Communion. The new situation to which we have referred and the progress in consensus which we ourselves have experienced, persuades us that all our Churches should join with us in this study process, on the broadest possible scale . . . that this is, indeed, imperative and possible!"

CONCLUSION

If it were an easy matter to appropriate the measure of unity which God wills for his children, the churches would not have remained apart so long and so stubbornly. Our sections have been dealing and wrestling with intractable problems, and they have done so in a mood and temper determined by the conviction that, "the call to Christian unity is clarion-clear." The results which emerged from our study together are not really a series of documents. Far more significant is the experience of a deepening of fellowship in a tremendous undertaking, and the growing assurance that we do not embark on it alone. "We have become . . . aware of the Holy Spirit, working in our midst, to create within us the will and desire to commit ourselves anew to the imperatives of the Gospel. We have come to see that the unity Christ wills for his Church can be realized only through that renewal of our lives whereby through grace we are delivered from the consequences of our imperfect vision and our sin. And we have been moved to ask what kind of unity it is that we envisage for the one family of God." For this experience we humbly give thanks.

SECTION 1. *Imperatives and Motivations*

Chairman: Bishop Francis Gerald Ensley
Secretary: The Rev. W. O. Fennell

The Situation:

The Gospel of one God commands unity and offers us power to achieve it. But in North America we know by experience that efforts toward unity have been very productive of new and acute divisions. We have learned also that for many Christian groups, the Gospel itself is claimed as the justification for continuing separatisms. Loyalties to Christ which presumably should bind us together into a single company seem instead to produce separation or at least aloofness from Christians of other persuasions and traditions. Motives are mixed and nowhere are they more mixed than in the service of God. They compete where they should coincide. We feel more closely bound to members of our own congregation than to those of neighboring congregations. We seldom consider that our obligations to other communions are as vital and compelling as our obligation to our own. The kind of unity we seek is a source of division as well as of cohesion. Others seek unity for reasons which to us are wrong, and they, in turn, cannot accept our own motives. Unity therefore requires mutual exploration of our conflicting loyalties and motives.

The Objectives:

a. to analyze our own motivations in the present movement toward unity, and to distinguish those motives which are derived from the Gospel from those which are opposed to it.

b. To discover the points at which present church loyalties tend to run counter to the demands for greater unity.

c. to learn why it is that for so many Christians loyalty to Christ is not adequately channeled into loyalties to Christ's Church.

d. to understand why current movements toward unity evoke deep suspicions and even sincere opposition.

e. to examine what basis we have for confidence that the true Church of Christ will find visible expression in this world.

f. to bring to bear on all these questions the teachings of Scripture on the nature of unity.

The Report:

I. THE GOSPEL IMPERATIVES TO CHRISTIAN UNITY

Our search for unity rests upon a necessity inherent in the very nature of the Christian Gospel; it is not just the result of *our* desire for unity or *our* will to find a fuller expression of Christian community. This is the truth which has become increasingly clear to us as we have attempted to understand why Christians have been and are being drawn closer to one another in ecumenical fellowship and conversation.

According to the testimony of Scripture, the oneness of God's people results from what God himself has done. The Gospel is, above all, an indicative—an announcement of who God is and the gift he has given us—before it is an imperative. It is, as the word "gospel" means, good news of the salvation God has wrought, of the new life he offers us.

When we respond in faith to God's gift, with the eagerness of a man who sells everything to obtain the pearl of great price, we acknowledge an obligation which is far more compelling than what we happen to feel or will, far more urgent than the practical considerations which may seem to bring us together. It is precisely because *God has made us one* that we are impelled to acknowledge, express, and seek our deepest unity.

At every point in the biblical story of God's action among men, upon which Christian worship and theology are based, the divine indicative stands behind and underscores the divine imperative.

A. *God Has Created Man for Unity*

The first great announcement of the Gospel is that God has created man as the noblest of his creatures, made in his own image. No exposition of the doctrine of creation would be complete without stressing that God has made man for community and unity, not for isolation and strife. Man's life is dependent upon God with whom he has communion and for whom he acts as regent over the works of creation (Gen. 1:27-30); and his life is also bound to that of another person, apart from whom he is incomplete (Gen. 2:18; cf. "male and female," 1:27). The truth of human existence is that man, by his God-given nature, is a social being. The glory and wonder of man's life is that God visits him personally (Ps. 8:3-8), blessing him with the rich and manifold gifts of the creation. And yet the tragedy of man's life, as sketched in lurid colors in Genesis, chapters 3-11, is that man has separated himself from God and his fellowman by his sin; he is anxious, lonely and lost—a man whose restless heart vainly attempts to find wholeness by his own desperate actions or to build a community which perishes quickly like a tower of Babel.

Thus our search for unity is basically a search for salvation: for the wholeness and community which God, the Creator, intends for man. From the indicative of God's act of creation comes an inescapable imperative: if man would act in accordance with his own God-given nature, he must seek unity.

B. *God Has Restored the Broken Unity of Mankind in Jesus Christ*

The Gospel of the New Testament is the heralded proclamation of God's saving action in Jesus Christ to restore and renew man's broken life by bringing him into a new relationship with God and with his neighbor. Jesus not only announces the good news of God's initiative to seek and deliver men, but he himself is the messianic agent of God's healing or saving activity. The salvation offered men is not that of individualistic bliss in another world, but eternal life—the life of God's kingdom—which begins now by participation in Christ's *ecclesia,* the community of the New Covenant. This corporate life is a foretaste and a promise of what God will give his people when their earthly pilgrimage is complete.

The gathering of God's people is proclaimed as the fulfillment of God's redemptive work begun in Israel's history. In the widening perspective of faith, it became clear that God had taken the initiative to restore man to his true being by calling a people unto himself. Delivering a band of slaves from the pharaoh's yoke, he bound them to himself in covenant and formed them as a community, separate from the nations of the earth. By ever-renewed acts of mercy and by strange works of judgment, he disciplined this people to understand the meaning of its calling and its inescapable unity as the agent of his purpose among men. To this people he gave the promise that through them all peoples of the earth would receive blessing (Gen. 12:2) and that through their corporate witness his salvation would reach to the ends of the earth (Isa. 49:6).

The Church is the people of God—renewed, reconstituted, and transformed. Since its character is given to it by the grace of God rather than by the action of men, it embraces all who in faith acknowledge Christ as Lord, regardless of race, class, nation or culture (Gal. 3:28; 1 Cor. 12:13). One of its distinctive marks is unity—the unity which is given by God who through Christ has made us one by breaking down the dividing wall of hostility and reconciling us to himself and to one another (Eph. 2:11-22).

The unity of the Church is both a gift and a demand. The Church is one as Christ is one (1 Cor. 1:12-13). In a variety of images this unity is portrayed in the New Testament. The true vine has many branches but it is one vine (John 15:5). The one Shepherd has many sheep but they belong to one flock (John 10:16). The Church is the household of God, in which the members of God's family are at home (Eph. 2:19). It is the Israel of God, the heirs of the promises and responsibilities of the chosen people of the old covenant (1 Peter 2:9-10). An outstanding description of the Church's unity is the figure of the Body of Christ (1 Cor. 12:12-31). It is by *one* Spirit that men are incorporated into the one body. Within the body there are many members, but all are coordinated by Christ who is the head. There are diversities of gifts and ways of service, but under the guidance of the Spirit these are enhanced by the supreme spiritual gift of love and contribute to the upbuilding of the Body. As a physical body is animated by the spirit, so the Church is a visible community in which the risen Christ is present in the midst of his people in life-giving and unifying love.

Thus the imperative to manifest our unity concretely and visibly in the world is based on the truth that God has made us one in Christ. Christ's sacrifice, which displays the infinite love and undeserved grace of God, places us under obligation to love one another, even as he has loved us (1 John 4:7-21). Any form of disunity that prevents the fullest expression of love in community and which promotes strife, jealousy, or factionalism is a denial of the full meaning of the Gospel.

C. *God Renews the Church for Its Mission*

Another announcement of the Christian Gospel, already anticipated in what has just been said, is that in Christ God has poured out his Spirit upon men, thereby unifying his people—as at Pentecost—so that they may proclaim the Gospel to all nations (Matt. 28:18-20).

The gift of the Spirit is, according to the New Testament, the sign that the New Age has dawned (Acts 2:1-36). The Church belongs to this New Age. The unity of its corporate life bears witness to the fact that God in Christ has already won the decisive victory over all the powers that set men at enmity against God and one another and thereby destroy the unity intended in God's creation. Its *koinonia*—that is, community characterized by love of God and love of neighbor—is a foretaste of the consummation when God will make all things new, when his kingdom will fully

come and his will be done. The Church is God's New Creation.
And "if any one is in Christ, he is a new creation; the old has
passed away, behold, the new has come" (2 Cor. 5:17).

The Christian, however, lives both in the realization of God's
victory and in the expectation that God's victory is yet to be com-
pleted. Disunity among Christians is evidence of the persistence of
sin after sin's power has been broken, of the temptation to walk
according to the flesh rather than according to the Spirit (1 Cor.
3:3), of the lingering of the old age even after the New Age has
been inaugurated. Thus Christ's people, as today, are broken,
divided, and scattered.

But the unity of Christ's people cannot finally be broken by our
unfaithfulness, for their unity is in Jesus Christ. Every branch of
the vine that bears no fruit, the vinedresser takes away, and
every branch that bears fruit he purges that it may bear more
fruit (John 15:2). The Church is renewed constantly by Christ's
indwelling Spirit, as the branches receive life from the vine. It
hears from him the command to love one another, as he has loved
us (John 13:34-35; 15:9-17). And through him it not only becomes conscious of its separation from the world but of its mission
to the world. Christ, who is ever present with his people, prays
for our unity—a unity which must be manifest visibly and cor-
porately to the world in order that men may believe the Gospel
(John 17). Indeed, the unity of Christ's followers will be evidence
to the world that God has sent his Son (John 17:23). The announcement that God was in Christ reconciling the world unto
himself has an imperative corollary: he has entrusted to us the
ministry of reconciliation (2 Cor. 5:18-20). In fulfilling its mission, the Church realizes its true unity and only through its unity
may it fulfill its mission.

Having listened again to the Gospel as witnessed by Scripture,
we affirm that the call to Christian unity is clarion-clear. We are
convinced that the urgency of the call does not arise merely from
the natural tendencies of our group life, from the demands of expedience or social necessity, or from our own will or designs. Unity
rests primarily on what God has done, is doing, and will do. By
his act of creation, he has made us for unity. By his redemptive
action in Jesus Christ, he has made us one. And by the continual
activity of his Spirit he renews our life in order that we may manifest our unity. Unity is not an option which we may take or leave;
rather, if we are faithful to the Gospel which we have received
and in which we stand, we must acknowledge that it is God's gift,

God's demand, and God's promise. Christian faith means receiving this gift, obeying this demand, and hoping in this promise.

II. OUR CONTEMPORARY RESPONSE TO THE GOSPEL

The imperatives of the Gospel, however, do not belong to an abstract realm of thought and speculation; nor are they meant merely for the time when the Gospel was expressed in the preaching and writing of early apostles. The Lord of history speaks to us in our time, as he has to his people in other generations, and he calls us to respond in the concrete situations of our contemporary world. To be sure, it is the same Gospel—the "everlasting Gospel" —that we hear, but its imperative becomes the more urgent and compelling because it is heard in the context of the concrete needs of daily life which call for action.

We live in an age when hostilities and fears have reached horrifying dimensions, and in which the Church must speak to a world convulsed in crisis. Men are influenced, and often victimized, by massive concentrations of power, by subtle and insidious forms of thought-control, by loyalties and movements which seem to have demonic power, by anxieties that lurk in the depths of lives empty of ultimate meaning. In the face of racial conflicts, of the allurement of secular philosophies, of the vast social changes brought about by the industrialization and urbanization of society, and of the resurgence of ancient world religions, Christians are summoned to respond obediently to Christ. In such a situation we are rightly chastened by the way in which our divisions stultify our witness. Churches stand empty because of the shortage of man power; new communities spring up and the Word of God is not preached in them; and our efforts are weakened or neutralized by the duplication of our programs and the waste of our resources. Amid the Babel of our time we speak with many voices, with the result that our testimony is drowned out by voices from the world, louder and more strident. In our fragmentary fellowship we dissipate our influence by tending our denominational fires or competing with fellow Christians, and we fail to speak to the massive social problems of our time. When people crave participation in an abiding community which embraces them in their loneliness and guilt, we deny them the sustaining comfort of the Christian fellowship. We nourish into growth churches in parts of the world where Christianity is at best a tolerated minority movement, only to find that our disunity paralyzes our coming to the support of their attempts to make a unified Christian witness. Thus we fail, in many specific ways, to respond obediently to the Lord who commits to us the ministry of reconciliation.

Yet it is in these concrete situations that the imperatives of the Gospel are reinforced and made the more urgent. We rightly deplore the gross inefficiency of our divided efforts, not because efficiency in itself is a Christian imperative, but because faithful response to the Gospel should make us careful stewards of our resources in order that our evangelistic work of preaching and teaching, of social action, and of world outreach may have its maximum effectiveness.

Thus in the thinking of our group we find it impossible to distinguish two types of imperatives: one rooted in the Gospel and the other arising out of our contemporary situation. Rather, we realize that the imperative of the Gospel comes to us in the concrete situations and realities of our time. It speaks to us with the accent of great urgency and pointed appeal precisely because it is made concrete in needs that are pressing, critical problems that call for action, and specific things that we know should be done.

III. Sources of Our Frustration

When the Gospel unmistakably calls us to unity, and when the imperative is reinforced by the concrete realities of our daily world, what deters us from giving Christ the full measure of obedience? Why do we not manifest, or even seek to appropriate, the unity which is God's gift to his people?

It is in the attempt to answer this question that we find it most difficult to assess our motives accurately. Without pretending to justify ourselves before God or to secure ourselves complacently in things as they are, it can be said honestly that our dividedness is not wholly the result of wilful perversity. In some degree, our condition is the evidence of our partial vision, for our lives are set within the limitations and conditions of time and circumstance. Often our minds have been conditioned by an incomplete interpretation of the Gospel which has been given in an area shut off from the larger life of the Church. Our entrance into the Christian faith has been through the door of a particular denomination or communion, and within this fold we have found our lives embraced by God's grace from infancy to death. And even when ignorance or circumstance has not obscured our vision, many have been aware that the Gospel is a mystery whose range and depth no finite man can wholly comprehend.

It needs to be said, too, that acquiescence in or defense of our divisions has often resulted from a genuine effort to be faithful to the Gospel. Devotion to specific doctrines or ecclesiastical practices has frequently been motivated by the conviction that Christian distinctiveness must be maintained, especially in our culture where American Christianity so easily merges with prevailing folkways and thought-forms. Fidelity has often taken the form of a reform movement which has had as its purpose recalling the Church to its true mission, and as we well know from our Christian history, these movements have led to expulsion or separation from the institutional Church. In other cases, movements toward visible Christian unity have been resisted by those whose fidelity to the Gospel prompts them to protest against what they fear may result in making the Church a huge corporation or a massive power bloc. Since the New Testament warns against the perils of infidelity, and insists that Christian distinctiveness must be maintained at all costs, we should respect the sincere motive of fidelity which presents both a problem and a challenge to Christians seeking unity.

And yet it is the power and subtlety of sin which obscures our vision and corrupts our commendable motives. Sin can make even the fidelity in which we seek to hold the Gospel a means which blinds us to the claims of more comprehensive truth and more active charity. It can take the desire for renewal and reform, so essential to the Church's vitality, and make the reformer strident in tone and the remainder of the fellowship stubborn in resistance. It can obscure our sense of mission, so that the claims of efficiency, to which we readily respond, become mere administrative ends instead of wise stewardship for the furtherance of the Gospel. It tempts us to confuse God's gift of unity with human institutional structures which by themselves are in danger of circumscribing the full life of the Church instead of bringing it to free expression. It shows itself in the personal and institutional pride, in the complacency and self-regard which deepen our divisions. It corrupts our genuine Christian desire to come together into fellowship into the preference or necessity of being with our own kind—our race, our nation, our social class. It constrains us to find new reasons for justifying and perpetuating cleavages which the changes of history have rendered irrelevant. And it is also sin which makes us impatient with each other and with the ways in which God works in human history; it prompts us to despair because we do not see our hopes immediately fulfilled; and it makes us fearful for the Ark of God, persuaded that its safety is in danger except upon our terms and under our safekeeping.

IV. THE SHAPE OF THE UNITY WE SEEK

In our study and self-examination we have been made acutely aware of these frustrating influences which prevent the manifestation of our God-given unity. But we have become even more aware of the Holy Spirit working in our midst to create within us the will and desire to commit ourselves anew to the imperatives of the Gospel. We have come to see that the unity Christ wills for his Church can be realized only through that renewal of our lives whereby through grace we are delivered from the divisive consequences of our imperfect vision and our sin. And we have been moved to ask what kind of unity it is that we envisage for the one family of God.

It is, of course, beyond the range of our study to attempt a detailed sketch of the kind of visible unity toward which the Gospel imperatives impel us. But we believe that, at the very least, our unity must take shape along these lines.

a) The unity we envisage will be a unity which gives visible expression to the fact that we do belong to the one houshold of God. Within that household there will be no barriers to prevent the members of Christ's family from entering fully into that community of shared life, worship, and witness which properly belongs to those who are his own. This will mean a unity in which every ministry is a ministry of and for all the members. It will mean an open welcome to all members of the family to the banquet table at which we receive and celebrate with thanksgiving our new life in Christ. It will mean that beneath all of our various confessions there will be a unity of the Church's declared faith.

b) The unity we seek will require the kind of structures and symbols which will act as living centers of loyalty, transcending the more limited loyalties which we have hitherto accepted in our denominational life. It may well be that we shall become more aware of the structures we already have in common: the apostolic Word, the ministry, the sacraments, the teachers of the Church of every age, the treasury of prayers, hymns and orders of worship of ancient and modern times. We see it as an evidence of God's gracious, unifying work among us that more and more we find in these a bond of unity, whereas before we saw in them only that which estranged us from one another.

c) Within these structures of the Church there will have to be freedom for expression of those insights into truth which the Holy Spirit gives to men as he chooses. Among the misconceptions prevalent among us, none is so groundless as the notion that unity must be equated with uniformity. God in his creation has made us different one from the other in order that our lives may be enriched with manifold variety. And just as the nations will bring their glory and treasures to the Holy City, so the churches will bring their insights and traditions for the enrichment of the total life of Christ's people. Nothing of lasting value in God's gift to us will be forfeited, though we may expect that, under the corrective of our different gifts and insights, the Holy Spirit may lead us into new apprehensions of the truth and more adequate ways to express our unity in Christ.

As we contemplate the unity which until now we have very partially manifested, we have asked ourselves in what practical ways we can more adequately express it. Various possibilities, operative at different levels, suggest themselves. We can learn to understand each other a great deal more fully, believing that out of increasing knowledge will come greater appreciation and a more appropriate measure of interconfessional courtesy. We can remove all deliberately created barriers which we have allowed to separate us, and we can scrutinize with tireless vigor everything that keeps us apart. We can seek areas where we can act together and so seal our common discipleship with a common witness before the world. And, greatly though we may prize tasks jointly discharged and worship shared one with another, there are some among us who feel pledged to nothing less than such a union as will mediate to us a fuller life in the whole Church and manifest unmistakably before the world the unity God has given us in Christ.

In confident expectation that God has richer blessings to bestow upon us than we can claim in our divided state, we shall in all humility bend every effort to be one, even as Christ and his Father are one; and we shall listen more alertly to what God yearns to say to his Church in our time, and through the Church to the world.

SECTION 2. *Doctrinal Consensus and Conflict*

Chairman: Dr. Edgar M. Carlson
Secretary: Dr. Walter N. Roberts

The Situation:

It has been supposed that conflict in the realm of dogma has produced the splintering of the Christian community, and that agreement in doctrine is the necessary first step in reunion. There are, however, among North American communions some which agree fully in doctrine and which yet are hostile to one another. And there are some formal creeds which diverge widely without producing sharp conflict. It has been suggested that a homogeneity in faith is developing in which the lines between churches no longer coincide with historical controversies. Also, there is some evidence that in all churches there is a contrast between the official and traditional formularies and the working faith by which Christians live, and that we are not as far apart in the latter as in the former. In some respects there is a remarkable consensus in basic convictions; in some respects, there are new conflicts which must be recognized. Where bitter controversies emerge, they tend to cut new paths not so much between one denomination and another as through all denominations. There are vigorous debates concerning what are the central doctrines, concerning the nature and meaning of doctrinal statements, and concerning the degree of importance to be assigned to them. Such factors greatly affect our conceptions of unity and of the road toward its realization.

The Objectives:

a. to study the degree and kind of consensus in faith which binds us together.

b. to examine the extent and significance of our common use of the historic confessions.

c. to discuss the degree of conformity and freedom in faith which should be considered essential to Christian unity.

d. to discover the points of deepest conflict in the realm of doctrines.

e. to distinguish the kind of consensus which should precede unity from the kind which can only develop after closer fellowship.

f. to explore the ways in which mutual allegiance to Jesus Christ should lead us to welcome diversities in the expression of this allegiance within each communion and across denominational lines.

The Report:

I. INTRODUCTION

In reporting the results of its discussions on "Doctrinal Consensus and Conflict," the members of this section wish first to record their gratitude for the privilege of having been participants in an earnest doctrinal discussion involving representatives of so many of the Christian communions. The breadth of its official and unofficial representation alone constitutes a significant historical event and an ecumenical accomplishment.

The section was specifically asked to study *a*) the degree and kind of consensus in faith which binds us together, *b*) the extent and significance of our common use of the historic confessions, *c*) the degree of conformity and freedom in faith which should be considered essential to Christian unity, *d*) the points of conflict in the realm of doctrine, *e*) the kind of consensus which should precede union as distinguished from that which can only develop after closer fellowship, and *f*) the diversity which is appropriate in view of our allegiance to Jesus Christ.

The section had at its disposal the findings of three study groups which had engaged in discussions and studies related to the specific assignment of the section over a two-year period (Saskatoon, Vancouver, Minneapolis). The Saskatoon group arrived at a very high degree of consensus, centering in the Person of Christ and the Word of God, and extending into many aspects of the doctrine of the Church. This group holds that "the unity we seek to express under God should be sufficiently elastic to permit varieties of doctrinal expression provided that they all maintain the Christological faith of the historic Church, with its biblical foundation." The Minneapolis group discovered by the use of its "check-list" a considerable homogeneity of doctrine running across denominational lines, a large agreement on the importance of doctrine to the unity of the Church, and at the same time a wide range of variant teaching both among pastors and laymen, even in the most doctrinally minded churches. It finds that "neither clergy nor laity feels any great urge toward organizational unity," and concludes that "the movement toward unity cannot rely heavily on the desire for unity in the contemporary churches," unless the churches become more aware than now of the "imperative" to unity growing out of "the very nature of the Christian faith." The Vancouver group notes that there is a large measure of agreement in the statements of Faith and Order meetings, but feels that they reflect "a tendency to be too complacent about agreement," and obscure the presence in our churches of "disagreements . . . far more fundamental than most of the statements of ecumenical gatherings would suggest."

In addition to the reports of the study groups, a statement on "Christian Unity as Viewed by the Eastern Orthodox Church," submitted by representatives of the Greek Orthodox Church in the U.S.A., was available to the section for study and discussion. It defined the general ecumenical position of the Eastern Orthodox Church with specific reference to the theme of this conference.

Of the four papers presented to the evening plenary sessions by chairmen of the respective Faith and Order Commissions, this section found Dr. Robert L. Calhoun's paper on "Christ and the Church" particularly relevant and helpful to this work.

II. Some General Observations

A. The members of the section are impressed with the gift of unity which is already evident in the willingness of all participants to engage in this theological encounter on an ecumenical basis. This is the fruitage of many years of Faith and Order studies and conversations.

B. Discussion in the section was characterized by a readiness to face central and crucial issues in the realm of doctrine instead of ignoring or by-passing them. There seemed to be a common feeling that sincerity in our desire for unity calls us not only to confront one another but to confront together the truth of the Gospel in all its fulness. We seemed agreed that "The way to the center is the way to unity."

C. The members of the section found that when they thus faced "the center" and spoke of "Jesus Christ," the "Word of God," the "Gospel," the "Church," there was a rather large body of common discourse which made for meaningful and fruitful discussion in spite of diversities in other areas and in the theological explication of this common vocabulary.

D. The section found the wide range of tradition represented by the membership both an obstacle and a challenge. The various traditions have developed differing and sometimes distinctive ways of clarifying and formulating the faith in theological systems and doctrinal statements. They have also developed varied institutional structures and practices, many of which have doctrinal implications. This variety adds to both the problem and the promise of fruitful communication.

E. As we have engaged in this discussion of "Consensus and Conflict," we have been made aware of the necessity of having some comprehensive perspective which can include both our consensus and our conflict without doing injustice to either. Such ecumenical discussions as that in which we have engaged may be particularly helpful in achieving such a perspective.

F. A pronounced emphasis which recurred throughout the discussion was the importance of the "servant-image" for the Christian Church, its theology and its mission. The judgment was expressed, and broadly affirmed, that in the Bible the image of the "servant" has a centrality and significance which Christianity in our time needs to rediscover. It was as the "servant of the Lord" that Israel was called upon to fulfill her destiny. Jesus Christ himself gloried in fulfilling the role of a servant who lived "to serve, not to be served." Paul interpreted the significance of the incarnation and work of Jesus Christ by affirming that in him the eternal Son of God decisively and exultantly took the form of a servant. In the Church of today as well as in the world of today, it is of first-rate importance that the significance of the "servant-image" be discovered by persons, groups, and institutions. It was held that unity will be promoted among the churches in their apprehension of Christian truth and in their dedication to the Church's mission under the Lordship of Christ when they take seriously the normative character of the "servant" for Christian thought and action.

III. DOCTRINAL CONSENSUS, CONFLICT AND DIVERSITY

A. *The Degree and Kind of Consensus in Faith that Binds Us Together*

We have found ourselves bound together in a common faith that impels us to a common witness, despite the variety of doctrinal standards found in our churches. "Faith" here means something more than "doctrine," though closely related to doctrine; it means the trustful response of the whole men to God's self-revelation in Christ. Primarily, the faith we share is a common commitment to the high calling of God in Christ Jesus, and a common mission to bring to all mankind the message of the great salvation he offers. When this faith becomes a message (*kerygma*) it demands an intellectual expression and begins to be articulated into doctrine. The articulation of doctrine must never become an idol (i.e., an end in itself) but is ministerial to the Church's inner life of worship and nurture and her outgoing mission to the world. The Church needs a massive and vertebrate form for her faith, and finds abundant material in God's self-revelation for such a reasoned-out message, but Christian doctrine must never be divorced from Christian devotion and obedience, and must therefore never wholly abandon the poetry of faith for the prose of doctrinal elaboration. If this partnership between faith and doctrine is maintained, we may expect consensus in faith to be accompanied by a high degree of consensus in doctrine, and this is indeed what we find among ourselves.

The center of our doctrinal consensus is Christ himself as the incarnate Word of God and the sacrificial Savior of the world in whom God bore the sins of mankind and founded a new humanity. At the beginning of the Faith and Order Movement, faith in the divine-human Lord and Savior tended to stand in a sort of splendid isolation, as the one clear point on which we were united. It is still the center of our consensus; but under the influence of the biblical renewal there is now a growing sense of its connection with other basic Christian doctrines: God's covenant with his people Israel, fulfilled and renewed in Christ; the Church as the new people of God, the Body of Christ, the community (koinonia) of the Holy Spirit, pressing on toward its consummation in a new community of mankind and a new heaven and earth. The stern events of our time have taught us to see new meaning in the dramatic conflict between the kingdom of Christ and the God-opposing powers, as portrayed in the New Testament; but our faith in Christ's ultimate Lordship over the world as well as the Church stands firm as the final capstone in the arch of faith that now begins to tower over the wreckage and confusion of our time. There has been a great recovery in recent years of the centrality of biblical revelation in Christian doctrine—though this has not penetrated all the curricula of Christian education—both as the record of the mighty acts of God leading up to our redemption in Christ, and also as the source of intelligible truths expressed in inspired words, whereby the message of our redemption can be spelled out. While we differ in our theories of revelation, reason and biblical inspiration, we are united in looking to the witness of Holy Scripture, confirmed and interpreted by the witness of the Holy Spirit in the Church, as the *sine qua non* of authentic Christian doctrine.

B. *Extent and Significance of Our Common Use of the Historic Confessions*

When we compare the actual *use* of historic confessions in different churches, we find them sharply divided between *creedal* churches, where they are largely used for catechetical instruction and in public worship, and *noncreedal* churches, where there is grave objection to using them at all—except as historical documents. When we examine the *significance* of the use of creeds and confessions, we find this sharp polarization much diminished. For example, some noncreedal churches of the "covenant" type express their opposition to confessionalism by declaring that they use creeds only as "testimonies, not tests" of faith. Yet there are churches of the creedal type which use the very same word "testimony," to define their own use of their historic confessions. All our communions agree that their creeds and confessions are subordinate to Scripture, at least in the negative sense that they must not contradict Scripture. They further agree that these confessions must be interpreted and reinterpreted in the light of Scripture under the guidance of the Holy Spirit. Those churches which make no use of historic confessions actually use "tests" or norms of other sorts (such as the Quaker "queries" or the "covenants" of other churches) to keep up standards of Christian commitment and Christian instruction among their members. We agree with the Lausanne call (1927) to re-examine the content, the historical significance and the meaning for us of the great ecumenical definitions of the early church councils; and we also agree that when the Church's very existence is challenged again, by anti-Christian trends and dangerously perverted versions of the Christian message, such threats need to be countered by similarly pointed confessions of the mind of Christ. A good recent example of such a contemporary confession, formulated with specific reference to the current renaissance of Hinduism and the deluge of communism, is that of the Batak Protestant Church in Indonesia.

C. *Conformity and Freedom of Faith*

The section wishes to reassert as sufficient ground of membership in the Ecumenical Movement the confession that Jesus Christ is "God and Saviour." While some of us are dissatisfied with this form of words, all of us recognize that loyalty to Christ as God's incarnate Word and our Savior is the very heart of our given unity. Every church will wish to supplement and interpret this central faith; none can repudiate it without ceasing to be united to her sister communions. This common confession is rooted in revelation as witnessed in Scripture and received in the Church through the Spirit. The authority of the faith, then, is located in the Scriptures, the historic tradition of the Church, and the continuing work of the Holy Spirit. Diversity of doctrine not contrary to this authority reflects the riches of God's grace and the diversity of his gifts to the Church. The unity we seek is not to be found in enforced conformity to a detailed, complete unchangeable system of doctrine. Our only absolute captivity is to Christ and his mission; this captivity sets us totally free to realize the purpose for which we were created. Freedom to interpret Christian truth in varied ways, as the Spirit guides us to apply it to changing situations and different men, is part of Christian liberty—and responsibility. Against what seem to be real perversions of the Gospel, all are bound to protest in the name of the truth; but none of our churches is so "authoritative" that it forbids all difference on special points of doctrine (theologoumena).

D. Points of Deepest Conflict

We have to distinguish between diversity, *creative* conflict which helps to get truth stated and *destructive* conflict which obscures the truth. Diversity and creative conflict spring from our finiteness; destructive conflict from our sin. Destructive conflict in matters of doctrine exists at various levels between member churches within the fellowship of the World Council of Churches, and also between the member churches and others which find it impossible to seek membership in it. All conflicts which keep churches in opposition are serious because they make it hard to hear the voice of Christ above the clamor of rival churches; but the latter type of conflict, which now keeps Roman Catholics and some Protestants out of official ecumenical confrontation, is most serious. Continued study and conferences are recommended, to see if it is really necessary for all such groups to stay out on doctrinal grounds, when other groups, quite as different from the Protestant majority (e.g., certain Eastern Orthodox churches) are already in. Conflicts also exist among the member churches in the World Council, sometimes dividing them from one another, sometimes cutting across denominational lines and sometimes reducible to differences of emphasis. Examples of such conflicts may be found in varying theories of religious knowledge, theories concerning the nature of the union between the divine and the human in Jesus Christ, varying concepts of the nature of the Church, and varying ways in which the Lord and Head of the Church is related to the concrete life of the Church and its members (e.g., in the various "means of grace" specially preferred in different communions). The conflicts center, as has often been noted, in the part of Christian doctrine dealing with the ministry and the sacraments, while they are at a minimum in the doctrine of God and the doctrine of Christ.

E. *Consensus Which Should Precede Unity and That Which Must Await Closer Fellowship*

There is, of course, a *given* consensus already existing, concerning which we have already spoken under (A). This given consensus does not yet fully express the oneness of the Church which it is God's will for his people to realize. We call attention, therefore, to those areas in which further agreement needs to be reached before we can move toward closer oneness. (The necessity of agreement will vary, of course, according to the nature of the unity we seek; "mutual recognition" requires less than "corporate unity.")

1. The nature of the Church, its ministry and its sacraments. Here greater agreement is needed, based on much further study and conference between the various types of churches, before some of them can consider intercommunion, and others can consider reunion.

2. The nature of the authority and inspiration of the Bible. Here is one of the chief causes of disunity among Protestants. The relations between the Bible and reason, and the nature of revelation (whether expressed in "propositions" or "events" or both) need particular study in this connection.

3. Finally, the nature of the unity we seek. On this, as noted above, will depend the degree of doctrinal unity necessary beforehand. It is quite plain that participants in the ecumenical movement are hoping for different outcomes. It is good to make these differences conscious and try to resolve them.

After the unity we seek (or which God wills for us) reaches each stage of realization, the ministry of the Holy Spirit will lead (in the process of growing together) to a profounder appreciation of the gift of the Church and a profounder understanding of the meaning of its worship, its sacramental *koinonia,* and its mission in the world. Some united churches have deliberately left the drafting of a longer doctrinal statement of faith until after they have merged upon a very simple "basis of union," including a short declaration of their common faith.

F. *"Diversities to Be Welcomed" in the Expression of Our Common Allegiance*

We have already distinguished "diversity" from "conflict" under D above. Our common allegiance to Jesus Christ means a loving obedience to him, which may be expressed in diverse ways. In his missionary work, the Apostle Paul became "all things to all men" that he might "by all means win some." We welcome such diversity in the life and thought of the churches, as a manifestation of the "fruits of the Spirit" and a contribution to the "fullness of Christ." Diversities of this sort are found in liturgical practice, in cultural tradition, in types of Christian service, in styles of Christian art, in ways of proclaiming the faith. Whether diversity in theological doctrine can be encouraged without endangering the Christian faith itself, is questioned by some of us. Diversity of faith has often resulted from diversity of theology. It is important to distinguish the divine revelation which is the center of our common faith from the human systems of theology which relate this revelation to contemporary schools of philosophy and changing world situations. The purity of the common faith is better preserved by encouraging creative conflict between theological systems than by prematurely finalizing any one of them. (Doctors of divinity are stewards of divine revelation, but the history of doctrine proves that they do not possess divine omniscience.) As Dr. Calhoun remarked in his address on "Christ and the Church," the mystery of God's infinite Being can never be fully resolved by finite minds, for "God as self-disclosed to us men remains mystery not only in some secrets of his Being that remain undisclosed, but also in his self-revelation itself." We cannot therefore hope or desire to eliminate all diversities from Christian doctrine. We walk together in the light of the same divine-human Face; we bow together before the same ineffable Mystery, content to argue with one another's best judgments, since none can claim to have plumbed the infinite depths of the Godhead.

In the work of this section we have repeatedly verified the Lausanne principle of "comprehension." That is, when the seemingly conflicting doctrines of different churches are carefully defined in face-to-face conference, they are first found to be less contradictory than they appeared to be, and then found to be diverse aspects of a comprehensive truth which all need to consider in order to deepen and correct their own favorite views. [See point B above.] As every American in our day needs to be a world citizen in order to be a good American, so every confessional theologian needs to be an ecumenical theologian in order to be a good representative of his own confession. The sparks of comprehension that flew between Baptists and Lutherans, Quakers and Orthodox will continue to illuminate the minds and hearts of all of us who took part in these discussions.

Not all doctrinal differences can speedily be turned into fruitful diversities so as to be resolved by mutual comprehension. The doctrinal differences concerning the ministry, the sacraments and others mentioned under D above cannot be overcome at this time, and constitute an impasse which must be examined and re-examined by all the methods recommended at the Lund Conference. However, the progress that has already been made by the Faith and Order Movement, and our experience in this section, give us confidence that here, too, destructive conflict may some day be transformed through creative conflict into a more comprehensive truth that will include us all. For us all, Jesus Christ is the Truth. Theology or doctrinal labor is the service of our minds humbly and joyfully offered to him, and therefore to one another. Our hope in seeking unity resides not in endeavors to master other men with our superior insights, but in love to serve our brother and to be served by him as servants together of the Word of God.

IV. RECOMMENDATION

The section records its conviction that there is need for a continuation and extension of the kind of theological exchange which has here taken place, to all sections of our continent. The work of the sixteen study groups which made preparatory studies for this conference give evidence of both the possibility and fruitfulness of such a project. It is hoped that the encouragement which has been given to Faith and Order studies through this conference will establish the work of Faith and Order as a proportionally larger part of the total ecumenical enterprise in this area.

SECTION 3. *Baptism Into Christ*

Chairman: The Rt. Rev. Stephen F. Bayne
Secretary: The Rev. George L. Hunt

The Situation:

In faithfulness to the eternal Gospel, churches have from the beginning obeyed the Lord's command to baptize. In this obedience they have found a mark of their oneness. "There is . . . one baptism" (Eph. 4:5). Some communions, to be sure, have insisted that their doctrine and practice alone is valid. Others, even though sharply divided on other grounds, have gratefully recognized in this sacrament a bond of union which the Lord gives to his whole people. In North America, once-bitter controversies over baptism have tended to lose their force, so that baptism is no longer as strong a bond nor as high a barrier as formerly. Yet whenever steps are taken toward closer fellowship, the divergent understandings of baptism and confirmation often recover their divisive force. When we probe together into the apathy that exists in every church, and into the widespread ignorance and superficial conceptions of the sacrament, we discover a common need not only to remove obstacles to unity but also to recover the oneness and the truth of this event. The churches need each other in recovering a sense of God's activity and purpose in baptism, and in determining what God requires of us by way of consensus and freedom in receiving his grace through baptism.

The Objectives:

a. to discover the extent to which Christian baptism is an element in our unity and disunity.
b. to listen together to Scripture for its teaching concerning the power of baptism to unify God's people.
c. to discern the recent changes in both scholarly and popular attitudes toward the significance of this event.
d. to examine the degree of consensus in the doctrine and practice of baptism which is necessary before greater unity can be realized.
e. to determine the degree to which the various communions now recognize as valid the baptism and confirmation of other communions.
f. to weigh the implications of this recognition in dealing with other obstacles to unity.

The Report:

PART I—AFFIRMATIONS OF AGREEMENT

(1) Baptism, acknowledged to be grounded in Scripture and the command of our Lord and almost universally practiced in some form in Christendom throughout the centuries, constitutes an important measure of unity and provides the opportunity for deeper mutual understanding.

(2) We affirm the primacy of God's act in baptism, which also involves the reaffirmation by the Church of its faith in the crucified and risen Lord and the re-enacting of his death and resurrection in the life of the Christian as the result of believing response to the same loving activity of God. In baptism, God comes to man with a gracious and redemptive purpose offering him forgiveness of sins and the new life in Christ and enabling him to grow by his grace and the gift of the Spirit into the fullness of his stature that he may be conformed to the image of his Son. At whatever point of time baptism is administered, we agree that growth into personal and intelligent faith, repentance and self-committal must take place if the full purpose of baptism is to be realized.

The primacy of God in baptism is variously expressed in the churches by the biblical concept of the covenant or by such terms as "prevenient grace" or "the initiating activity of the Spirit." However expressed, in as far as baptism involves any kind of human response or activity, it must be interpreted as response to what God has already done in Christ. The principal agent in the regeneration of men is God, not man. Any interpretation of baptism, which reduces it merely to a sign of human commitment or testimony, leaves out of account an essential element in the New Testament conception of baptism.

(3) While some would insist that immersion is the more fitting mode, both for scriptural and symbolic reasons, we agree that the spiritual event is the decisive factor. Note was taken, however, that some churches would insist on immersion as the only valid form of baptism, believing this to be not only symbolically appropriate, but required by the authority of the New Testament itself.

(4) All churches regard baptism as the means of entry into the universal Church and not only into membership of a particular denomination; the full implications of this are not always realized. The impossibility in a divided Christendom of finding our unity in one outward and visible Church obscures for Christians the fact of their real unity in Christ through baptism.

(5) We are concerned, however, that there is in our time a widespread carelessness or apparent slackness in regard both to the practice of and the teaching concerning baptism. Despite its widespread observance, the significance and unifying effect of this ordinance or sacrament has been obscured for several reasons. Among the most important are the present divided state of Christendom, the influence of secularism, the lack of adequate instruction, and the difficulty of the contemporary mind in understanding religious symbolism. We are clear that we must devote our-

selves to a fresh examination of and submission to the biblical teaching concerning baptism. We must also make a reassessment of our own traditions in order to arrive at a more adequate understanding of what God intends in this ordinance or sacrament for the new life in Christ of the believer.

PART II—STATEMENT OF DIFFERENCES

We all agree that the children of Christian parents are entitled to share in the promises of God and to enjoy the benefits which belong to the covenant people. Some believe that such children do in fact so share, whether or not they are baptized prior to their confession of faith.

(1) Those who affirm only *believers'* baptism emphasize the necessity of personal faith and decision as conditions of God's activity in bringing the new man into existence. Man's freedom to respond to the grace of God is grounded in God's own creation of man and does not constitute any merit on his part. His freedom is not a freedom to save himself but the freedom to cast himself upon the mercy of God in Christ for forgiveness and renewal through the Holy Spirit. Exponents of this view maintain that biological metaphors, such as rebirth and the Pauline image of dying and rising again can only be satisfactorily understood when a personal relationship between God and man is assumed in which man has a real part to play. This is not to make man the author of his own salvation but to insist that God is saving persons. Sinful man is able to respond to the grace of God by an act of faith which is truly his own, though impossible without the prior activity of God.

The distinctive mark of those whose traditions include *infant* baptism is that baptism is the outward sign and seal that the child has now entered into the fellowship of the covenant people and/or the means of grace whereby the child is grafted into the Body of Christ. The significance of baptism is not to be found immediately in anything done by the child. The faith of the Church, together with the vows and promises of the parents and/or sponsors, presents the child to God who accepts him or her in baptism into the Church, thereby effecting or declaring God's eternal and gracious acceptance of the child into the covenant relationship with himself. It should, however, be noted in churches which practice infant baptism that confirmation or public profession of faith means the responsible renewal by the person of the promises and vows made in his or her behalf at baptism.

(2) A point of real tension was discerned between those who regard the very act of baptism as the occasion for the specific ac-

tivity on the part of God in effecting the regeneration of the individual and those who hold that baptism symbolizes a spiritual change which has already taken place as the result of believing faith. Some would assert the necessity of water baptism for salvation, whereas others would regard baptism of the Spirit as possible and indeed actual before the immersion in water. Though all agree that God is not limited by his sacraments, some would link the act of baptism with remission of sins and the new life in a much closer relationship than others. We note the distinction between those who hold that baptism with water merely points to the activity of God's grace and declares it and those who hold it to be the effectual means whereby the spiritual change is brought about. This underlies the distrust of many in regard to the word "sacrament" understood in this latter sense and their preference for the word "ordinance." It was observed that neither of these terms is applied to baptism in the New Testament.

(3) Most of our significant differences appear to be rooted in our different views of the Church. All hold that God's gracious and redeeming activity in Christ is the ultimate ground and origin of the Church. However, our varying and sometimes conflicting understandings of the meaning and nature of baptism reflect our differences with respect to the Church, its authority and order, the requirements for membership in it, the nature and place of its sacraments or ordinances, the agencies and organs of its continuing historic life in the world, and the means used by the Holy Spirit to sanctify its members. These and the like differences profoundly affect our understanding of baptism and seem to make it unlikely that a study of baptism alone will offer any final guide in our search for unity. "The question of the Church has precedence over the question of baptism," in the words of a recent study in this field.

PART III

It would be untrue to our discussion, however, to end our report on a negative note. If we have found that our study of baptism led us only to face once again the stubborn problem of our divisions in the doctrine of the Church, we have also found that the question of the Church looks differently to us now that we have become more aware of our deep unity in baptism. Christians are one in our baptism into Christ. This unity, often formless and voiceless, yet presses two gifts on all who share it. One is a fresh and deep understanding of the greatness of Christ's Church and the failure of many of our present practices in baptism and in church membership and life to measure up to that greatness.

The second is a sharper sense of urgency in our ecumenical task. The very fact of the unity already existing among Christians who share one baptism and the new life expressed by it and growing out of it gives an almost irresistible impulse to press forward afresh in our assault on the root differences between us. Sharing these two gifts from our study, we are led therefore to propose these questions to the clergy and laity of the churches—to the communions in baptism in every allegiance.

(1) Of the churches which practice infant baptism we ask— How far among you is obedient use of every gift and resource of the Church made in order that the infant may reach that point of faithful personal response and witness which would be the proper fulfilment of his baptismal vows? What is the responsibility of the Church to the baptized person who does not become a believer?

(2) Of the churches which practice only believers' baptism, we ask—Is sufficient justice done among you to the fact that God's Grace is active in and through the Christian community from the very beginning of a person's life, preparing him for the full confession and experience of the faith? What is the responsibility of the Church to the unbaptized child of Christian parents?

(3) Finally, we ask all Christians—Do we in our lives bear witness to our baptism into the death and resurrection of Christ? In what ways do we show that we are not our own but disciples of our Sovereign Lord?

SECTION 4. *The Table of the Lord*

Chairman: Dr. James I. McCord
Secretary: Dr. Howard G. Hageman

The Situation:

The Lord's Table unites us. ". . . we who are many are one body, for we all partake of the same loaf" (1 Cor. 10:17). At his table, Christ mediates to us the reconciling love and power of God. Here he forgives our sins and breaks through our enmities. Holy Communion is not first of all a problem to be solved but the solution of all earthly problems, through the grace of the Lord Jesus Christ. Nevertheless we find ourselves divided at his table and by his table. We are sharply at odds over the meanings and functions of the bread and wine, over the conditions which determine their distribution, over those who rightly administer or receive. Nor can we agree whether joint participation in the

Eucharist is to be considered as a step toward unity, or as a goal to be reached only when the churches have in fact become one Body in doctrine and life. These differences are accentuated by many others—deep chasms in basic convictions about the triune God, about the world and its history, and about the redemptive work of Christ. Every area of Christian thought and life is involved in this matter.

The Objectives:

a. to seek to understand the beliefs and practices of denominations other than our own regarding the Lord's table.

b. to share with one another our convictions about Holy Communion as a bond of unity and to gauge the extent to which a common meal already exists.

c. to accept together the burdens which division brings to all those who "draw near with faith," and to understand together that division.

d. to discuss the bearing which the recognition of one baptism has upon our refusal to recognize one table.

e. to explore possible steps toward more appropriate and more inclusive observance of the sacraments among our churches, in mutual faithfulness to the demands of the Gospel.

The Report:

PART I—PREAMBLE

In faith, hope, and love we have met at Oberlin, discovering anew what Christians have discovered before, the richness and depth of our unity as brethren in Christ. Yet all of us are painfully aware that it is at the table of the Lord, given to us as the continuing sacrament of unity, that Christians in history have been divided from each other and continue to be separated. In our present situation we face a distressing predicament; on the one hand we recognize the long history of controversy which has surrounded the Holy Communion, obliging each one of us to adopt positions and hold convictions which conform with the confessions and traditions of our churches; on the other hand we acknowledge a heightened awareness of the judgment upon our separate tables and our inability to join with each other in celebration of the Supper of the Lord.

We rejoice, therefore, that in such a dilemma we have been able to converse with one another meaningfully about the Eucharist. Our ability to speak and to listen to one another is, we believe, the result of the guidance of the Holy Spirit of God Who has not ceased to speak to the Church and to lead her into all truth. We would, however, record our belief that this leading of the Holy Spirit has been mediated to us in several ways.

a) In the tragic situation of man in our time, we who believe in the reconciling power of the Gospel of Jesus Christ, the central fact proclaimed at his table, have been forced to listen anew to what Christ would say to his Church.

b) In the liturgical movements present in all our churches with their renewed interest in the worship of the triune God by his redeemed community, we see evidences of a return of all the churches to deeper concern with the Lord's table.

c) Above all, in the Church's reading and rereading of the Bible in our ecumenical situation and in the many new areas of insight gained into the life of the apostolic Church we acknowledge the prompting of the Spirit of Christ.

In this new situation we believe that all who consider the Holy Communion in its relation to unity share these common concerns:

1. A concern that our eucharistic faith and practice should in the deepest sense of the word be biblical; not in the sense of using the Scriptures as an arsenal of texts to support our points of view, but in the sense of seeking a fuller understanding of the sacramental life of the apostolic Church; in this common concern we all read the Scriptures freely and freshly as a shared book;

2. A concern that the table of the Lord should have its unique place in the common life of the Church, both in her internal strengthening and upbuilding in Christ and in her external mission on the geographical, social, and ideological frontiers of the faith;

3. A concern that we shall see in the Eucharist primarily what God in Christ is doing for our redemption as we look back in faith to what he has done and forward in hope to what he shall do.

Impelled by these motivations, sharing these concerns, and above all in obedience to the Lord of the Church, we who have been together at Oberlin present our agreements regarding the table of the Lord.

PART II—AGREEMENTS

1. At the table of the Lord the Church remembers in thanksgiving and gratitude the life, death and resurrection of Jesus Christ (1 Cor. 11:24). What is meant by this commemoration is more than mere recollection of a past event. Our agreement is based on a fresh understanding of the biblical doctrine of God and history. The God of the Bible has not only acted decisively in the past through Christ's atoning death and resurrection; he continues to act in the present; he will continue to act in the future. Therefore, the faithful commemoration of what Christ has done for us is at the same time an action in which Christ mediates himself to us in the present moment. This is the same Christ who will in the last day share with his church the victorious completion of his purpose (Heb. 13:8).

2. Jesus Christ on the night in which he was betrayed chose bread and wine as the elements for the first Eucharist at the Last Supper. Rejecting any one-sided preoccupation with the elements in isolation, we agree that in the entire eucharistic action the whole Christ is personally present as both subject and object, i.e., as the One who is at the same time the Giver and the Gift.

3. In view of our belief in Christ's active presence in the whole eucharistic action, we agree that this action is our participation in his risen life and the fulfillment of his promise to his church.

4. Christ's presence at his table follows from his promise and command. It is only in repentance and faith that the believer as an "empty vessel" receives the fruits of redemption, including the forgiveness of sins, justification, sanctification, newness of life and communion with his brethren. The Holy Spirit bears witness in the present to the reality of these fruits and directs our hope to their realization in the consummation of God's purpose (Romans 8:16-17). The Holy Communion is a means of placing us in the presence of Christ in a total way. In his presence we are judged as well as forgiven (1 Cor. 11:17-34).

5. The indispensable quality of the Eucharist derives from the once-for-all character of the atoning death and resurrection of Jesus Christ as it was prophetically and proleptically set forth in the Last Supper and remembered by and represented in the Christian community. "This do in remembrance of me" (1 Cor. 11: 24-25; cf. Luke 22:19) calls us to the table where he has covenanted to meet us. As a consequence of our meeting him at his table we are made aware that he confronts us in other situations where we must respond in faith and love.

6. The Eucharist is therefore in the center of the response of the worshiping church to God's gracious activity in Christ. That which is offered and received in the Eucharist is central to the Christian life. It is important that all elements of proclamation— worship, service, obedience, and mission—be understood in their unity (2 Cor. 9:12-13). Liturgy in the narrow sense is not enough; the service of God by his people in their witness in the world and in winning others to Christ is inextricably bound up with their eucharistic life. The preached word of God is not to be set over against the Supper of the Lord. Both are commanded by Christ; both are involved in his work of redemption.

7. There is a growing realization of the eschatological nature of the Eucharist. "You proclaim the Lord's death until he comes" (1 Cor. 11:26) points unmistakably to the relation between the Supper and the Parousia. Our communion with Christ at the table of the Lord is thus both a present participation in his risen life (1 Cor. 10:16) and a foretaste of the messianic Feast (Mark 14:25; Rev. 19:7-9).

8. In the Eucharist God's covenant with man is renewed as revealed and sealed in Jesus' sacrificial surrender of his life to God and for man. It points continually both to the constancy of God's faithfulness to his covenant people and to the relationship maintained by the renewal of the life of faithful obedience through the power of the Holy Spirit. The new age has broken through; God in Christ makes all things new. It is to this covenant life that we, as heirs of God and joint heirs with Christ (Rom. 8:17) are called and come in the Holy Communion. We are "a royal priesthood, a holy nation" (1 Peter 2:9), called to offer to God our sacrifice of praise and thanksgiving, ourselves, our souls and bodies. By personal participation in the body and blood of the One Lord Jesus Christ, we are strengthened for life in the corporate community of the new covenant and enabled to discern our oneness with each other. The blessings we receive at the Lord's table empower us for our witness and work in the world into which we are sent.

PART III—AN APPEAL TO THE CHURCHES

All that we have gained from our discussions at Oberlin is only a preface to the larger task which still confronts the churches in their eucharistic life. This task, put in its simplest terms, is the heightening or, in some cases, a recovery of an utter seriousness toward the Eucharist as the sacrament of communion between

Christ and his Body and the sacrament of unity in the Body.
We are convinced that this task can be greatly aided by the process of ecumenical study, the process, that is of surveying our respective traditions, of facing seriously the crucial problem of intercommunion, of taking upon ourselves the pain of our division at
the table of the Lord, of searching and finding new agreements
in our understanding of the gracious mystery of Christ's act and
promise in Holy Communion. The new situation, to which we
have referred, and the progress in consensus which we ourselves
have experienced, persuades us that all our churches should join
with us in this study process, on the broadest possible scale—that
this is, indeed, imperative and possible. The benefits of such a
sharing would be twofold—a greater vitality in understanding
and fellowship in the whole realm of eucharistic action, and also
a powerful impetus to seek the fullness of communion with all
our fellow Christians. And from both these benefits would flow
new power, new courage, new clarity for the church's mission
and outreach in this distraught and broken world, for which
Christ's Body was broken and his blood shed.

Professor Sittler spoke for us all when he said to us, "The celebration of the Supper of the Lord is indeed recollection, Eucharist,
the seal of forgiveness of sins, and the gift and nurturing of life
in the Lord of the feast. But it is something more; something immediate and poignant in the history of all the embattled 'little
flocks' of the first century, known again in our day by millions
in shattered and cut-off lives in cells, rubble, behind wire and behind curtains. It is the proclamation of engrafted membership in
a kingdom not born of history, and therefore, not at the mercy of
history's demonic tyrannies. The somber chalice of the table of the
Lord has in our day again become a defiant sign uplifted, the
believer's toast of terrible joy."[1] It can also become the gift of hope
and anticipation to those whose hunger and thirst is for "the unity
of the spirit in the bond of peace" (Eph. 4:3).

In all our discussions we have been acutely conscious of the
difficult problems of order and ministry as these are related to
the due administration of the sacraments. We recognize that these
cannot be separated from the full meaning of the Eucharist or
from the problems of Christian unity. But we have found it possible to express our common understanding and fellowship apart
from and prior to agreement on all matters of order. It may be

---

[1]From: *The Shape of the Church's Response in Worship* by Joseph Sittler, address given
September 6, 1957, Cf. p. 114.

that the time is not yet ripe for a really fruitful exploration of these long-standing disagreements. But the time for that *is* coming and will be hastened as Christians in all the churches engage in some such enterprise as this one in which we have received so rich a blessing and such a sure token of our community in Christ's self-giving love.

It is our hope that all the churches will take up and carry forward some such process of study and search. We earnestly invite them to encourage critical and appreciative conversation between themselves and Christians of other traditions, to stimulate the reading *together* of that history of our salvation that judges all our separate histories, to bend every effort to the end that all Christians may come to share the imperative for the oneness which is ours by God's gift and by his will.

We commend to them the guides and materials that have shaped our own conversation, but we urge them to experiment for themselves in new ways of search and exploration in this great central area of our common Christian concern. And if we are faithful and serious in such a study, we can "grow up in every way into him who is the head, into Christ, from whom the whole body, joined and knit together by every joint with which it is supplied, when each part is working properly, makes bodily growth and upbuilds itself in love. (Eph. 4:15-16)[2]

[No members of the Society of Friends or the Salvation Army were present in the discussions of Section 4. The position of these groups involves a basic assumption which was not fully recognized by those who produced the report. We find great inspiration in the new depth of meaning which the report of Section 4 gives to the act of communion with our Lord. However, we wish to interpret this report in accordance with our belief in the non-necessity of the outward elements of bread and wine to mediate the living presence of Christ to the believer in the act of communion with him.

> Written by T. Canby Jones in consultation with all of the Quaker delegates and one of the Salvation Army delegates.]

---

[2]In our discussion at Oberlin we were guided by an excellent orientation paper prepared by the Austin Study Group. Any further consideration of our report would be greatly enriched by referring to this orientation paper. Copies may be secured from Dr. James I. McCord, Austin Presbyterian Theological Seminary, Austin, Texas.

REPORT OF DIVISION II

The Nature of the Unity We Seek
In Terms of Organizational Structures

CHAIRMAN: DR. ROBERT TOBIAS
SECRETARY: DR. GEORGIA HARKNESS

The theme of our studies in Division II is "The Nature of the Unity We Seek in Terms of Organizational Structures." We do not presume to set forth a full ecclesiology, and we recognize certain differences of conviction, as yet unabridged, at many crucial points. Nevertheless, we have agreements of profound importance to ecumenical fellowship and action.

We believe that the Church is founded on the mighty act of God in Jesus Christ. Without underlying foundations in faith and conviction, organizational structures in the Church tend to become pragmatic, as in any social institution, based at best on considerations of expediency and at worst on self-interest and a struggle for personal or corporate power. We therefore are constrained to declare our faith as to the nature of the unity on which any ecumenical or truly Christian organizational structures must rest.

I. THE NATURE OF CHRISTIAN UNITY

A. *Our Unity in Christ.* Our basic unity is in Jesus Christ, the Son of God and our divine Lord and Savior. We believe that the Church, as the fellowship (*koinonia*) of Christ's followers throughout all time and in every place, has been called into being by God. While existing in the world and in its visible forms enmeshed in many aspects of social culture, it is more than a social institution. It is an ordered community whose Head is Christ, and it is the Body of Christ.

B. *Our Unity in Mission.* As the Body of Christ, the Church has an apostolic task. This is to witness to the Gospel and to bring its redeeming power to bear upon every aspect of human life. For this task it has been given an ordered life of Word, sacraments and ministry which is to be exercised in and by the power of the Holy Spirit. Because of human sin and error, no denomination or congregation, as no Christian, fulfills this mission perfectly; yet every church by virtue of its very nature has this responsibility. To the fulfillment of this mission, all organizational structures must be directed.

C. *Our Unity in Visible Structure.*

1. The Church by its very nature exists in history with a visible structure, derived from the historical character of the divine revelation given in Christ. By his commission to the apostles to proclaim the Gospel and to administer the sacraments, Christ gave visible means by which he reveals himself to the faith of the Church. The unity of the Church is both visible and invisible.

2. We believe the visible reality of the Church involves its given function as well as organizational embodiment. At the dimension of given function we have a large measure of agreement. At the dimension of organizational embodiment we may have varying structures but do not regard these as insuperable barriers to union.

Stubborn differences, however, separate us in our understanding of another matter involving both these dimensions. These have to do with the Church's order, and particularly the sacraments and the ministry. For example, some of us believe that apart from an "historic episcopate" and multiple sacraments there is no true Church. Others of us hold that an ordered ministry and two sacraments are essentials of the Church. Still others believe that the significance of ministry and sacraments lies in the spiritual end they serve, and may not be essentials of the Church in any particular form. In all these concepts there are basic concerns about order which call for fuller understanding and common study, if we are to move toward unity in visible structure.

3. Ecumenical character is basic to the nature of Christ's true Church. This includes such fellowship, co-operative effort, and concern for the reunion of the divided Church as may be open without violation of Christian conviction.

D. *Our Unity in Authority and Freedom.* Authority exercised in and by the Church proceeds from the sovereign God who has made Christ the Head of the Church and Lord of all. God declares his authority through the Scriptures and through the testimony of the Holy Spirit in the Church. In the exercise of this authority, the Church is motivated by the love which established it as a holy fellowship in which all are members one of another. Freedom in the Church is the responsible right of the people of God to seek and to do the will of Christ under the leading of the Holy Spirit.

E. *Our Unity in Worship.* Christian worship is response to God's redeeming work in Christ. It is the service of God in life and rite, ordered by the means of grace which he has provided. Within the fellowship of Christ's followers there is a rich variety of forms of worship. We believe that God does not require of us a single way of worship. No diversity in our several forms and rites can alter this fundamental unity. From this common service to God in Christ any unity in action must proceed.

II. IMPLICATIONS FOR THE CHURCHES

Certain implications for the churches have been suggested in the foregoing statement of the nature of our unity. We must now indicate these more explicitly.

A. *The Life of the Congregation.* The individual Christian has membership in the Church Universal through the local congregation. The unity sought in the congregation must not be parochial, but be appraised in terms of the unity to which the Whole Church is called. So also the meaning of the unity we seek in the Church of Christ must be considered in the light of the unity we both find and seek in the local church.

Although many forces, both theological and sociological, influence the nature of the congregation, its basic unity lies in commitment to the faith of the Church in Jesus Christ. Both the manifest unity of the Church and the major problems confronting churches as they seek to heed our Lord's call to unity must be concerns of the congregation. This demand can no longer be evaded or left solely to larger ecclesiastical units.

A congregation reveals its ecumenical spirit when it engages in tasks which are basic to the life and service of any church, and furthermore pursues these as far as possible in cooperation with the members of other denominations. Among these are (a) ecumenical worship, study and service, with steady inculcation of a sense of belonging to the whole Church of Christ; (b) evangelism, both as a dimension of the total activity of a witnessing Church and with special reference to the missionary outreach of the Church; (c) social action in the alleviation of suffering, especially that caused by hunger, homelessness, poverty and disease; the reconciling agency of the Church in industrial strife; concern for community welfare and for social justice; a Christian critique of basic social structures and the establishment of a responsible society under the Lordship of Christ; (d) education and action for peace in international issues; (e) encouragement to Christian family life and a common bond of church membership within the family; (f) elimination of discrimination based on race or class distinctions, both in the fellowship of the Church and in community life as a whole; (g) Christian education in all its varied aspects. As Christians of a congregation engage faithfully in these enterprises their vision is enlarged, and as they do these things with other Christians, ecumenical fellowship is deepened.

B. *Co-operation in State and Local Councils.* The emergence and expansion of many state and local councils in recent years is both an indication of an existing unity among the churches and an instrument for its increase. While they are not a church or the Church, they have in them something of the nature of the Church, for in their existence they bear witness to the conviction that in co-operative Christian effort, the unity of Christ's Church is manifest beyond the boundaries of the congregation and the denomination. Heretofore, councils of churches have principally been regarded as instruments for cooperative activities among the churches. However, there is emerging a concern for their theological implications, and a call for a serious study of faith and order in relation to them. This may well lead to the furthering of a deeper unity.

Councils have rendered great service in encouraging greater unity of spirit as well as effectiveness of action within and among congregations. Their place is recognized within the American scene. For their fullest usefulness they must have the responsible support of local congregations. Possible limitations lie in the danger of inducing complacency on the ground that such cooperation is enough; fragmentation when only a portion of the Christian community is represented; and the cultivation of a merely social fellowship that is mistaken for Christian unity.

A development sometimes aided by the churches through such councils is the establishment of community or federated churches where the local situation seems to call for it. While this development may provide a basis for a significant form of ecumenical fellowship, there are, nevertheless, theological and structural problems which arise. For these reasons the matter requires further serious consideration.

C. *The Balance of Freedom and Authority.* Authority in church government exists for the orderly functioning of any group, whether in the congregation or a denomination. It must be both directed and limited by the purpose of bringing to all Christians the freedom that is in Christ. Separated from this objective, it becomes a form of dominance which is at variance with the very nature of the Christian *koinonia.*

Churches of episcopal, presbyterial, and congregational polity, with combinations of these elements, are represented in this conference. We recognize that all of these forms of polity have deep rootage both in historic tradition and in the faith of their adherents. We point out (1) that there can be no large measure of organic union without a resolution of these differences in a more inclusive whole, and (2) that more general understanding of the grounds of difference would be a significant step toward Christian unity.

D. *Plans of Union.* Any plan of organic union, representing, as it well may, the conviction that spiritual unity requires visible expression, must be based on a clear understanding of the faith of the whole Church. Its proponents ought to view the necessary and often painful readjustments with Christian love and in obedience to the leading of the Holy Spirit. Where churches possess a similar understanding of the nature of the Church and of the ministry, steps toward organizational unity may be called for as a fuller expression of the deeper unity which is our common goal. Such steps, however, should be preceded by careful consideration of relevant theological and sociological factors, and by efforts toward a more widespread ecumenical consciousness and sense of responsibility throughout the churches.

Together in this conference as we have studied the nature of the unity we seek in relation to order and organization, we have seen anew the necessary and, we believe, the God-given place of such structures as instruments for the fulfillment of his purpose. But above all, we have seen that

> The Church's one foundation
> is Jesus Christ her Lord.

To Christ, who is the Lord of us all, we dedicate such human foundations of Christian unity as he may enable us, in our weakness but in his strength, to lay to the greater glory of God.

III. RECOMMENDATIONS

A. *Recommendation Concerning an Ongoing Theological Study in the Area of Order and Organization*

Studies on such themes as "Our Unity in Christ and Our Disunity as Churches," or "The Church, the Churches, and the World Council of Churches" presuppose some differentiation of dimension in our total Christian life. In its preparatory studies for this Conference the Toronto Study Group distinguishes between two dimensions of the Church's existence: that of "primary order" and "secondary organization," between an "ordered structure which at all times and in all places serves as the means by which God constitutes the Church as the Church and an organization which under particular circumstances gives effective expression to some aspect or another of the primary structure . . ." (p. 4).

Are there criteria for a distinction between "primary order" and "secondary organization"? What are the implications of such a distinction for the churches in the determination of their own life and structures?

What are the implications for the churches in their relations to one another and to the whole Church?

Believing that study in this area may lead to further clarification of issues and focus for our conversations, the Conference requests the U.S. Conference for the World Council of Churches, in consultation with the National Councils of Churches in Canada and the U.S.A., to make provision for an ongoing deliberative theological study in the area of order and organization, and suggests that the Toronto paper be included among papers to be studied.

B. *Recommendation Concerning an Ongoing Study of the Ecclesiological Significance of Local, State, and National Councils of Churches*

In the multiple denominational structure characteristic of North American church life, councils of churches have been created along structural patterns roughly parallel to denominational patterns, from local parish to world confessional body. These councils have been conceived of largely in terms of co-operative action. The significance of their existence, however, clearly has implications beyond the realm of action, particularly for the churches' self-understanding.

What does it mean theologically that the churches have deemed it necessary to create councils of churches and other bodies, to fulfill certain of the Church's imperatives?

What does it mean in terms of the relation between church and church? What does it mean in terms of the relation of churches to *the* Church, of the mission of the Church in the world and the adequacy of churches as presently organized?

If, as the Lake Geneva Orientation Paper states, it is "the role of a council of churches to enable its members to manifest their oneness in Christ in the geographical community," what are the implications for our present multiple structural pattern within any given community?

The conference believes that these and related questions need thorough consideration by the churches based on careful research and deliberative preparation, and therefore requests the U.S. Conference for the World Council of Churches, in consultation with the National Councils of Churches in Canada and the U.S.A., to make provision for an ongoing study of the ecclesiological significance of local, state and national councils of churches.

C. *Recommendation Concerning the Establishment of Facilities for Continuing Faith and Order Studies in the U.S.A.*

There are doubtless other areas in the life of the churches in the U.S.A. which would benefit from the kind of study generally associated with Faith and Order.

Division II, whose area of responsibility at this conference has to do with organizational structures as related to unity, believes that some more permanent structure is needed for the proper consideration of matters related to Faith and Order. Presumably, responsibility for such studies in the U.S.A. should be lodged in the framework of the National Council of Churches as the common organ of its constituent churches, it being understood that any general conference to be convened shall be normally held on a North American basis.

The Conference, therefore, requests the U.S. Conference for the World Council of Churches and the National Council of Churches to consider the creation of appropriate agencies (staff, committees, offices, etc.) as may best serve the churches in the U.S.A. in their common concerns for aspects of Faith and Order peculiar to the American scene, and as may enhance their participation, separately and together, in the concerns for Faith and Order of the whole ecumenical movement.

SECTION 5. *The Life of the Congregation*

Chairman: Dr. Emlyn Davies
Secretary: The Rev. Richard D. Isler

The Situation:

In North America the "congregational type" church has flourished; here, too, churches which have been "noncongregational" in type have tended to develop in this direction. And whatever the historic type may be, for all churches membership in a given congregation has been the Christian's chief link to "the One Holy

Catholic Church" in which we believe. Each congregation is a school where we learn about both our unity in Christ and our divisions. Here we experience the intricate interplay of motives and forces which encourage or inhibit unity. Here we confuse that unity which is of God with the manifest varieties of unity which are of men; here we encounter both that diversity and freedom which are gifts of the Spirit and those divisions which root in our corporate sin. Just as in New Testament times, where the church in Corinth was the Church only through its participation in the One Body, so today each genuine congregation participates in the ecumenical reality. But organization into congregations has often introduced rivalry between different congregations, sometimes within the same denomination, sometimes between congregations of rival denominations. Local congregations, which are expressions of an ecumenical reality, often work to destroy it. The organized life of the congregation is a testing ground of ecumenicity. It has a mission in which the whole Church participates, just as the mission of the whole Church is its mission. Everywhere in North America the congregation stands on the frontier between the Gospel and the world.

The Objectives:

  a. to share our understandings of how and when a congregation becomes genuinely ecumenical.
  b. to assess the nature of the unity and the diversity which have been the active goals in the life of our congregations.
  c. to ask how far congregations are at present agencies of unity or of division in the communities in which they operate.
  d. to relate the unities realized by congregations to the quest for unity on the wider scale.
  e. to compare the accepted church-disciplines and self-disciplines in the life of a congregation with those which are needed in relation to other congregations and traditions.
  f. to explore the potential contributions of the parish to the ecumenical movement and vice versa.

The Report:

INTRODUCTION

We speak as representatives not alone of the One Church but of our separate denominations and local congregations in the North American scene. We begin by calling attention to the fact that while there are many forms of church organization on the

North American continent, the Christian's membership in the "One Holy Catholic and Apostolic Church," in which we believe, is through the local congregation. It is therefore important that we appraise the meaning of the unity we seek in the Church of Christ in terms of the unity we both find and seek in the local church.

We discover two types of forces for unity in the local units of the Church which, for lack of better terms, we shall denote as sociological and theological. It is necessary to distinguish between the two, although they overlap and interweave in the actual life of any church. It should be further noted that God is sovereign of all history and is at work in and through both the sociological and theological.

Among the sociological forces for unity in the local church are racial and cultural homogeneity, economic and social ties, and common possessions and activities. These and other such forces are of deep importance and demand far closer study and more careful examination than is usually given by local congregations. We would urge all congregations to study themselves in light of the various social forces which help shape their nature. It is important to note that many of these forces may be divisive in one context and unitive in another, or unitive in the life of a particular congregation and yet clearly divisive in relationships beyond its own life.

Despite the importance of the sociological, we find the forces most crucial to the unity of a Christian congregation and to its ecumenical mission are theological in nature. These forces manifest themselves in the faith, worship, and concerns of the congregation leading both to internal unity and ecumenical consciousness and participation.

UNITY IN FAITH

A local congregation participates in the life of the One Holy Catholic and Apostolic Church when it commits itself to the faith of the Church. While every congregation, in conformity with its general church discipline or by its own decision, is free to amplify and interpret this basic faith, it will be obedient to it since it reminds the local congregation that the very source of its existence is the act of God in Christ Jesus. It is through our common relatedness to a common Lord that our unity is to be found. This is a distinctive mark of an ecumenical congregation.

UNITY IN WORSHIP

A local congregation is ecumenical as it truly worships God as Creator, Redeemer and Sustainer of the world. In unity with all other such congregations it celebrates its faith in God's call in Christ through the appropriate proclamation of the Word, liturgy, and sacrament. It will open its fellowship to all and include within its petitions and stewardship the welfare of all people.

UNITY IN CONCERN

A local congregation is ecumenical when it accepts the responsibility of proclaiming the Gospel in areas of common concern. Primary among these is to keep before its people both the God-given unity in Christ and the divisions which separate both individual Christians and churches. The local congregation must seek constantly that grace of God whereby alone the congregation and the whole Church can be delivered from the sin and agony of disunity. It will accept the unity it has found through worship, study and service both as a gift of God and as a means of grace for obedience to his will toward perfect oneness.

A word of warning must be sounded. Although the churches have been led by God a long way toward greater unity over the last half century, the hardest part of the journey clearly lies ahead. We do but trifle with the meaning of ecumenicity unless local congregations address themselves to the major problems facing the churches as they seek to heed our Lord's call to unity. Our churches continue to be separated on such grave issues as mutual participation in the sacraments, the recognition of each other's ministry, even the matter of the qualifications necessary for the individual Christian to move from one congregation or one church to another. The open conflicts between churches in the formulation of doctrine and government of the church only further serve to illustrate the scandal of our divisions. The difficulties in issues like these must neither be minimized nor be permitted to drive Christians to despair of the hope of finding a solution to them by and in the grace of God.

Such problems can be faced properly and completely only when they are concerns in the life of every local congregation that believes and prays and works for the unity of all God's people. The matters that separate members of the Body of Christ must be accepted by local congregations as evidence of our unwillingness to obey his will to Oneness and of his love and mercy in refusing to acquiesce in our separateness. They must be studied with care not alone in company with those who agree among themselves, but across every line of disagreement if we are ever to be brought to the point of full obedience to the God and Father of all. As an important step in this process the local congregation will participate actively in the various organized expressions of the ecumenical movement, such as the councils of churches, local, national, and world.

A concern of the congregation wishing to be ecumenical will involve its witness. It will in its corporate and personal life both celebrate the glory of the Gospel and seek to share it with all who are outside the church at home and abroad. It will reaffirm the position of the Second Assembly of the World Council of Churches that "Evangelism is no specialized or separable or periodic activity, but is rather a dimension of the total activity of the Church. Everything the Church does is of evangelizing significance."

The local congregation will concern itself with and accept the responsibility for Christian education and culture through home, school, and community.

A local congregation manifests its ecumenical concern when it recognizes that there is no area of life which is not touched by the Gospel of Jesus Christ. It will cultivate an informed social conscience and lay upon its members the earnest responsibility for a fuller justice in which all may share. It will confront such problems as the creation and maintenance of international peace, racial equality and justice, industrial harmony, and other similar areas of tension with the full Gospel of Jesus Christ.

CONCLUSION

As a Christian congregation is laid hold upon by God as revealed in Jesus Christ, it will inevitably recognize itself as but a unit in the whole people of God. The heeding of God's call naturally forces a congregation to seek fellowship, inspiration and sustenance from the whole Body of Christ. Without this relationship the congregation is incomplete, and under the inspiration of the Holy Spirit will know itself to be so. These relationships will involve neighboring parishes, denominational organizations, interdenominational agencies, and, in fact, persons and groups wherever they may be found who are similarly under the kingship of Christ. In addition, such a congregation will recognize its responsibility to all men and institutions within the geographical community in which it finds itself.

It has been said that the ecumenical movement is inevitable and involvement in that movement for the local congregation is necessary because the congregation thereby becomes more efficient and can accomplish certain objectives it could not in isolation. To be sure, at times such involvement results in these by-products. The congregation, however, is involved in the movement not by any act of expedience, but because God's people is one people and God's Church, One Church. The cross of Christ binds all his disciples together no matter how man may resist.

The ecumenical task is beyond man's capabilities. It is a task, the consummation of which is in the hands of God as he draws all men unto himself. Saying this, however, in no way relieves the individual of responsibility, with God's grace, to attempt to restore the unity which has been lost. The individual is related most basically to the Body of Christ through the local congregation. We are therefore bold to say that the task most imperative upon the local congregation in our time is the ecumenical task. No longer can this work be placed to one side or assigned to larger ecclesiastical units alone. It must become central to the life of the Church, the churches and the individual Christian.

SECTION 6. *The Work of State and Local Councils*

Chairman: Dr. Elmer J. F. Arndt
Secretary: Dr. W. B. Blakemore

The Situation:

To a degree greater than in any other country, the churches in the U.S.A. have developed councils of churches as instruments of co-operation. The number and strength of these councils have grown steadily, as have the fields of action in which competition has been replaced by co-operation. In many cities the obstacles which have prevented co-operation on the national or world levels have been by-passed or overcome. For many Christians, the work of these councils has helped to define the nature of the unity we either should seek or should not seek. For some, this work marks steady advance toward unity. For others, it offers a substitute for genuine unity which may in the long run retard unity. For some the success of the councils has been achieved by giving priority to pragmatic and expediential factors at the expense of the essential issues in faith and order. For others, the experience in councils has disclosed a genuine unity in faith, in fellowship, in service, yes, and even in order. Whatever may be the accurate appraisal, the relationship of the state and local councils to the national and world councils has not received adequate attention.

The Objectives:

a. to assess the actual and potential contributions of local and state councils to the development of greater unity in faith and order.
b. to distinguish the forms of co-operation which delay genuine oneness from the forms which impel us toward a deeper togetherness.
c. to discuss the most fruitful ways of linking together movements for local co-operation and movements for national and world co-operation.
d. to appraise the bearing of federated churches and community churches upon the search for greater unity in faith and order.
e. to explore together those points where loyalty to Christ prevents us yet from working together in fulfilling a joint mission in our own home town.
f. to ask whether the concern for unity in faith and order should now become a recognized function of state and local councils.

The Report:

Today over forty denominations totaling more than 40,000,000 communicants are represented in nearly 1,000 local and state councils or federations of churches. Besides the employed staffs of these councils, over 500,000 lay men and women fill positions of leadership and service in these councils or in programs which they sponsor.

While some of these councils date back to the beginning of this century or earlier, the most rapid development of state and local councils has come in the last ten years. Their appearance is evidence that many churches have sensed an agreement in their mission and have been ready to work together. Not only have these councils been agencies through which member churches have expressed unity; the councils have also contributed to the unity of the member churches. In one sense the councils have been constituted by the churches and from this viewpoint they have responsibilities toward these churches. In another sense the councils have come into existence as a response of the churches to an underlying given unity, and from this viewpoint the churches have responsibilities toward the councils.

The councils are instruments through which denominations, congregations and individual Christians are brought into a closer relationship to the whole Church and to the wholeness of the Church. While councils of churches are not the unity we seek, we believe that either they have a place in that unity or help in its discovery. In some sense, through their councils churches remind themselves that they are in a larger unity of "the Church." Therefore, while councils or federations are not a church nor the Church, they have something of the nature of the Church about them. They are a continual reminder of a unity in Christ which is wider than that of the congregation, the denomination or a national or regional church.

Heretofore, councils of churches have typically been regarded as instruments for co-operative activities between the churches. At their meeting in June, 1957, the Association of Council Secretaries listed approximately a dozen areas of activity typical of local, state and national councils. It has become increasingly obvious, however, that these council activities have theological implications and that these activities cannot be furthered effectively unless, at local and state levels, the churches through their councils engage in serious discussion of matters that are central to the faith and order of the Church of Christ. Only by the help of such discussion can we hope that the activities of councils may truly be activities worthy of "the Church." Only as there is in local, state and national councils, as well as in the World Council, a vigorous engagement with concerns of faith and order will the councils and the churches with them move toward the unity we seek by common engagement in activities appropriate to the Church in its wholeness.

To be most helpful the concern of the councils with doctrine and order should be nothing less than a renewal of the mind of the whole Church in North America. This concern should be carried forward jointly in all parts of the continent. We therefore urge the churches to use their councils at every level (local, state, national and world) to devise ways whereby the churches can join together in the consideration of matters of faith and order. We call the attention of the churches to the fact that the Association of Council Secretaries is prepared to move forward in this area of study and service. While councils themselves do not initiate unity negotiations among denominations, they may provide opportunities for the fruitful exploration of faith and order issues involved in the renewal and unity of the life of the Church.

There are certain localities in North America where social and religious circumstances create a predisposition for the formation of types of congregations known as "federated churches," "community churches," "union Protestant churches," "interdenominational larger parishes," denominational congregations practicing an "ecumenical ministry" in the local community, and so on. These kinds of congregations have often appeared because there are conditions under which none of the traditional denominational structures for congregations seems adequate. Each of these newer forms of congregation is a response to a particular circumstance, and while each reflects some aspect of the ecumenical ideal, no one of them can be considered the unity we seek. However, their variety is an encouragement to the whole Church to venture upon those inquiries into faith and order which will lead to a better understanding of the Church.

By a consideration of matters of faith and order which will result in renewed conceptions of the Church, a renewal of the Church in all its parts may be possible, and to the possibility of this renewal the churches must become open. Social beliefs influence social realities. A continuing reconstruction of our beliefs about the Church is essential to free the churches and councils from obsolete institutionalisms into newly effective programs and structures.

It is only as we achieve a proper understanding of the faith and order of the Church—what it is in its being—that we can properly assess the activities of councils and the structures of contemporary organization.

For instance, if it is true to say that a function of the Church is to seek its own unity, that function becomes a criterion by which the activities of councils may be judged. But it is also true that the activities which councils have developed as they have responded in a Christian spirit to the needs and pressures of the world about them is a judgment upon the churches in terms of the proper functions of the Church. In other words, the emergent programs of the councils must, as the acts of Christians, be examined positively for indications of the function of the Church as well as judged by criteria derived from Scripture, tradition or theology. The experience to date, of state and local councils in North America, confirms our belief that the following are among the proper tasks of the Church and that, under present circumstances, these tasks can be carried out most effectively only by congregations and denominations working together through their councils.

a. It is a proper task of the Church to seek its own unity.

b. It is a proper task of the Church to provide for the manifestation of the wholeness of the Church in each and every local congregation.

c. It is a proper task of the Church to provide the ministry of reconciliation in the community.

There are existing areas of conciliar co-operation such as worship, Christian nurture, institutional ministries, and social reconstruction, whose further development requires discussion and decision in the areas of the faith and order of the Church.

It is only when questions of faith and order have been thoroughly examined that persons, congregations or denominations are justified in refusing co-operation. We believe that with respect to any proposal of co-operative action the burden of proof for an adopted position lies equally upon those who refuse co-operation and those who urge it, and that joint engagement in discussion of faith and order is therefore not an option for Christians, but a part of a divine imperative.

It is possible now for us to indicate some of the ways in which the councils of churches or other religious structures may delay the achievement of genuine oneness.

a. The success of particular programs already established may lead to a complacency in which these are felt to be a sufficient expression of unity.

b. There is a strong tendency for councils or associations to be content with representing only a portion of the Christian community (such as a particular class, community, profession, confessional family, or race) and to mistake these narrower ranges of inclusiveness for wholeness.

c. Councils, by providing opportunities for shared service, create units of very intense comradeship. This intensity of fellowship is too often mistaken for an adequate expression of Christian unity.

d. There is a fourth inadequacy which limits the effectiveness of councils and which points to a special problem of the conciliar movement. Councils of churches often are able to communicate with the churches only at the denominational

level. They have difficulty in communicating ecumenical
concerns to congregations and to persons. Inadequate corre-
lations of personnel, programs, and structures amongst congregations, denominations and the several levels of councils
have created serious frustrations in communication within
the Christian community in North America and between
the parts of that community and the world Christian community.

These problems challenge the churches to seek more effective
unity in their practice and relationships. The motivation to resolve practical and structural problems rests in a concern for the
renewal of the Church. A widespread discussion of the faith and
order of the Church by the churches in North America is an essential part of the preparation for that renewal. Of all presently
existing structures, the councils of churches provide the best and
most available vehicle for widespread faith and order studies.
By initiating those studies the churches will take a major step toward the transcendence of our present disunity by the unity we
seek.

SECTION 7. *Authority and Freedom in Church Government*

Chairman: Dr. Truman B. Douglass
Secretary: Dr. Robert T. Handy

The Situation:

Congregations are never wholly autonomous units. Nor are
they related only to other congregations in the same neighborhood.
They are bound in some sort of organizational structure within
the tradition and life of a historic denomination. It is, in fact,
this wider church fellowship which usually founds and nurtures
the congregation as a local expression of its life. Through this
denomination a congregation accepts and seeks to fulfill its mission to the world. Conversely the mission of the denomination is
channeled through the same organs into the work of the local
congregation. The interlocking structure of authority and command is simultaneously a structure of service. It is typical for
American churches both to insist on effective rationalized administrative agencies and to resist any infringement by these
agencies on local sovereignty. Our denominational "machinery"
is very highly developed and intricately integrated to insure effective administration. Yet the exercise of administrative authority

tends to be limited by the co-operation of the governed, by the control of finances, by the demands of pragmatic expediency, and by the personal dynamism of the leader. All denominations, caught in uneasy balance between the necessities of authority and the necessities of freedom, face similar problems of using the "power-structure" in the dual direction of a greater internal cohesion and of a greater unity with others in the ecumenical task. Their members may be fearful of the "authoritarian tendencies" of their own denomination, yet they usually are more suspicious of the monolithic tendencies in any search for ecumenical unity.

The Objectives:

a. to study the power-structure of our denominations as it actually operates in the American scene.
b. to appraise the degree to which church authority depends upon voluntary support, and the extent of similarity among the denominations in this respect.
c. to determine the degree to which, regardless of official doctrine and polity, nonconstitutional forms of authority affect the actual functioning of the churches.
d. to explore to what extent and with what validity, the fears of "monolithic" authority and power constitute an obstacle to the unity we seek.
e. to discuss how diversity, flexibility, and freedom may be genuinely protected in any structural expression of Christian unity.

The Report:

Authority exercised in and by the Church proceeds from the sovereign God who so loved the world that he gave his only-begotten Son Jesus Christ to be our Savior and established him as Head of the Church and Lord of all. God declares his authority through the Scriptures, through the Church, and through the testimony of the Holy Spirit. Authority exercised in the Church in his name is derived from Christ through men called and sent by him and mediated by the continuing life of the Church.

Although many different religious traditions and kinds of Church government are represented in this conference, we are agreed that the exercise of authority in the name of Christ is essential for the sustaining of the Church's life, the strengthening of its witness to the Gospel, and the furthering of its mission. In the exercise of this authority, the Church is motivated by the love which established it as a holy fellowship in which all are members one of another.

The grant of authority is explicit: "All authority in heaven and on earth has been given to me. Go therefore and make disciples of all nations, baptizing them in the name of the Father and of the Son and of the Holy Spirit, teaching them to observe all that I have commanded you; and lo, I am with you always, to the close of the age" (Matthew 28:18-20).

Freedom in the Christian Church is the responsible right of the people of God to seek and to do the will of Christ under the leadership of the Holy Spirit. "If you continue in my word, you are truly my disciples, and you will know the truth, and the truth will make you free." (John 8:31-32)

Authority exercised by the Church over the individual is directed and limited by God's purpose to bring freedom in Christ to mankind. Each church, in accordance with its own ethos, recognizes that it must bring means of spiritual growth and development in the family of God to the members of the family according to the particular needs and abilities of each member.

There are wide divergencies, however, among the churches of North America as to the locus of church authority, its scope and functions, and the means by which authority is exercised. Some churches hold to a form of government that may be set in a certain classification, while others have forms that represent a combination of or variations from the classical church polities.

Churches of episcopal, presbyterial, and congregational polity have the characteristic ways of exercising authority implied in these three words. In many of these churches, the location of authority is an expression of a view of the nature of the Church itself and therefore a doctrinal matter. In some churches, however, the location of authority is regarded less dogmatically, so that they can accept in one communion and fellowship quite different arrangements for preserving the doctrine and discipline of Christ.

In churches of historical episcopal polity the bishop is the primary guardian of the church's faith and discipline. Yet in no case does he possess arbitrary and absolute authority. He acts within a framework of doctrine and law that has been transmitted through the church's life across the centuries, and it is his duty to adhere to the church's teaching as he has received it. He is subject to the authority and discipline of his brother bishops, and to a pastoral relationship with his clergy and people which places important limitations on what he does and why he does it. The historic episcopate is also found in a constitutional form in churches which have provided a voice for clergy and laity within the process of defining doctrine and exercising discipline.

At the other extreme stand the churches of congregational polity, in which the individual congregation provides the locus of authority in deciding questions of doctrine and discipline. In many of these, the authority of the congregation is regarded as a doctrinal matter, based upon beliefs as to the testimony of Scripture about the nature of the Christian Church itself. Yet here again, the congregation is constrained by its obligation to be loyal to the Gospel of Jesus Christ, and its consensus is not regarded as a matter of human opinion but of the revealed Word of God appropriated under the leading of the Holy Spirit. The congregation itself is not regarded as one more church, but rather as one more embodiment in time and space of the Church universal. Its association with other congregations in voluntary conventions and councils is not an "extra" but a fitting expression of its Christian life.

The primary characteristic of presbyterial polity is a system of government appointed to preserve the unity and purity of the whole Church in harmony with and under the authority of the Scriptures. Presbyters or elders, selected from and approved by the people of the congregations, together with the ministers, ordained and installed by presbyteries or classes, govern in ordered groups at several levels such as sessions or consistories, presbyteries, classes, synods and assemblies; the larger body or a representation of it exercises authority over the smaller, and the representation of the whole exerts authority over all the parts.

In all three systems, the governing bodies rely on the Holy Spirit to guide them in reaching decisions in harmony with the Gospel.

The Holy Scriptures are normative for all the churches. Some churches recognize tradition as an additional authority, while others insist upon the Scriptures as the only rule of faith and practice.

Various adaptations of these three historic polities exist, and a church of one polity may incorporate elements of recognized value found in other polities without any sense of disloyalty to its own tradition.

Many North American churches have developed administrative agencies which may or may not be directly administered by the same authority as that which decides questions of doctrine and discipline. These agencies tend to play a large part in the life of their church and to develop similar structures designed to achieve the goals of efficiency and democracy, in the sense of responsiveness to the desires of the broad constituency of the communion they serve. Where such agencies are regarded as a direct activity of Church government, they may become the major activity of government, bringing about a substantial functional similarity between churches whose polity is fundamentally different. The work of the administrative agencies is work of the Church, on a scale unprecedented in Christian history. Besides providing service to local congregations, they help to extend Christ's ministry into areas that the congregations themselves would not or could not enter.

In order to carry forward such activities as missions, education, social service and evangelism, these agencies engage in the raising and spending of money and direct the work of clerical and lay personnel. Their structure is similar not only to corresponding agencies of other churches but to nonreligious voluntary agencies in North American culture, and represents the currently effective means of marshalling large resources to do a large job rather than a significant change in concepts of the basic government systems of the several churches. Such organizations would be capable of modification or abandonment if circumstances required, and yet by their important services they exercise a strong continuing influence on Church thought and action.

In concentrating on their own areas of responsibility, the administrative agencies might be expected to occupy the position of vested interests impeding the support of agencies for interchurch cooperation. Experience indicates, however, that their leadership is often in the forefront of the ecumenical enterprise, and the secretariat of the churches is usually alert to opportunities of joint action for the advancement of the Church's mission to the world in all its aspects.

To look to similarities in church power structures as a bridge to the overcoming of differences of polity is, however, a superficial approach to the problem of the exercise of authority in the Church.

The need of wide support for the agencies' programs has important effects, both good and bad, on the life of the church they

serve. They tend to strengthen the position of the laity throughout
the church governmental structures. Desire to protect their own
programs sometimes tempts them to exert pressure against explicit doctrinal positions and against the exercise of corrective discipline in their church. Within the local congregation similar forces
are at work, setting objectives of growth and financial prosperity
before the local church in terms that have a social or economic
motivation as well as a religious motivation.

As means expressly designed for action in the churches' social
setting, these agencies are important means for Christianizing
North America, but they could defeat their primary purpose if
the opposite effect of Americanizing the churches became a stumbling block to the exercise of the doctrine and discipline of Christ.
The local congregation may be in even greater danger of becoming an institution that compromises the Gospel for the sake of
maximum institutional success in its community. The similarities
achieved by the churches of North America in the institutional
dimension could run the risk of reducing the Gospel and sacraments of Christ to the rituals and pious principles of a mere
fraternal association.

Churches with a compromised Gospel would have no compelling reason either for staying apart or for coming together. Their
unity would not be the unity in Christ which we seek. Hence, the
nature of the unity to which we believe Christ does call us must
be sought not primarily in our cultural similarities, but rather in
the differing convictions we tenaciously hold as men under authority from Christ in his Church.

In this light, we find important significance in the fact that
most of our churches—whether of episcopal, presbyterial, or congregational polity—are speaking the same language when they discuss the place of authority in the Church. Our standard caricatures of types of polity not our own have been found to be
erroneous. The episcopate does not consist of a grant of unlimited
power to one man. The presbyterial system does not trace its
authority to powers delegated by men to other men, nor does the
congregational system represent an ecclesiastical expression of
political democracy, establishing what is true by a mere popular
vote.

Each system finds its Christian authority in the sovereignty of
God as revealed in Jesus Christ, in the commissioning of the
apostles, in the continuing life of the Church, and specifically in
the action of the Holy Spirit in the agents of church authority

characteristic of its own system. Each depends on the Scriptures for the verification and illumination of its understanding of the Gospel. We have discovered that the difference between our several traditions are family differences, and though we as yet do not know how they may be resolved, we have found new meaning in the fact that no man can say, "Jesus is Lord," but by the Holy Ghost.

Jesus is not made Lord by the decision of a bishop nor by the vote of a representative or popular assembly. If bishops, presbyteries, and congregations declare his Lordship, it is the same voice that is speaking—the voice of the Holy Spirit.

This does not mean that any of us has come to regard the question of the location of authority in the Church as a matter of indifference or of unlimited variety. Each of us in our several traditions carries memories of Christian history which convince us that other authorities than the one on which we rely may be false to their vocation of exercising the authority of Christ. We remember usurpations, rebellions, perversions, and apostasies of former times, and though we write off ancient battles as long ago forgiven, they are not forgotten—and they are not wholly forgiven. To see the Christian past as others see it may be a necessary step in our understanding of the Christian present and in our moving forward together into the Christian future.

In North America, each church is in certain respects a "free" church, a voluntary association before the law in that no man can be required to join it or continue in it. But the concept of a church as deriving its authority from its members is, in the opinion of most of us, a misstatement of the case. Our churches neither claim nor attempt to exercise authority over nonmembers. But acceptance of membership constitutes an acceptance of an authority other than the individual's own opinions about what is true and good.

If, as in the congregational system, a man has a direct voice in the congregation's decision, he is participating in a process expected to declare God's will, not man's, and the same would be true if he were to become a participant in the episcopal or presbyterial process of decision.

The need for effective resistance to the secularizing of the Church's concept of authority may be an important contributing factor to the discovery of the unity we seek.

Here we must make mention of a religious position held by some, that no church system has any authority over the right of the Christian man to believe and act as he believes God would have him believe and act. Such a view does have room for the concept that the Church is a voluntary association possessing only the authority delegated to it by its individual members. In this view, the location of authority is the individual Christian; rather than the congregation, the presbytery or the episcopate.

While the reconciliation of this view with any of these three polities is a difficult problem, there is a point of contact in that every church recognizes a vital personal relationship of the individual to Christ, together with the supreme importance of conscience under the Gospel as the individual's guide in belief and conduct. In addition, the element of consent under the Gospel is and has always been a factor in the exercise of Church authority; and the consensus of the faithful on the acceptance or rejection of a decision or decree has in all Christian ages been a genuine part of the Church's governmental process.

In attempting to discern the vision of the unity we seek, some of us look for agreement in doctrine and sacraments without being greatly concerned about the merging of governments. Others hope for a union of administrative and governmental units in a system allowing great diversity in doctrine and sacraments. Each of us tends to regard the system under which the Gospel has been brought to him as the one that ought to be most suitable for the Church of the future; and each of us, in discussion with others, has developed a renewed appreciation of his own church's polity.

Yet, the imperatives of "One Lord, one faith, one baptism," as well as "one flock and one shepherd" do not permit us to be content with a degree of unity that falls short of God's will for his Church as revealed in the Scriptures. Wherever we have closed the door to our Christian brother, we have given offense to Christ himself. Knowing this, and knowing our inability to achieve unity by our own wit and wisdom, we pray that God may show us the nature of the unity to which he calls us and may hasten the day when our Lord's prayer for unity will be fulfilled.

SECTION 8. *The Variations in Denominational Polities*

Chairman: Dr. David W. Hay
Secretary: The Rt. Rev. Robert T. Gibson

The Situation:

Because of their inheritance and faith, the churches of North America are ordered in very different patterns. There are the familiar contrasts between episcopal, presbyterial and congregational polities. There are also subtle differences of convictions as to whether particular forms of order may be essential to the life of the Church. Some view Christian unity in terms of a spiritual fellowship which is quite independent of organizational structures; others hold that some cohesive structure is required before greater unity can be realized. There have been repeated efforts to combine the distinctive values of episcopal, presbyterial and congregational systems into a single order. North American churches are kin to churches in which these efforts have been consummated in new forms of government (e.g., the United Church of Canada, the Church of South India). Various denominations are now engaged in weighing particular proposals for corporate union. All are being asked to study plans for "a federal union" of many churches. For each proposal there are proponents and opponents. In each plan, there are opportunities and risks.

The Objectives:

a. to examine the ways in which the Church is an invisible reality, and to relate these invisible and visible aspects to one another.
b. to explore the distinction between that order which is essential to the Church's life and that organization where diversity and flexibility are to be encouraged.
c. to discuss the ways in which Church order should be determined by historical continuity with Jesus Christ and his apostles.
d. to weigh the advantages and disadvantages in current plans for greater unity in organization.
e. to evaluate the experience of churches which have tried to weld together episcopal, presbyterial and congregational polities.
f. to discuss the ground for widespread demands for rapid advance toward organic union and for equally widespread fears of such advance.
g. to examine those institutional factors which impede or enhance the movement toward unity.

The Report:

The findings of the members of this section have been guided to a major extent not alone by the assigned "objectives" of this conference but also by the orientation papers prepared by study groups in Chicago and Toronto.

Our reported findings fall naturally into two parts:

1. *Regarding the nature of the visible Church and its organizational structure which underlie all denominational polities.* This part consists of theses, with which most of us can agree, which are in substance a brief abstract setting forth the central argument of the Toronto Report, revised and amended as a result of our group discussions.

2. *Regarding the considerations for any plan or plans of union in North America.* This part consists of the implications for the churches which most of us agree are the logical outcome of our discussions together and of our conclusions in Part One.

PART ONE

I. *The Visible Church and Its Order*

The problem of "Church Order" can only arise because the Church on earth is necessarily a visible society, ministering to the world and the invisible life in Christ.

The mysterious reality of the Church's life is accessible only to the vision of faith but the existence of the Church in time is bound up with certain historical institutions whose roots lie in the divine purpose and action. Visibility and historicity are thus integral and essential to the life of the Church. We differ in our identification of the factors which constitute the *esse* of the Church. All Christians we observe, however, appear to find it necessary to take serious account both of the invisible grace and of the visible sign as factors in the making of the earthly, historical Church. To this extent the visible fellowship and its essential activities are a "sacrament" or efficacious sign of the Church's hidden nature as the Body of Christ.[1]

In considering the visible aspect of the one Church a distinction must be made between the visible means by which God continues his Church in being and the transitory forms which come and go within historical change. Wide diversity makes it clear that few of the external structures can be universally necessary to the Church's existence, but the very visibility of the Church as continuously identifiable in history requires some outward forms as

---

[1] This report is written from the point of view of those Christians for whom sacraments are a necessary part of their life in Christ. The members of Section 8 fully recognize that there are groups of Christian people who do not make administration of sacraments a part of their corporate life. We sincerely regret that there was no representative of such a group associated with us in discussion, and we do not intend by any conclusions here set forth to pass judgment upon the reality of anyone's Christian life or service.

enduring elements. The distinction between these permanent and temporary forms is here formulated as a distinction between "order" and "organization."

II. *The Problem of Order and Organization*

Since order is the visible form of a human community it must be pictured as a kind of organization. The problem then is one of distinguishing between a "primary" organization (or "order") and a "secondary" organization (or "organization"). We seek principles of discrimination between such a primary organization as is essential to the continuous existence and identity of the visible Church, and the variety of structures through which this "order" can be made operative.

An example of such a distinction can be shown in the Lord's Supper, or Eucharist, as included in the essential order of the Church. For the action of the Church to be identifiable as the Eucharist it should be celebrated with the elements used in the Last Supper and with an appeal to the original institution. No particular liturgical rite, however, can be regarded as essential to eucharistic order.

This illustrated distinction should be applied in all cases to avoid two opposing errors: (1) the "platonizing" of order out of existence by making the distinction between order and organization absolute and total, and (2) the enslavement of the Church under any and all conditions to a particular organizational pattern.

III. *Order and Function in Society*

The use in the New Testament of such terms as "people" and "members of the household" to refer to the Church and its members points to an analogy between the Church as visible, historical community and the other social groups in which men live. The analogy of the family thus commends itself as shedding light on the Church's visible structure and especially on the distinction between order and organization, although no analogy can provide a complete parallel to the unique historical community of the Church.

The regulation of family life in the institution of "marriage" is an instance of "order" or primary organization. The minimum definition of marriage, which will distinguish it from casual cohabitation, involves its recognition as an ordering of sexuality in such a way that the family discharges certain essential functions by means of which a man and a woman are effectively related to each other and to their children. Over against this essential order we can set a variety of organizations (e.g., monogamous, polygamous, polyandrous) which may serve the functions of marriage in particular situations. Here are real distinctions at the sociological level between marriage (order) and different patterns (organizations) of the marriage relationship.

There is still the problem of the boundary between the essential order of marriage and the varying social forms it may take without losing its identity. Because there is no absolute opposition between order and organization the problem is a complex one. But to this essential distinction between constant *function* and diversified *embodiment* we may usefully look for the principle of discrimination between order (or primary organization) and organization in the secondary sense.

IV. *Order and Function in the Church*

Applying this principle of discrimination to the problem of order and organization in the Church, we note that the Church has to do with the fundamental relation of man to God. Just as casual sexual intercourse does not in itself constitute a marriage, so the mere meeting of human beings to talk or think about God does not constitute them into a Church. On the contrary, the Church is God's creation possessing a divinely given order in which man is related to God on the basis of God's action. That order is constituted by certain essential functions just as the essential functions of the order of marriage effectively relate a man to wife and children. It appears that there are three distinguishable functions which together define the essential order of the Church.

First, the Church must preach the Gospel of God's action, for apart from the confession and proclamation of the Gospel the Church must lack one of the primary elements of its functional order.

Second, the Church must administer the sacraments, in which divine action in history is mediated to men through visible, tangible signs. Without these efficacious signs of the grace which sustains the Church and the Christian in faith and love, the Church would lack another essential element of its functional order.

Third, the Church must necessarily be maintained and governed as a visible fellowship, in and by which the Gospel is preached and the sacraments are administered, and through which human communion with God is expressed and shared. This third essential element of its functional order is thus a ministry. As to whether this be the ministry of all in the exercise of which some are set apart, or whether there is a particular ministry which is authorized by God to perform this essential function in and for the visible fellowship, there is a differing opinion. Nevertheless it appears that the entrusting of the essential ministerial function to particular persons within the fellowship is a distinct element of Church order. This agreement does not extend to the recognition of a ministry ordered in any particular way as essential, nor does it involve unanimity of understanding as to how the authorized ministry is related to the congregation of the faithful.

The above affirms that the Church is constituted by God, Father, Son and Holy Spirit, through a particular order which distinguishes the Church from every other "religious society," and that this order consists of the Gospel, the sacraments, and the ministry of Word and sacraments. Over against this essential *order* we should set the variety of possible *organizations* through which these constant, essential functions may be performed under varying conditions.

Since these enduring functions of Gospel, sacraments and ministry must be expressed through some particular usage, it is difficult, as in the case of the family, to find the boundary between the essential order of the Church and its varying organizational expressions. No definition, however, should obliterate the distinction between the constant *function* and its diversified or transitory *embodiment*.

V. *The Question of Apostolic Order*

The inherent reference of the preaching and the sacramental actions of the Church to the divine action in history, implies that there must be a historical element in our definition of the Church's functional order. The Church's function is to communicate a unique divine action in history which we call the Gospel of Jesus Christ—to proclaim that Gospel history, to represent it in its sacraments, and to maintain a fellowship rooted in that history and devoted to its proclamation and "extension."

The Church's functional order is thus grounded in the "apostolic tradition," which embodies the particular historical revelation from which the Church's universal mission springs. This is clear in the case of the Gospel proclamation. The message is not a generalized affirmation of divine activity but a witness to God's saving work in Christ. Consequently, the Church cannot function as the Church unless it confesses the Gospel as proclaimed and presented in the apostolic *kerygma* (preaching) and the apostolic Scriptures. We are concerned, therefore, with the primary principle to which both "apostolic" Scriptures and "Apostles' Creed" bear witness—namely, the unique position of apostolic tradition as the visible foundation of the whole structure of Christian belief, worship, and life. Apostolic witness pertains to the essential order of the Church because the function of proclaiming the Gospel is defined in terms of the apostolic proclamation of the Gospel.

The same principle applies to the Christian sacraments. The Church cannot function as the Church unless it administers the sacraments instituted by God and transmitted to each successive generation from the apostolic Church itself. The apostolic "signa," then, pertain to the essential order of the Church, because the Church's function of celebrating them is defined in terms of the divinely ordained "representation" of the events to which the Gospel bears witness.

The same principles apply to the "apostolic ministry," even though more complex questions are forced on us by the radically differing conceptions of the role of the ministry in the Church. The basic questions have to do with the kind of ministry the Church must have if its fellowship is to be truly an apostolic *koinonia* (fellowship).

All differing theories and practices of the ministry claim some apostolic precedents or authority. Since diversity of doctrines of Church order at the level of the ministry is obviously such as to make any compromise formula impossible, we are strongly challenged to a deeper searching at this point of essential function. We may claim at least that there is a common substratum on which all views ultimately rest. This common ground can be stated in the proposition that the Church cannot function as the Church unless it maintains the ministry, and not just any ministry, but the true Christian ministry which Christ wills for his Church and to which the apostolic tradition bears witness.

The Church has certain functions which it must perform in obedience to its Lord and apart from which it cannot rightly claim to be the Church. At the same time it is clear that a wide variety of modes of performance is quite compatible with the integrity of the essential functions. Applying the distinction between primary function and secondary mode, we suggest that the criterion of *essential functional order* defined by *apostolicity* as our principle of discrimination between order and organization will lead to certain preliminary conclusions. We shall be led by this criterion to recognize that, while catechisms, liturgies and polities belong to the sphere of organization, the apostolic tradition of doctrine as embodied in Scripture belongs, together with the sacraments and the ministry, to the Church's fundamental order. This must inevitably find expression in a more or less explicitly organized pattern of instruction, worship and government, and we can never expect to find order in a state of naked innocence, unhampered by the clothing of secondary organization. Nonetheless, it is the visible body of order as such that belongs to the *esse* of the Church, while organization can be changed again and again without touching the essence of the Church's divine mission.

PART TWO

As a result of our discussions we find ourselves for the most part agreed upon the following consideration for any plan or plans of union in North America:

I. That any plan of union is important in at least this respect: as a judgment that "spiritual unity" (conceived as invisibility) is not enough. Our unity in Christ must find some kind of visible expression.

II. That any plan of union must seek to represent the faith of the Una Sancta. It is not enough to ask whether a given statement of faith expresses the particular preferences of particular groups of Christians. Rather it must ask: What is the faith of the Christian Church? What does it mean to be one in Jesus Christ? And this is to say we believe that any plan of union must be ecumenically responsible. It must seek to make clear its understanding of the Scriptures and of the ecumenical symbols as elements of visibility.

III. That any plan must make clear that the nature of the Church and of the ministry cannot be dissociated from the faith of the Church, that though there are wide differences in our understanding of order, order cannot be reduced to organization. Since order must manifest itself visibly, churches with closely similar understandings of order can scarcely avoid the imperative to work toward organizational unity, without prejudging the nature of the ultimate unity which we believe God seeks for all of the churches.

IV. That since the apostolic character of Church order is recognized by all of us as essential to the nature and unity of

the Church, any plan of union needs to clarify the question
of the way in which apostolicity is related to historical continuity.

V. That any plan of union must respect the belief of each tradition that God has had reason for calling it into being and
that the *koinonia* (fellowship) of the Holy Spirit in which
alone the Christian life can be nurtured has not been the
exclusive characteristic of any one kind of organization.

VI. That just as certainly any plan of union ought to reflect an
attitude of profound repentance for our long persistence in
separateness and disunity and the conviction that God is
now calling us to realize our deeper unity.

VII. That any plan of union in North America, as in any other
region, must recognize the nature and effect of social and
cultural factors in the development of the churches within
that cultural area, even as we must recognize that all such
factors have their profound theological significance. For
example:

1. That any plan of union for the churches in North America needs to face the nature of the influence upon the
churches not only of the concept of a free society but
also of the tendency to see the churches as bulwarks of
such a free society and as providing an undergirding of
the American way of life as against threats of communism and every other form of totalitarianism, even as
Christians in Europe must face the theological implications of the pressures for establishment of, and of the
concern for, European unity, and as Christians in Asia
must face the theological implications of their growing
desire for their integrity and dignity as national communities, and of their encounter as minority groups
within their nations with other living religions. In all
such considerations we cannot avoid the judgment of
Almighty God upon any motives for unity that cannot
possibly be regarded as Christian.

2. That ethnic and cultural pluralisms have been powerful
influences in the proliferation of sects and in the maintenance of disunity in North America, and that this
situation is itself a judgment upon the incompleteness of
our *koinonia* (fellowship) in Christ which, when genuine,

is neither stopped nor embarrassed by differences in class, race, or culture.

3. That the ordering of church life in each of our American traditions has yielded in significant ways to the influence of democratic ideas (even as those ideas have been stimulated by Christian understanding), indeed often with actual changes in the conception of order and polity, and yet that the recognition of such changes does not alter the truth that the ordering of the Church (whatever the particular form) is itself required by our faith and is rooted in it.

4. That though the easy mobility of both clergy and laity from one church to another in North America may be interpreted as meaning that matters of faith and order are not, after all, of basic importance, yet its deeper import may be that such mobility reflects a kind of American dilution of Christian faith into "religion in general" and the assumption that personal feelings of "natural piety" and "the good life" are quite sufficient, though we would not deny that some mobility may well represent the conviction that the really primary Christian tradition underlies all our particular traditions.

5. That though such phenomena as community churches which have been characteristic of the North America situation have taken seriously the demand for unity in Christ, their significance, like that of any congregation, must be judged not by any ideal of merely good fellowship of congenial persons but by the meaning of *koinonia* in Christ and the seriousness with which they acknowledge the nature of the Church.

VIII. That because the movement toward ecumenical consciousness is not characteristic of particular congregations, our churches in North America need to be trained in ecumenical consciousness and responsibility, and that this training must be increasingly realized before any plan or plans of union can hope to be truly effective.

REPORT OF DIVISION III

The Nature of the Unity We Seek In View of Cultural Pressures

CHAIRMAN: DR. MERRIMON CUNINGGIM
SECRETARY: THE VERY REV. JOHN B. COBURN

The task assigned to Division III was the study of the bearing of cultural factors on the unity of the Church. In light of necessary limitations of time and program not all the cultural factors relevant for the conference theme could be investigated. The four sections composing the division were instructed to direct their attention specifically to the following four areas: the mobility of the population, governmental policies and programs, forces at work on the college campus, and racial and economic stratification.

Despite the diversity of subject matter, the division can report certain threads that run throughout the concerns of its constituent sections. Some of these common themes consist in convictions that we share, some are no more than tentative conclusions, and some are simply queries that point the path to further consideration. Our identification and definition of unresolved questions may indeed be more important to the ongoing search for unity among the churches than the somewhat easier identification of matters of consensus.

Yet concerted affirmation is the place where we begin. We affirm at the outset the importance of considering the cultural factors in a Conference on Faith and Order because these factors constitute the setting of the churches in society. Cultural factors affect the behavior of the churches, and thus produce an inevitable effect not only upon the pattern of their relationships to one another but also upon their polities and doctrines. Careful sociological analysis of these cultural pressures is called for, and the sections are aware that we have made only a beginning upon this task in this conference.

But the concern that motivates us is a theological concern, and the analysis must be theological as well as sociological. In this respect as well, only a beginning has been made in groups studying Faith and Order. Our interests are in the world because God is in the world, and the commission of Christ to his Church is to go there. We stand therefore in what might be called a missionary situation and our motivation is the missionary imperative.

It is important to explore carefully what we are trying to say. We are *not* saying that the cultural pressures themselves are of God, any more than we would say that all that impinges upon an individual from the outside society is of God. We *are* saying, however, that churches, like individuals in this respect, must respond to the raw material of their situation in society. Cultural pressures may or may not be of God. Although we may differ among ourselves as to how to distinguish between those that are or are not of God, we agree that they can be recognized by the churches and used of God, for both cultural forces and the Church are under the governance of God. The cultural situation determines some of the conditions in which the churches must work out their own destinies, separately or together.

Again, we are *not* saying that the cultural factors represent a pressure toward unity, for we know that often they represent temptations to continued disunity. We *are* saying, however, that whether the immediate effect of the recognition of and response to these factors leads toward unity or disunity, they make up the social milieu in which the churches now exist. They are factors that Christians must know and that the transmission of the Gospel must take into account. We rejoice that the Faith and Order Movement has been broadened in this conference so as to include the concerns of Division III, and we call sharp attention to their relevance for the life of the churches.

An examination of the bearing of cultural pressures on the unity of the Church drives us first to a consideration of the nature of those pressures. The material is vast, even in the few facets of it which were assigned to our sections, and if our concern were sociological only we could easily get lost in it. The reports of the individual sections, together with the preparatory material, furnish indispensable data, and only a hint of their significance can be given here. Here, for example, are some facts which illustrate the significance of the problem of mobility: one out of five people in North America moves every year; from 30 to 50% of the membership of average congregations come from some other denominational background; 50% of the present membership of the average urban church has been added within the past ten years. The abandonment of old churches, the need for establishment of new churches, the growing heterogeneity of local congregations and the consequent homogeneity among the family of churches are only some of the elements of impact.

Or consider the endless area of contacts between the churches and government on national, state or provincial, and local levels. Strategies and more than strategies of the churches are involved in various ministrations to and benefits received from governmental entities. Questions are inevitably raised as to whether churches should accommodate their pattern of relationships and service to governmental policy, and whether they should use government for their own benefit. The ministry to personnel of the Armed Forces, to take an illustration, is only one problem, yet note its dimensions: 3,200 chaplains are now in the military establishment of the United States; in the six-year period from 1951 to 1957 the religious facilities for the Air Force alone cost $19,652,000, and the Air Force has now "programmed" additional religious facilities costing $15,000,000 for a single year. Or, again, 36,000 persons were baptized by military chaplains in one recent year. These persons are being brought into the Christian life but not thereby automatically into denominational life despite the conscientious efforts of chaplains in this regard. This is a taste of the terrible urgency of our topic.

The other two sections of Division III provide data similar in their scope and poignancy. The forces at work on the college campus cannot be ignored by the churches. The Church and the university are already engaged in fruitful ecumenical encounter. The opportunities for communicating the Gospel were never greater. The churches' care of students, growing as it is, hardly keeps pace with the growth in student bodies themselves. From 2,000,000 in college in 1954 the number, it is estimated, will increase to 6,000,000 by 1970. One fact of the 1954 picture can highlight the problem: 127,000 students in that year were on the campuses of state teachers' colleges where there was at work at least one Protestant staff person; but this left 164,000 in other state teachers' colleges without any on-campus Protestant ministry.

And what shall we say about the economic and racial stratifications of our day and their meaning for the unity of life and witness of the churches? The front pages of our newspapers pose the problem for us every day. For example, the composition of few of our churches is mixed racially. Many of those few which claim a cross-section are actually one-group churches that have representatives of other groups only on a token basis. Though the local congregation, as was noted above, tends to become heterogeneous in denominational background, it is developing a considerable homogeneity in racial and economic, and thus social, background.

In appearance and patterns of relationship some of our local churches are hardly distinguishable from social clubs. Such facts as these, which represent only a sampling of what is available, constitute part of the substance of our concern.

We do not label all such facts as good or bad. They may be one or the other, and often something of both. We do maintain, however, that their examination by our churches is imperative. In a bewildering variety of ways they make their impact upon the life of the churches, and particularly upon churches in their relationship with each other. And what of this sense of community that we have in part and long for more fully? An examination of the bearing of cultural pressures on the unity of the Church forces us, secondly, to an analysis of the nature of the unity we seek. Our conclusions held in common with Divisions I and II can be succinctly stated. First, our unity is in Christ who commissions us to go into the world; nowhere else than in Christ do we find unity or can we hope to find it as completely. Second, its existence needs to be made visible; it must express itself, if it is real, and become manifest in our own life and time. In the third place, it is not uniformity that is our goal; the unity we seek is the diversity in unity that allows place for various forms of worship, polity, interpersonal relations and service.

There are three further affirmations about the nature of our unity which grow more directly out of our theological concern for the cultural factors of our day. Fourth, the unity we seek must be locally identifiable and operable. The problems that our culture represents, though often derived from world or national conditions, are also felt where we live, always in local situations, always in concrete concerns. The effectiveness of whatever manifestation of unity we have or will create will turn on its being applicable to the individual problem, such as mobility or racial stratification and to the particular setting, such as the campus or the military base. It is not enough for Christian unity that it find expression only in supralocal terms and forms.

Fifth, real Christian unity is more a process than a condition. It is primarily a sense of relatedness, a knowledge of belonging; and more, it is the exercise of that sense and that knowledge. If unity is only status or condition, if its manifestation is taken for the thing itself, then we might be tempted to allow the cultural pressures we feel to call it forth. We might think *we* could build it; and we might try to build it out of necessity or expediency.

But this will not do, for our sixth conviction about the nature of the unity we seek is that this unity is and will be the gift of God. When the churches co-operate with each other for reasons of expediency or necessity—that is, purely in response to the cultural pressures that are felt—what significance, what real gain, is there for Christian unity? Our answers to this question are unclear, and differing opinions exist among us. But to the related question, "What must bring this unity about?" we reply in one voice, "God alone can bring it to pass." In its essential nature the Church is not a function of society. Although we are engaged in sociological as well as theological analysis, our concern in all such analysis is theological. The unity we seek is the gift of God. This does not mean that man should do nothing, for it is our Christian belief that God works through human life and actions. It does mean that merely human structures and manipulations are not decisive.

These six do not constitute all the aspects of unity, but they are, we believe, indispensable. Unity will be more than we have set forth, as the reports of the other two divisions will make clear. Our conviction is that it must not be less.

But that it not be less there are barriers to be overcome and obstacles to be removed. These barriers and obstacles to the unity we seek may be identified in many areas of the Church's life and thought, as again the reports of the other divisions will undoubtedly touch upon. It is the peculiar responsibility of Division III to try to identify the barriers implicit in the response of the churches, or lack of response to the cultural pressures of our society. Here once more, treatment in depth is desirable, yet not possible within the scope of this report. The obstacles we observe will simply be listed.

First, there is ignorance, or perhaps even worse, unwillingness to understand. The churches have not yet bothered to study as thoroughly as they must the problems, for example, of mobility, or of their relationship to government and to higher education, or of economic and racial stratification. Second, there is exclusiveness: the desire to perpetuate denominational values in isolation and to strengthen denominational loyalties as ends in themselves—disregarding the character and force of the cultural pressures upon them. Third, there is the adoption of cultural, secular values. A preoccupation with the values of comfort, congeniality and success tends to dilute the prophetic concern with the disunities of society as well as of the churches. Finally, there is the absence of a climate of acceptance in local congregations and of an authentic ecumenical atmosphere among the churches as a whole. Just as the sense of relatedness is more important than any and all manifestations of it in church councils, co-operative endeavors, and even organic unions, just so its absence on all levels is the greatest single obstacle to the realization of the unity we seek. The lack of a dynamic sense of relatedness may blunt the force that the cultural pressures should exert upon us, but this is its lesser fault; its greater evil is that it frustrates the promise "that they all may be one."

The discussion of these matters as an essential concern of the Faith and Order Movement has only now been undertaken; and much greater progress can be expected as the discussion is continued more widely within the churches over the years.

A part of the difficulty in this discussion lies within ourselves: we are not yet ready to face up to the implications we already see. We are defensive where tradition and emotional attachment as well as conviction are involved. On the one hand, for example, many laymen and ministers can cross denominational lines and acquiesce in a unity of doctrine or polity rather easily because they have relatively little deep commitment to such divisions; whereas others are more rigid in such concerns because basic personal associations and status are involved. On the other hand, many laymen and ministers are more flexible in matters of class and race and social station, for they have little at stake in personal security there; whereas others react negatively in these areas because their involvement is deep. In one fashion or another we resist the direction of our own insights and study.

Or the problem may be the tensions inherent in our topic. Though proclaiming our concern to be theological in character, we have yet maintained that we are involved in two types of analysis, both theological and sociological. There is thus created a tension of two poles of interest that have not yet been brought into fruitful juxtaposition in most church circles. Take the two positions: (a) "The churches must be seen as over against the cultural factors and forces, in opposition to, let us say, the standards of university or of government"; and (b) "The churches must enlarge the possibilities of adaptation to the cultural factors and forces, and active cooperation with, say, forces within the university or government." Each of these positions has been represented in Division III; each has validity in certain situations; and we have come to no consensus. The conditions that determine which should prevail in different situations require clearer definition. As part of our experience, therefore, we report this tension to the conference.

Yet other implications and conclusions are more affirmative and are ready to be offered. First, it is our judgment that the circumstances of our common cultural situation are compelling us to strive for a manifestation of unity in measure and degree that goes beyond our own present desires and strivings. Second, such pressures toward unity as are placed upon the churches by the cultural factors we have examined signify that the churches have sometimes allowed the initiative toward creating manifestations of unity to be taken away from them. This must not be; for the initiative must lie with the churches if the unity thus manifest is to be the real unity that is from God rather than the spurious unity that is of man.

This means, in the third place, that if we are to respond to the cultural pressures of our time in the light of the unity we seek, the churches must recover a profound sense of mission, of their corporate mission to society as the bearers of the Gospel of Christ. They must look upon the moving millions, the thousands on our campuses and in governmental service, the whole communities caught in the bonds of economic and racial stratification, as mission fields not yet white unto harvest but desperately needing the watering and tending of the churches' ministry. Out of such a concern as has been felt in all sections of Division III there might come, in the providence of God, a new and powerful missionary endeavor in which the churches begin to find the unity they seek in the service of the Lord they profess.

There is a final conclusion to offer. This conclusion has to do with the correlation we believe we have discovered between the manifestations of unity on the one hand and, on the other, the effectiveness of the churches' witness. It is a simple correlation: the degree of the manifestation of the unity we seek determines in substantial measure the degree of effectiveness of the witness. Two words of caution for understanding this conclusion may be helpful. First, we are not relinquishing our belief, noted above, in the dynamism of diversity; the manifestations of unity may and undoubtedly will be varied. Second, it *is* the *unity we seek,* not just any kind of unity, not merely the welter of cooperative efforts that now go on in its name.

We have come full circle in our statement to the Conference, for this final conclusion points directly to the proposition with which we began: that the concerns with which Division III has been charged and privileged to deal are altogether proper concerns of the Faith and Order Movement. We believe that, in recognition of the cultural pressures upon us, we must allow God in his good time to use us together in unity. We must prove not only loyal to our separate churches but also to his Church, the unity of which we seek and which he alone can give.

SECTION 9. *The Mobility of the Population*

Chairman: The Rev. Walter Kloetzli
Secretary: Dr. Rembert E. Stokes

The Situation:

The unity we seek directly depends on the commission which Christ has given to his Church. This commission assigns to us all a single mission. But this mission in turn is conditioned by the contours of contemporary society. Nothing more deeply affects the shape of that society than the process of migration which is proceeding in an unprecedented and accelerating degree. New suburbs and cities are arising. These areas are the scene at times of keener competition among the churches, at times of co-operative planning, at times of new forms of federation. They sometimes form a vacuum unfilled by any organized Christian work. Among older parishes, the movement of laymen contributes both to the erosion of denominational lines and to their accentuation. In some cases, the majority of members in a given congregation have transferred from other denominations. A similar fluidity characterizes the ministers and the theological teachers of the churches. The causes and results of this osmosis are difficult to assess. Does it indicate or portend the evaporation of denominational differences, the popular ignorance of these differences, or their accentuation? We encounter a basic homogeneity among North American denominations as well as a vigorous heterogeneity. Such factors clearly condition the character both of the unity we have and of the unity we seek.

The Objectives:

   a. to appraise the extent of mobility (population, laymen, clergymen).
   b. to examine the kind of cooperative work adopted for reaching the new residential areas.
   c. to assess the results of mobility upon parish life and upon denominational policies.

d. to weigh the dilemmas and opportunities presented by the increasing homogeneity and heterogeneity among the denominations.

e. to apprehend the subtle effects of mobility upon conceptions of the nature and mission of the Church.

f. to discuss how far the Christian duty to strengthen community in social life demands that denominational differences be overridden in new areas.

g. to discuss the strategies by which the churches may develop unity in mission to a rapidly changing society.

The Report:

A. THE IMPACT OF MOBILITY

1. North Americans are a people on the move. Excepting only our Indian neighbors, we or our forefathers moved here from another land. All of us must move off this earth to go to our eternal home. In between one in five of us moves every year. Moving vans, trailer courts, traffic jams, booming new communities and dying old ones dot our landscape. Ribbons of roads and highways, railroad tracks and charted air lanes speed us on our way.

2. We move from south to north, from east to west, from farms to cities and from cities to suburbs. Others of us move in the reverse directions. Some move upward on the social ladder; others fall backward. The adult North American who still lives in the home where he was born is a rare phenomenon indeed! The magnitude and extent of our moving about is described more precisely in the appended paper, drawn from the preparatory papers submitted to stimulate our discussions in Section 9 (cf. pp. 275-288). Such movement from place to place is not new in human history. What is new is its volume, its individual character, and the proportion of people it involves.

3. This pattern of movement we call mobility profoundly affects the church, her ministry to people, and the unity she seeks. Mobility brings problems to the church of the revolving door which in a year transfers as many members as she gains and in ten years loses half of her members while gaining a new half. Mobility brings problems to the southern or eastern "sending" church and to the northern and western church in the area of new residence, to the open country and small town church bidding farewell to her youth and to the city church called upon to wel-

come scores of newcomers, to the venerable central city church dismissing her young adults and to the bustling suburban church which receives them.

4. But mobility also offers opportunities to the church. It gives her a second chance to reach previously unreached persons. It gives her opportunity to show the migrant new meanings for the experiences carried into the new setting. Mobility may help to deepen his faith and to strengthen his spiritual life. It compels the church to rethink her practices, her traditions, even the form and content of her message. It opens up new avenues of co-operation, new evidences of unity, and a renewed urgency for dedication alone to the Lord and his services.

5. Our gracious God will give to his studying, trusting and praying children sufficient of his wisdom to transfer the problems they sense into the opportunities he offers. In this Spirit, and compelled by a sense of urgency, we approach the challenge which mobility poses for the nature of the unity we seek.

B. THE NATURE OF THE UNITY WE SEEK

6. The nature of the unity we seek is the Church, united in answer to God's purpose, in which the Living Lord, Jesus Christ, the Hope of the World, the ultimate security, is central.

7. The nature of the unity we seek is a church whose outward unity of visible structure, as well as the unity of love we now have as a gift of God, will be recognizable as home to men as they move from place to place around the world. She will be a church in which the Word of God is studied and known and loved as the common ground of authority, and in which the sacraments or ordinances are administered in such form as to further, not impede, our unity in Christ, and yet provide the deepest expression of personal relationships with God and our brothers.

8. The nature of the unity we seek is a church, in which there is a continued openness to the Holy Spirit in personal prayer and corporate worship which is meaningful and helpful to all devout men. She will be a church which proclaims the whole Gospel to the whole world. The faithful dispenser of her message will proclaim the mighty Acts of God: the Creation, the Law, the Incarnation, the Atonement, the Resurrection, the Ascension, and the Second Coming. Her preachers also will discipline themselves with the various methods available to preach the Old and the New Testaments, the prophets as well as the apostles. The uprooted and oppressed people in modern life need to hear the whole Gospel dispensed with power.

9. The nature of the unity we seek is a church, renewed, whose parts recognize the truth in the positions held by other parts, with all their common heritage and history in Christ, so that each recognizes that she can understand herself only in relation to others, and in humble penitence, and with a spirit of reconciliation overcome selfish partisanship, so that common counsel and comradeship supercede church rivalries. Our concern is for a deep unity where each person, congregation, or larger body finds fellowship, not in sentimental combinations around a lowest common denominator of belief, but by fidelity to truth sought with recognition of and repentance for long cherished prejudice.

10. Finally, the nature of the unity we seek is a church, renewed, in which we are fellow laborers with God. "Except God build the house, they labor in vain that build it." Personal ministry must take precedence over brick and mortar, advertising techniques and promotion stunts. Church success must not be measured by increase in numbers or bigger and better budgets, but by loyal devotion to him who "suffered, died, was buried, and rose again" for our redemption. Christians are always on the march. We are strangers and pilgrims here, yet we also are called to serve as lights whereby men may see our good works and glorify our Father which is in heaven. We are thus busily engaged yet never thoroughly at home in this world, for we are passing on toward and awaiting the home life beyond this world and history. The past must not fetter but enrich. The future must not be feared but welcomed!

C. The Mobile Person in His New Environment

11. It is easy to succumb to the temptation to generalize about mobility, its effects, and the people who move. Actually there are many people who move within a particular year. There is the young couple setting up their first home. There are those who retire from the farm to the small town or city, the southern Negroes who move north, the immigrants from overseas, the families who move to the suburbs, the junior executives for whom promotion means transfer to a new location, the clergyman accepting a new charge. There are those, as in sales or service trades or in transportation, whose work calls for intermingled periods of travel and "at homeness." There are year-round mobile people who follow the agricultural harvests, who move in trailers from one construction job to another, who sail the seven seas, or who follow the birds to warmer or cooler climates as the seasons change. Mobile people wear many faces and garbs.

12. How mobility affects a person also varies. One person quickly will grow roots and become a part of the new environment, as does a successfully transplanted tree. Another never comes to feel himself a part of the strange new place but is more akin to a potted plant temporarily set on a ledge until a better place is found. A third person may become demoralized by his move. He is akin to the shrub from which the soil fell away in the transplanting process, so that its roots had no continuing support from the old to the new site.

13. For some persons, in other words, mobility may be a negative and demoralizing experience in their lives. For others, mobility may be an avenue to a new, rich and creative life, full of rewards for them and their families and rich in the blessings they bring to their neighbors in the new environment.

14. Although recognizing the dangers of generalizing, it does appear that those people who have become uprooted by geographical and social mobility, apart from the common needs of all men to be loved and to have meaning, have accentuated needs of belonging and stability. These transplanted people also have the need for cultural continuity expressed in language, the emotional tone and forms of worship. The Nashville Study Group has reported:

The loyalties that move us most profoundly are associated with concrete symbols. including objects and experiences. A building, a group of people among whom one finds acceptance and status, family association, satisfying educational experiences that stretch our minds, enjoyment of the security of the familiar, music, and hymnody—these are only a few.

15. When one whom we have begun to call the "mobilite" comes into a community in the midst of serious deterioration of physical plant and economic and social structures, he seldom finds the "deep roots of belongingness and acceptance which can come only with time and experience." In meeting the needs of the "mobilite" in such an environment, it becomes the task and the challenge of the church to promote spiritual and social security in the midst of these unstable social and economic conditions, to combat the hostility of the "mobilite" by finding for him acceptance, to offer him community in which he can worship, serve and find fulfillment and growth.

16. The church offers to the person in his new environment a link across the miles. It can be his old and familiar tabernacle in his new campsite. In worshiping with kindred Christian spirits

he figuratively joins hands with relatives and friends "back home."
They gain a warm feeling of assurance from the knowledge that
in his new home their loved one can find in his church spiritual
counsel, strength, and a continued relationship with Christ like
that which he knew when he lived among them.

D. Congregation, Denomination, and Community

17. One of the truths about mobility's effect upon the nature
of the unity we seek seems to be that the destinies of congregation,
denomination, and community are increasingly bound together in
one bundle of cause and effect. As mobility brings to a community
changes in age, sex, race, social and economic conditions, all three
parties are forced to examine their concepts of the Body of Christ
and its mission. If the new understandings widen the circle of the
Church and move it toward a sense of mission to all men, Christian unity will be advanced. If the re-examination results in nar-
rowing our concept of the Church and restricting its mission to
that of a membership club, all levels of our unity suffer. These
results flow from examinations by any one of the three parties
involved—congregation, denomination, and community. The results are aggregated when more than one party moves in the
same direction.

18. When mobility increases or decreases the population level
in a community, Christian forces may respond by increasing their
co-operation. However, they may respond also by increasing their
competition and thus weaken our co-operative unity, reduce our
ecumenical conversations and strain the love which unites us.

19. Community changes, in part or largely induced by mobility,
confront the church with certain imperatives. Each imperative is
a task for the local congregation. At the same time, all are too
big to be dealt with effectively by any one church or any one
denomination. They demand co-operative structures and unified
channels of Christian involvement. Among such imperatives for
the church are:

    a. To utilize and contribute to the life-preserving forces of the
    community, e.g., health and welfare resources, bridge-build-
    ing between groups, acculturation processes, esthetic values
    of life (art, color, literature, vegetation).

    b. To assist in and/or stimulate conservation programs for ex-
    isting neighborhoods. One function of religion is to conserve.
    It can help the "mobilite" achieve a wholesome image of
    himself, of his neighbors, and of the community. It can
    stimulate and participate in actual programs for physical

and social conservation (not exclusion) of the neighborhood and its values.

c. To participate in the renewal of older communities. Man must be born again; the old shall become new. Change in an individual's life is facilitated by changes in his environment. The church can stimulate and participate in programs for renewing the physical plant of community which may take actual funds and leadership from the church, e.g., the Baltimore Plan.[1] The church can envision and provide leadership for renewal of neighborhood as "community."

d. To help shape physical, social, and value structures of new communities, e.g., suburbia, redevelopment areas. One function of the church is to be prophetic, to strain mightily that the desert may blossom as a rose. New communities require men to build their relationships from a new beginning. The church may be physically excluded from our new communities for years if it is not included in original planning. Such new beginnings offer the church a significant opportunity for shaping a responsible society.

e. To impart durable values to "mobilites" and contribute such values to social structures in transition. There are imperishable spiritual and moral values of which the church is the guardian. A community in transition may lose its integrating value system as well as social controls. At such times the church must be the rock of ages and the hope of society.

20. Studies have revealed that one result of North American mobility patterns has been to increase the denominational, social, and racial heterogeneity of our congregations. For example, it appears that on the average 30-50% of our local membership will be out of different denominational traditions. As a consequence of such mobility, denominational distinctiveness may become blurred, congregational life may be enriched as new members bring with them their varying traditions, and the family of churches may become more homogeneous. The impact of mobility in this area seems to raise the question of what differences, if any, really matter? In the eyes of the community and of increasing numbers of individual church members there are apparently few. The sharing of different experiences and traditions as a result of this membership mobility is a powerful force for unity amid di-

---

[1]Protestant churches envisioned, initiated, and partially financed a project which physically renewed a slum area in Baltimore, Maryland, and rejuvenated the citizen morale of the neighborhood. This was the prophetic forerunner of the official "Baltimore Plan" and the federal government's Urban Renewal Program.

versity. For example, it was one of the determinative factors in shaping the United Church of South India. On the other hand, membership mobility sometimes blurs the sense of the church's divine mission and requires a recapturing of the urgency of the truth that *no* man shall be separated from the love of God in Christ Jesus.

21. Mobility with its resultant transfer of members from a church of one denomination to a church of another highlights the urgent necessity for systematic instruction and preparation for church membership. Such instruction normally will be denominationally oriented, but it should at the same time emphasize membership not in the institutional church but in the Holy Catholic Church, the Body of Christ.

22. Membership instruction especially helpful to a mobile person should seek to give information and a sympathetic understanding of all the major families of Christendom, their history, traditions, polities, and distinctive teachings. It should give an introduction to such matters as forms and elements of worship commonly used. It should also acquaint prospective members with such commonly accepted doctrines as atonement and God's reconciling activity in the world, stewardship and man's responsibility for all that God has entrusted to him, and the power of the Holy Spirit to enable men to lead lives more akin to what God wills.

23. Denominational loyalties, it must be said, are valuable resources which should be conserved and which God can use constructively to further the outward evidence of the unity he created. Denominationalism need not imply harmful competition, and when such competition does occur, it is to be deplored. Strong and secure denominations with a loyal band of faithful members who are truly dedicated to the Lord's business can be among the strongest forces for true and effective Christian unity.

E. ECUMENICAL CONCERNS

24. Emerging from this vortex of congregation, community, and denominational forces are indications of areas within the church where our unity urgently needs to be manifest in cooperative action. Some such areas are:

a. Leadership recruitment and training (clergy and laity). For example, the challenge of tasks in the whole Church is sufficiently exciting and demanding to attract the best youths and adults. Today's tasks demand intensive training and retraining of churchmen which may be accomplished by co-operative programs.

b. Federation of efforts at the parish level; e.g., sharing staff, jointly employing specialists, larger parish plans, joint leadership and budget, group ministry.

c. Church planning; e.g., redefinition of comity, participation in government and civic planning by the church.

d. Joint capital fund-raising; e.g., opportunities and responsibilities raised by the impact of mobility are costly beyond present concepts, but not to accept them is even more costly. Foundation and other nonchurch sources are more ready to contribute capital funds to joint projects than to denominational efforts.

e. Research, ecumenical study (role of Councils, resources of WCC Study Department), and face-to-face conversations.

25. There are also questions and issues raised which specifically need theological clarification. For instance:

a. We are already one in Christ and the Body of Christ. These are gifts of the Holy Spirit. Mobility tends to increase the heterogeneity of the local congregation and the relative homogeneity of the various congregations and denominations. Is this, too, a gift of the Holy Spirit?

b. Are the respective roles of sacraments and ordinances commonly accepted in the church altered in any fashion by mobility? What impact do changes wrought by mobility have upon the unifying or dividing forces of the sacraments and ordinances?

c. What does the rate of turnover of clergy say about our concept of vocation and the effectiveness of a church's ministry to mobile persons? Does mobility of clergy from one denomination to another enhance our sense of unity or our sense of differences?

d. Changes in community and culture, and in the duty and response of the church to these changes, suggest the need for a more relevant contemporary expression of commonly held doctrines and of such concepts as the nature and mission of the church, the nature and destiny of man, and the full implications of the term "responsible society."

SECTION 10. *Governmental Policies and Programs*

Chairman: Dr. Roswell P. Barnes
Secretary: Dr. Alford Carleton

The Situation:

Religious institutions in North America are deeply involved in complex relationships with governmental institutions—local, state, national. Governmental programs and policies increasingly affect the policies and programs of the churches. One clear instance is provided by the armed forces and the church's ministry to them. Many ecumenical dilemmas and opportunities are provided by the various degrees of nondenominationalism, interdenominationalism, and denominational co-operation, as well as by the potential emergence of an "armed forces religion." There is a constant movement of laymen and clergymen into and out of governmental service where a kind of church unity-disunity obtains which is quite different from that in civilian life. Tension points may be discovered wherever governmental agencies deal with the churches (e.g., chapels, hospitals, prison camps, defense areas, industrial and atomic plants, Voice of America). It is difficult in these intricate involvements to distinguish between true and false ecumenicity. It is also difficult to distinguish that unity which God demands from that unity which emerges out of a nationalistic Americanism, in which every religion is expected to enhance the interests of the state. From the least tangible level of subconscious motivation to the most tangible level of administrative action, the quest for oneness in Christ's mission is influenced by the governmental situation as regards work among the servants of government (one of the largest "mission fields") and as regards the impact of the Gospel upon popular idolatries both inside and outside the churches.

The Objectives:

a. to understand the present situation vis-à-vis governmental policies and programs.

b. to appraise the extent of true and false ecumenicity within the chaplaincy.

c. to determine how the experience of chaplains in ministering to all may contribute to a common mission to civilians.

d. to understand the unity which is demanded if the mission of the church to the nation is to be effective.

e. to explore the points where Christian unity and American unity converge and diverge.

The Report:

The Section on Governmental Policies and Programs consisted of thirty men and women, with a broad range of professional experience—doctors, lawyers, editors, professors, clergymen (including chaplains in the armed forces) and full-time administrators of various religious organizations. Many of the group had firsthand knowledge of one or more phases of the type of problem under discussion, both as citizens and as members of the church. Some had been members also of the group in Washington, D. C., which made the preparatory study of this subject, and we had in our hands the report of that group. In our discussion it became clear that this is a very important and far-ranging topic, that only a beginning has been made in its consideration, and that, if the unity given us in Christ is to be apprehended, nurtured, and made effective in all our life, much further study must be given it.

DEFINITION OF OUR FIELD OF RESPONSIBILITY

As only one of several sections into which the conference is divided, our particular responsibility has been to consider the relationships between church and government, not in the abstract sense of "Church and State," but in the complicated interplay between the churches and the programs and policies of governments. Even those relationships were explored principally as to their bearing upon the nature and the effectiveness of the unity which we seek.

In view of the basic constituency of the group, and of the necessity of dealing with questions involving specific governments and their policies, the illustrations considered by the section were further limited to matters involving the churches in the United States and in Canada.

At the same time, the desire to restrict the subject in view of limits of time could not justify the section in omitting reference to the whole range of such relationships—local, state or provincial, national—nor in forgetting our responsibility as part of the ecumenical church for situations anywhere in the world.

Furthermore, the number and extent of these relationships is increasing as the role of government grows. Governments, in the intricate involvements inherent in a complex society of interdependent interests, have often turned to the churches for consultation and guidance on problems involving moral issues, and in many areas of common concern. Government needs and has the right to expect the counsel of the Church.

The Church, likewise, has the right to expect to be heard, not only when approached by government, but also when it feels that conscience has been infringed, that the religious life of the nation is being ill-served, that its witness to the world is imperilled. There are times when the Church hears the divine call to speak to government or nation with a prophetic voice. This is especially the case when nationalism threatens or denies higher loyalties.

When a nation believes that destiny has called it to some purpose defined in terms of high ethical and moral ideals, the government and the people generally tend to expect that the churches will allow themselves to become instruments of national policy and allies of the government. In such a situation the churches are expected to achieve unity among themselves in order to strengthen the national unity. Particularly in a time of national crisis, as in a war, the authority assumed by government makes extraordinary demands for unity in all aspects of the national life, including the churches. At such times, also, the churches must endeavor to declare to the government and nation the whole counsel of God. Communication between Church and government moves, therefore, in two directions.

CONCEPTS OF UNITY

Without intending to infringe on the responsibility of the conference as a whole, this section found it necessary, in order to give clarity to its thinking, to distinguish at least four major concepts as to the manifestation of the unity given us in Christ.

1. The dynamic sense of the fellowship of all believers;
2. Co-operation in witness and service;
3. Consensus of view and/or practice, in certain essentials;
4. Organic union.

It is recognized that these are not mutually exclusive, and more than one of them will be found to have a vital bearing upon many of the relationships here under discussion.

A PARTIAL LIST OF CHURCH-GOVERNMENT CONTACTS

When the section examined these relationships in some detail, it realized the enormous range of its assignment and the great significance of further study in this field. It calls attention, therefore, to the multiplicity of the points of contact between churches and governments in the United States and Canada, which give occasion or opportunity for the manifestation of Christian unity in witness or service. Some of these are points at which the churches must, in our society, carry on their activities or operate their institutions in accordance with specific laws and governmental policies. Others are points at which they feel called to support, to encourage or to request particular actions or enactments by the state. Others, again, are points at which they feel it necessary to resist governmental proposals or policies.

A partial listing of such occasions (at one or all levels of government) includes the following which were cited in our discussion:

1. Civil and religious liberty, including freedom of speech, assembly and publication, and the liberty of the Church to be the Church.
2. Legislation and policy regarding public education generally, and especially regarding religious instruction in the schools.
3. National and international broadcasting.
4. Programs of international aid and relief, problems of refugees, and international exchange of persons.
5. Policies affecting the church's prosecution of its world-wide mission or its relation to churches in other countries.
6. Matters of international justice and world order.
7. Chaplain service in the armed forces and in public institutions.
8. Provision of churches and/or religious ministries in government-controlled areas: e.g., Canal Zone, national parks.
9. Presentation of the views of the churches regarding legislation, through legislative or parliamentary committees, or royal commission.
10. Consultations between representatives of the churches and administrative officials of government.
11. Legislation and regulations concerning welfare services and institutions.
12. Enactment and enforcement of laws regarding racial discrimination and other social problems, such as juvenile delinquency, gambling, drug traffic, liquor control, prostitution, obscene publications.
13. Some aspects of taxation problems.
14. Laws regarding zoning, housing, and the use of land.
15. Pastoral services to the large number of Christians serving in government, on matters related to their vocation.

This is only a partial list, but it is sufficient to suggest a very large and significant area of practical contact and mutual influence between churches and governments.

CHURCHES' UNITED ACTION

At many of these points some or all of the churches represented in the Oberlin Conference have associated themselves with one another for more or less united action, in *ad hoc* combinations or through their councils of churches. Sometimes these associations have been entirely on the initiative of the churches; sometimes indeed enterprises of mutual concern urged upon government by the churches. Sometimes they have been in response to the situations in which the churches found themselves confronted by government action. Such united action by the churches has often been welcomed by government. We have become aware of very few situations in our two countries in which it has been arbitrarily imposed by government. Sometimes it has been imposed by circumstances, the force of which was recognized by both government and church. In our time both Church and state have been compelled and impelled to enter upon new responsibilities.

Church and government are not necessarily either sympathetic or antagonistic toward each other. Always Christ is Lord both of the Church and of the world, and both Church and government stand under the judgment of the Word of God. This section however, has not been concerned with judgment upon church or state. Our question has been the bearing and effect upon Christian unity of the churches' united response to governmental policies and programs.

SOME EXAMPLES

As in the discussions of the Washington Study Group, so this section found the chaplaincy an important illustration of developing patterns of co-operation, with some of their implications for the nature of our unity still to be discovered. Although there are some important differences in the organization of the work of the chaplains to the armed forces of Canada and of the United States, in both countries this has been recognized as an inescapable obligation of the churches to men under circumstances where governments must determine many conditions of the enterprise. It is notable that tens of thousands of men and women of the armed forces, and their dependents are here brought into active Christian life. It is inevitable that, in spite of careful provision to maintain services according to the rites of any church to which a man may belong, the pressure of circumstances—including the will of many of the Protestant personnel of the armed services—is for common forms of worship, religious education and fellowship, recognizably Protestant but not according to the regular practice of any one specific denomination. The significance of this continued consensus of usage and practice in a "general Protestant service" for the nature of the unity we seek is doubly marked in the case of families for many years associated with armed forces chapels who may lose recognizable attachment to any particular communion.

In view of the great number of men whose religious life has been significantly affected by this experience in the armed forces and their numbers reinforced by the mobility of the population as a whole, it is not surprising that the same question of "nondenominational churches" has raised itself in national parks—another place where access to people is controlled by government—in the Canal Zone and in other "churches overseas," some of them very flourishing and effective Christian bodies in areas where the witness and the unity of the Church are particularly vital matters.

A different set of relationships in which the churches' action has been voluntary but dependent on government regulation is exemplified by the programs for the admission of refugees in both Canada and the United States and for the use of surplus commodities, made available by the United States Government, to meet critical situations overseas. In this field it has been ecumenical Christian agencies such as Church World Service and the Division of Interchurch Aid and Service to Refugees of the World Council of Churches, that have been given co-ordination to the program. Moreover the volume and the geographic extent of the enterprises have given added stature to the agencies concerned. At the same time, it should be recorded that in the case of the use of surplus commodities this extensive program through the churches but based on government policy and conducted "in the name of the American people," has raised serious difficulties for sister churches concerned with the distribution and has been subject to the charge of the use of the churches as instruments of national policy. Our responsibility as Christians, therefore, requires us to be constantly alert as to the full implications of the involvement of the churches in these programs and to review from time to time the regulations under which they operate.

Another aspect of this problem of the confusion of Christianity with "the American way of life" is the program of religious broadcasting through the Voice of America, and portions of the People to People program. When these programs are rightly conducted, the cooperation of the churches may be appropriate. Only slightly misdirected, such efforts may easily become the cause of charges of cultural imperialism against "Christian America."

The organized common approach of the churches to governments for the expression of the concern of Christian people in appropriate matters of legislation and administrative decision has been steadily increasing in both Canada and the United States. For over fifty years churches in these countries have been working together in their approaches to government and particularly in the area of social concern. There has been a lesser amount of interfaith co-operation in this area, but no adequate study of this has been made. The growing body of experience in these matters has had important meaning for the unity of the churches, as well as for their relationships with government.

Implications for Christian Unity

Associations of the churches made necessary or expedient by government policies or programs affect our understanding of Christian unity and our quest for it in a variety of ways. Obviously they affect the relations of the churches with one another in our own countries. Co-operation of the churches in a common enterprise brings them together, and gives to all participants in it a broader Christian experience and greater mutual understanding. It enforces the interdependence of unity and mission, and it manifests a measure of unity in witness and service. When the common enterprise involves habitual common worship and common activities and practices of evangelism and congregational life, as in the chaplain services in the armed forces, the increase of fellowship and understanding must reach into the depths of Christian experience for both ministers and people. All this inevitably contributes to greater expression of Christian unity in the first three of the concepts of unity suggested earlier in this paper.

At the same time, these united undertakings prompted by government policies and programs raise or sharpen, for the churches, some serious questions of motive, basis, and results. What *are* the motives for them—institutional advantage, or Christian witness and service? If only the former, we must ask whether such motives are adequate for Christian unity, or can provide the foundations for a unity that will be lasting. Experience suggests a negative answer. What is the *basis* for this co-operation—expediency only, or some common faith and conviction and a common obedience to our Lord? "Life and Work" cannot be separated from "Faith and Order," and loyalty to truth is a constant obligation. What are the *results* of our co-operation—a clearer apprehension of truth, or a blurring of our insights? These are questions which ought to be asked and answered, and which will probably be given various answers. Yet, the churches' obligation to mission remains imperative, and the quest for the right manifestation of unity must continue.

The relations of our churches with those of other countries will also be affected by the activities we are considering. The response of the churches in our countries to the policies and programs of our governments may fortify and support the churches of other countries and strengthen our fellowship with them; or, as already noted, that response may sometimes be misconstrued or misrepresented in countries where relations between Church and government are quite different from ours, and so may make for disunity among Christians in the ecumenical fellowship. We must often weigh the one possibility against the other, and our decisions must be made with a full sense of responsibility to the world-wide Christian community.

Our study has reminded us that we cannot evade our obligations to Christian witness and service in obedience to our Lord Jesus Christ. It has enforced upon us a keener realization of our unity in mission, of our common responsibility in society, of the need for greater unity as and for a more effective witness and service in the world, and of the fact that such unity requires organization. It suggests that we may learn much about the nature of the unity we seek by making the venture of uniting in mission, and indeed that there are some things about our unity that we shall not learn until we do make that venture.

We cannot regard response to governmental policies and programs or to any pressure of outward circumstance as a primary source or motive of Christian unity. Our unity is given us in Christ, and the ultimate constraint to its manifestation is an inward impulsion, arising from the very nature of the faith and experience we have in him. But this is reinforced by the compulsion of outward circumstances, and the pressure of governmental policies and programs, calling forth our united response of support or of opposition, may be the providence of God. Truth demands discerning insight and discrimination in deciding what our response should be. But does not our duty to our Lord require us also to ask why we should so often need the prodding of governmental policies to spur us to unity of effort in his service? Here, as elsewhere, unity awaits the renewal of the Church in devotion and obedience to her Lord.

SECTION 11. *Forces at Work on the College Campus*

Chairman: The Rev. Henry E. Horn
Secretary: Dr. Preston T. Roberts, Jr.

The Situation:

An ever-larger proportion of the population, both non-Christian and Christian, spends an ever longer period in higher education. Educational institutions, increasingly pluralistic in structure and influence, develop policies vis-à-vis the churches which have an important bearing on the unity and mission of the churches. Many of the impulses toward church unity have come from academic circles, and many experiments in cooperation and/or unity have been tried on the campus. But the situation on the campus is extremely fluid. Few people know exactly what the situation is or what are its implications for the nature of the unity we seek. In spite of the fact that the ecumenical movement has been deeply affected by the work of educational institutions, there has never been a direct exploration in ecumenical conference of our corporate responsibility for campus life or of the bearing of academic institutions on the unity of the Church. Yet this segment of American culture is highly influential in shaping the dominant patterns of national and church life.

The Objectives:

a. to assess the present level of interdenominational conflict, co-operation and unity on the campus.
b. to appraise the potential contribution which the experience of college workers may make to the ecumenical movement among the churches.
c. to examine the institutional factors involved in the official relationships of the denominations and the schools.
d. to discuss the form and structure for greater unity among the churches in their presentation of the Gospel to students, to faculties and administrators, to the corporate educational world.

The Report:

The Church and the university[1] stand together in God-given encounter in society and within the university community itself. Both are of God's creation, a creation now in need of redemption. The Church bears within its life the Gospel; the university is pre-eminently the bearer of intellectual virtues, i.e., the disciplines of knowledge and the qualities of mind essential to any search for truth. Each needs the scrutiny of the other's gifts for its wholeness. Here then is the given unity we have: the given Gospel, the given intellectual virtues and the given encounter within the university community.

What then is the unity we seek? The unity we seek is a redeemed community where the clear and unconfused proclamation of the Gospel is carried out in a climate of mutual understanding, respect and acceptance, in which both the Gospel and the intellectual virtues are recognized, treasured, and used to God's glory for the recovery and maintenance of the wholeness of life. Then the Church and the university will stand in a relation of "double humility," each under the scrutiny of the other: the Church, an affirming community to which inquiry belongs, and the university, an inquiring community to which affirmation may and does belong.

We must, however, confess with penitence that the encounter given by God is weakened and sometimes destroyed by the babbling voice of a divided Church, often lacking the discipline of the intellectual virtues, as it speaks with uncertain word within the university community. This inability of a divided and consequently fearful Church constitutes the challenge and call to repentance and amendment of life. Not until the Gospel speaks clearly to the university through the kind of redemptive community we seek can we expect the university to recover a sense of the wholeness of man and the wholeness of truth.

As in all ecumenical encounter the first need seems to be one for understanding—understanding as between Church and university: understanding on the churches' part of their common Gospel and mission; and understanding on the university's part of its true nature and heritage to relate the whole of truth to the whole of man. With understanding will come mutual respect, confidence, and courage to face the encounter between Church and university.

---

[1]Throughout, the term "university" has reference to all institutions of higher learning.

Meanwhile Christians, sensing the Gospel's need to be embodied in a *koinonia,* have attempted in various ways to establish such a community on the campus.

Action along these lines has generally taken one of three main forms (see Appendix):

a. Denominational ministries (chaplaincies, university pastorates, church student organizations, etc.) which establish their own communities within the university.

b. Loosely knit or federated fellowships for study, worship, and witness in which it is intended that the tensions of ecumenical encounter be retained. (YMCA, YWCA, SCA, SCM, etc.)

c. The university or college churches[2] which for the sake of community on the campus cut through the faith and order tensions which continue to divide the churches outside.

All of these need further careful scrutiny from a faith and order standpoint for none seems fully to accept or do justice completely to the unity that we have or to the unity that we seek. The only certainty at the moment is that there must be *koinonia* on the campus. How the kind of unity we seek is to be achieved in this setting constitutes an urgent question for faith and order.

We remember that the modern ecumenical movement is indebted for much of its leadership to persons who learned as students to work together across denominational divisions. They often forged new patterns of unity to heighten ecumenicity and contributed greatly to the prophetic witness of the Church. We rejoice in the continuing leadership given by the World's Student Christian Federation, and we look with interest and satisfaction upon its initiation of a three-year emphasis on the life and mission of the Church. We hope that this program of study and leadership training will advance ecumenical understanding through the world and deepen student loyalties to the whole Church and its mission.

In summary, the nature of the unity we seek is such that:

a. it will clearly declare the unity given to us in our one Lord and reduce the scandal of our divisions;

b. it will facilitate a clear and unconfused proclamation of the Christian Gospel;

c. it will provide for deeper ecumenical encounter between members of the different Christian traditions;

---

[2]Not to be confused with the official college chapel which has regular religious services.

d. it will enable the churches to co-operate more effectively with the university administration and faculty in matters of common concern;

e. it will enable the churches to support campus-centered Christian communities of faculty and students as well as our congregations around about the campus, which witness in our separate traditions;

f. it will make possible a united penetration of all parts of the life of the university with the Christian message;

g. it will enable the churches together to provide professional Christian leadership to the hundreds of campuses now without such special ministry and to the sharply increased numbers of students expected on most campuses in the near future.

Having observed the several responses to the call to unity, both national and local in character, we make the following recommendations:

a. That the conference steering committee provide for the appointment of a commission (1) to review the report of Section 11 at the Oberlin Conference and the orientation paper prepared for it, and (2) to outline clearly the theses and issues for the Faith and Order Movement involved in cooperative Christian endeavors in institutions of higher learning both in the United States and in Canada. We believe that the continuation of close association and communication between existing campus Christian movements and the ecumenical movement in the churches is essential.

b. That the churches be encouraged as they appoint and assist in training professional personnel for this mission field in higher education, (1) to see this area as a major challenge for influencing our culture, (2) to provide an orientation ecumenical in spirit and adapted to the special needs of the field, and (3) to devise ways of keeping the workers involved in the ongoing, normal stream of church life for mutual support, encouragement and communication.

That hearty support be given by churches to the plans and programs now arising in the colleges and universities which are ecumenical in content or in possibility.

d. That encouragement be given to all efforts within student Christian organizations which seek conversation with campus programs not presently related to the United Student Christian Council and the World's Student Christian Federation, particularly with the International Fellowship of Evangelical Students (and their member movements in North America, the Inter-Varsity Christian Fellowships), and with the Baptist Student Unions (Southern Baptist) in the United States.

Campus Programs

I. United States:

(1) The Student Christian Associations (YMCA, YWCA): These voluntary lay movements pioneered in student Christian work and are active in bringing students of varied denominational backgrounds into a program of Christian activity, stressing student responsibility in the determination and development of the program.

(2) Denominational Programs: We are encouraged to find that denominational work in the universities, in foundations, and parishes is often marked by strong ecumenical concern. We are happy also that the denominational agencies and the student YMCA and YWCA are working together in the USCC and SVM and other agencies.

(3) Co-operatively Sponsored Programs: In these cases a group of denominations and sometimes the Christian associations join forces to provide support for clergy or lay leaders to serve an interdenominational student constituency.

(4) University and Church Partnership: This form of work represents a combination of the chaplaincy and the Christian association with Church support that deserves special note. Under the leadership of the Chaplain who is university-appointed the Christian association is the voluntary, on-campus association of Christian students. Denominational staff are nominated by the churches and confirmed by the university. Denominations are represented on the board of Christian association.

(5) College and University Churches[1]: Leadership of these churches (chaplains, college pastors) is appointed and supported by the college and university administrations. Despite certain ambiguities in ecclesiology occasioned by them, the fact of their existence needs to be noted for the issues raised in them for faith and order. A study of the mission and task of the college church now being undertaken deserves our careful attention, especially as it may

---

[1]Reference is made not to college chapel programs but to churches which contain a membership and program.

point to ways through which college churches may establish responsible relationships to the historically continuous churches.

(6) The Intervarsity Christian Fellowship: This organization, related to the International Fellowship of Evangelical Students, brings together students of different denominations in a program which stresses sharply conservative theological commitment. Although it is often separatist, in relation to other campus religious programs, it does provide a community for students of many different denominational backgrounds.

(7) Interconfessional Christian Councils: The organizational forms devised by Christian organizations to heighten co-operation and unity between campus groups are varied in type and in quality of work. While these councils sometimes foster Christian co-operation on campus, resulting in the promotion of Religious Emphasis Weeks and other programs, they are at other times plagued by inherent inabilities to turn co-operation into significant ecumenical endeavor. We agree, however, that in them there is to be found a great ecumenical potential.

(8) The Faculty Christian Fellowship: This organization and others similar to it are providing excellent opportunities for faculty members of varied religious heritages to meet together to give attention to the problems of the university and to the meaning of the teaching vocation in the light of Christian faith. We agree that the need for faculty encounter is great.

(9) The Departments of Religion: We note also that the academic work being done in departments of religion in the colleges and universities often makes splendid contributions to the cause of Christian unity by means of the introduction of students of many denominations to the common store of knowledge we have through the Hebrew-Christian heritage.

II. Canada:

The Student Christian Movement of Canada, formed after World War I to combine the activities of Student YMCA and YWCA and the Student Volunteer Movement, has remained until very recent times the only agency of the churches for Christian work among students in Canada, operating along the above lines. It has remained a vigorous force, but the smallness of its membership has given rise to concern among the churches as to whether they should not add their own denominational ministrations for their own students.

SECTION 12.   *Racial and Economic Stratification*

Chairman: Dr. J. Oscar Lee
Secretary: Miss Isabel Rogers

The Situation:

The mission of the Church to America is radically conditioned by the presence within both the Church and society of racial and class stratification. Some Christian communities are limited in membership or control to a single race or to a single economic class. In society there are accentuated tendencies both toward and away from integration of races and classes. These same tendencies appear in many areas within the churches. Demands for greater inclusiveness confront both congregations and denominations; they evoke great resistance, and even when welcomed, they pose complex problems of ecclesiastical and psychological adjustment. They place in fresh context all questions of the nature of the Church and the shape of its unity.

The Objectives:

a. to examine the degree to which the unity we seek must include the development of more inclusive congregations and denominations.

b. to explore the opportunities for moving toward greater catholicity in bridging the cleavages in American society.

c. to assess the perils and perplexities involved in multiclass and multirace churches.

d. to understand the conflict between the image of the Church which is held by local congregations and the image which is held by Christian theologians.

c. to measure the distance between denominational pronouncements and congregational acceptance.

f. to move toward a fuller comprehension of what unity in Christ means today for the oneness of American races and classes.

The Report:

Thirty-eight of us, representing twenty denominations, every section of the United States and Canada, and three races, meeting as a section of the North American Faith and Order Study Conference at Oberlin have wrestled with the problem of the Church and racial and economic cleavages.

As Christians we recognize that neither our church nor society is as it ought to be. Whereas society has many hopes for its improvement, Christians have in the Gospel of reconciliation a steadfast assurance that God can and will purify for himself a people and create a society wherein righteousness will dwell. It is to this people, the Church, that the ministry and message of reconciliation for a lost world have been entrusted. Yet as we in the churches look at ourselves, and then at the society about us, we confess that our *ministry* of reconciliation lags far behind our *message* of reconciliation. While we affirm the equality of all men in Christ, in actual practice our churches have generally accepted, supported, and sanctioned the racial and economic stratifications found in the social order. This disrupts the unity we seek.

THE UNITY WE SEEK

Our unity is in one Lord and one Spirit, although we may express this unity in diverse forms of worship, church organization, relationships between persons, and service. It requires our response in faith to the Lord of the Church, and a universal and inclusive acceptance of one another as persons. This unity is grounded in our encounter with God in worship but must always include our neighbor in a fellowship of Christian love and concern. Unity does not rule out disagreement, struggle and tensions—which may indeed have positive value—but in the power of love it enables a person to communicate with the other in understanding and respect.

Unity is a process. It makes no claim of having arrived. Rather, we are conscious that sin breaks unity and that God's grace is necessary for constant renewal.

BARRIERS TO UNITY

Christian unity is broken by racial and economic barriers drawn by both majority and minority groups. For example, our local congregations often fail to accept as persons those whom God has created in his image. We are conscious of race and economic class. If inclusiveness is a reflex action of faith, many in our congregations must not be new beings in Christ. For only the New Man can say, "As God has accepted me, though unworthy, so I must accept my neighbor, without asking whether he is worthy of my acceptance, and without asking whether he is like me."

The readiness of Christians to adopt secular values in judging the vitality of our churches is another barrier to Christian unity. We Christians want our churches to be "comfortable," like a club where we can relax with people like ourselves. We want our churches to be "successful" in competition, numbers, wealth, prestige. We are often so anxious to promote our success and comfort as congregations that we are not willing to take the risk of becoming racially and economically inclusive. Our ministers are under pressure from within and from without to serve these desires. We do not quite believe in seeking first the kingdom of God!

As congregations we maintain our own exclusiveness by our failure to relate ourselves to the neighborhood about us and to the needs of the persons in it. In a situation of great mobility our services are likely to follow those who have moved away, overlooking those nearby who may be of a different race or class. Or we retreat from a situation of need in a changing neighborhood to a newer area where "our own kind" of people live. In the suburbs our congregations too easily acquiesce in the pattern of residential segregation and make little effort to challenge it.

POSITIVE APPROACHES

In the light of this analysis we suggest several possible Christian approaches to the problem:

1. We need to know what the Church is. The Church derives its life from God as Source, from its God-given mission to proclaim and live the Gospel of Jesus Christ, and from its ultimate fulfillment in God. Therefore, the congregation which knows itself to be born of God is secure and in this security is an accepting community. It knows that Christian love can no more tolerate artificial barriers between persons than could God's love tolerate the real barriers which separated us from God.

2. Christian worship provides the power for the Church to be the Church. In worship God meets us both as individuals and in the company of our brothers. Here we know that Christ draws no racial or economic distinctions among persons.

3. We must recover the role of the minister as priest and prophet. As priest he creates a structure of trust and good

will strong enough to sustain differences which arise when he speaks as the prophet.

4. We need to see persons as beings of worth in themselves rather than as members of races or classes, and treat them as such.

5. As individual Christians, we need to expose ourselves to persons of other racial and class groups at work, at play, along the avenue, in the restaurant.

6. Small fellowship groups within the local church, motivated by Christian love, can be the means whereby we can come to understand and accept persons of other races and classes.

7. A concerned church will seek to know the make-up, problems, and needs of its neighborhood by making use of census data, information gleaned from Chambers of Commerce, community improvement groups, and city planning councils, as well as data gathered from surveys by members of the congregation.

8. The congregation as a responsible group in the neighborhood must act to solve problems and to meet the needs of its area. This may be done through taking well-considered stands on issues in the light of the Christian Gospel, by the influence of its members in various community groups, through cooperation with existing community agencies whose purposes include better housing and living conditions, equal job opportunities, better health, etc., and through support of legislation and judicial decisions favorable to inclusiveness.

9. Our denominations for the most part have adopted statements favoring inclusive services to all people. These denominations need to bring their practices into line with these statements if the congregations are to be fully supported in their efforts to achieve inclusiveness.

Christian love constrains us to find each other both at the level of social satisfactions and at the level of man's encounter with God. The Christian ethic insists that we rise above current social patterns to create a social structure in which each can belong and participate as a child of God rather than as a victim of prejudice.

PART THREE

Appendixes

APPENDIX I

SUPPLEMENT TO REPORT OF SECTION 9

THE IMPACT OF MOBILITY AS IT AFFECTS THE WORK OF THE CHURCHES IN THE U.S.A.[1]

Introduction

No analysis of the American scene is complete without some understanding of mobility as a factor in the social situation. From the very earliest days, mobility has played an important role in American life but with the rapid changes which have taken place in recent years, its significance has increased and it has assumed new patterns.

Perhaps no institution feels the effect of mobility more than does the church. The basic patterns of belief and the religious attitudes of people—the very foundations of faith and order—are subjected to new influences and new social and environmental factors which may strengthen them, weaken them or leave them in a state of chaotic confusion.

If the relationship between mobility and Christian unity is to be considered thoroughly, it seems necessary to give some background information on mobility, its dimensions, patterns, processes and effects.

A. THE VOLUME OF MOBILITY

With the continuing expansion of the national population the church is confronted with unprecedented opportunities for growth and development. The population increase from 1940 to 1950 of 19,000,000 was the largest ten-year growth in our nation's history. Two comparisons will further dramatize this phenomenon— the growth from 1930 to 1940 was only 9,000,000—and the increase since the 1950 census is already over 19,000,000 (with still better than three years to go in this census period). The population experts forecast 228,000,000 by 1975, and 336,000,000 by the year 2000. Further elaboration is not necessary to warrant the statement that we have "fields white unto harvest."

Recent studies of the Bureau of the Census indicate that one out of every five persons in continental United States moves during the course of a year. About two-thirds of these people made

---

[1]This paper consists largely of excerpts from the following preparatory papers for the Oberlin Faith and Order Conference:

J. Leslie Dunstan—"A Report on a Study of the Mobility of Church Members"
Yoshio Fukuyama—"Some Theological Implications of Mobility"
Walter Kloetzli—"The Effect of Mobility on the Individual and the Church"
Meryl Ruoss—"The Effect of Mobility on the Community"
Lauris Whitman—"Mobility—Its Scope and Dimensions"

changes of residence within a county and approximately one-third crossed county lines. There were over five million people who moved from one state to another during the most recent year studied. However, there is no equal distribution of migration throughout the country. Some states are primarily on the receiving end of the process. Others are more aware of the results of out-migration. During the ten-year period from 1940-1950, twenty-five states lost more people than they gained through migration. Among the states that showed gains, California and Florida accounted for more than two-thirds of the net population gain by migration. New York, New Jersey, Ohio, Michigan, Maryland, Washington and Oregon also showed substantial population increase as a result of in-migration. Some of the states which experienced losses as a result of out-migration included North Carolina, Georgia, Kentucky, Tennessee, Alabama and Mississippi.

B. PATTERNS OF MOBILITY

American people are on the move. They are moving from one job to another, from the cities to the suburbs, from the country to the city and from one section of the nation to another.

There are certain rather clear migration patterns in the United States at the present time. One is the pattern of movement from rural to urban areas. Another is from South to North, as the predominantly agricultural South loses people to other states. It is also true that the westward migration tends to continue with the resulting rapid growth in the Pacific Coast States.

While the major patterns of migration, involving long-distance movement, are more spectacular and attract more attention, the migration in metropolitan areas and within states is often as important in terms of its meaning for such a conference as this.

One of the major characteristics of this migration is movement from the city proper to the suburbs. The suburbs in our metropolitan areas are growing much more rapidly than the central cities. Much of this growth, although not all of it, can be attributed to migration in general and to movement from city to suburbs in particular. During the last ten or fifteen years the rate of movement from urban centers to the peripheral areas has been accelerating rapidly. The Census Bureau provides data on 168 metropolitan areas which had a total population in 1950 of 85 million people. Fifty million of these people lived in the central cities while about 35 million lived in the suburban areas around them. During the decade the central cities showed an increase in population of approximately 14% while the suburbs were gaining by more than 35%. An illustration or two will show how this works out in particular situations. The San Francisco-Oakland area had a total population gain of 53% from 1940 to 1950. The central cities gained 24% while the suburban areas increased by over 100%. During the same period, the Sacramento suburbs increased by 117% while the central city recorded an increase of less than 30%. The population of San Diego, itself, increased by 65% while its suburbs gained approximately 160%. While it is true that the difference in the rate of growth between the central city and the suburbs is due to several factors, a great deal of this difference can be traced to migration from the city to the suburbs.

Internal migration in the United States results in changes in the age, sex, race, social, and economic characteristics of the population in both the areas of origin and the areas of destination. For example, farm youth generally tend to enter nonfarm labor markets after the age of 15. The most frequent pattern in this instance is to respond to labor needs in nearby cities, or industrial areas. Their migration is not typically long distance.

In thinking about the relationship of mobility to Christian unity, it is important to remember that migration is but one aspect of mobility. Equally significant, and closely related to migration, is social mobility. By this we mean changes in social status of movement from one social class to another. This, too, is an important aspect of American life and one which is related in numerous ways to the life of the churches.

A special concomitant of mobility in certain areas is the phenomenon known as "commutation." This specialized pattern of mobility is a common characteristic of our urban areas. It demands specialized services for increasingly vast numbers of people which place unique demands upon the physical plant of any community. In both the communities of origin and destination the demands for parking, transit, traffic flow and control become monsters that absorb resources and energies of a community all out of proportion to more vital values.

C. Motives for Mobility

Internal migration in any given area or community is very sensitive to the economic factors at work in the area. For example, urban population growth tends to be more rapid in prosperity than in times of depression. Closely correlated to this is another point. The "pull" of urban opportunities for employment, vocational advancement, etc., seems to be a much more important factor in city-ward migrations than the "push" of rural population pressures. It is generally agreed among demographers that migration is primarily for economic reasons. People tend to move from areas of high fertility and low economic opportunity to those of low fertility and high economic opportunity. Migration is seen as the method by which the labor force adjusts to employment opportunities in different geographic areas.

A recent statement by a government official indicated that the basic, underlying cause of migration is the dynamic nature of our economy. Rapid changes have been taking place in the patterns of industrial deployment and the concentrations of job opportunities. There has been steady decline in the number of people on farms and a shift from agricultural employment to other occupations. There have been new developments in industry which require persons of special aptitudes, interests and training and these persons must locate where the opportunities exist. There is the increasingly common practice of moving staff members and junior executives from place to place so that the "organization man" has become a man on the move. The development of Social Security and pension and retirement plans, along with the increase in the life span, have increased the number of people who retire and move to locations more suitable for living in retirement. All of these, related in one way or another to the social and economic dynamics of our way of life, play a part in creating the migration situation which we face today.

Increased income, improved educational levels, new job opportunities, ease of transportation and other factors play a part in our patterns of social mobility. For most people, the goal of upward social mobility is being realized to some extent. There are many people, however, for whom their level of living and their standard of living remain far apart and they show little indication of change in social status.

Many aspects of social mobility are closely related to migration. Change in place of residence may be motivated by a desire for a change in status and may actually result in such a change. Without doubt this is one of the principal reasons for the movement to the suburbs which has been cited earlier. It may be just as closely related to a family move across the continent. However, such a move may not result in upward social mobility, as has been learned by many a family which has moved from a low income southern farm to the depressed inner-city area of a metropolitan community.

Mobility can sometimes be an escape from a present situation. What with the relative ease that exists today for moving to and fro it is not surprising to find people moving simply because they are "fed up" or want to try some new area. A recognition of these tendencies certainly cautions the Christian church to preach the "full-orbed" Gospel rather than a shallow success and happiness message.

D. Effects of Mobility Upon the Person

It should be remembered in discussing mobility that, whether we are talking about migration or social mobility, we are talking about changes that affect people. These people are either church members or potential church members. The changes which they make bring them into new and different cultural patterns and often expose them to churches with worship, programs and theological emphases, which are foreign to their background and experience. In many cases, the most difficult adjustment to the new situation will be the adjustment to the church life which they find. And this applies to the new social status situation as much as to the new community, itself.

A comparison of family life in a relatively stable rural community with that in a highly urbanized setting is extremely interesting. In the former, individuals are known as persons—in the totality of their setting—work, play, family, community activities, etc. "Everyone knows all about Tom Smith." When Tom Smith moves to the big city, he very often becomes lost in the crowd. Status is on the basis of symbols (car, house, job title, etc.). The people with whom he comes in contact know only a part of him.

Many of the day-to-day casual relationships of the rural setting are absent in the urban scene. In their place there stands a multitude of impersonal, anonymous contacts. Thus many of the "supportive" ties which help him to have a sense of "belongingness" are lacking. Tom Smith and his family are placed much more on their own resources. There are not a few analysts of modern life who attribute much of today's pressure for conformity to the attempts at "quick belongingness." Being constantly "on-the-move" or "subject-to-moving," Tom Smith and his family try to become part of their new neighborhood by having interests and tastes common to their neighbors. The deep roots of belongingness and acceptance which can come only with time and experience seldom develop. To add further to the complexities of modern life—even if Tom Smith were to remain in one homestead for the better part of his life—at least in the urban areas he would find neighbor after neighbor moving on. A lack of belongingness often causes a lack of involvement in community affairs. The mobile modern easily gets the feeling that "this is not my community" or "these are not my concerns." Thus the tendency is to become divorced from community responsibilities, social problems, etc. "Let those who belong here take care of things."

This situation is further aggravated by the fact that there are definite patterns of geographical distribution for our denominations. Migration frequently takes a person into an area where there are no churches of his own denomination and leaves him in a position where he must choose another denomination or withdraw from active church participation.

In the midst of this shifting setting men seek to find a faith for life. They seek stability amidst mobility, order in the midst of what seems to be a chaos. Then, too, they seek a foundation and guide for their existence in the ever-changing world about them. The Christian church to many people represents almost above all else a "port in a storm," a haven. Thus the demand is made on the church to maintain the status quo, to preserve peace for the members, and to help shut out the cares of the world.

E. EFFECTS OF MOBILITY UPON THE COMMUNITY

In what follows there are stated general effects on communities that are applicable to areas which might experience net loss of population due to mobility as well as to the more general experience of areas having a net gain of population due to mobility. The effects on communities are classified under three categories, namely, a) effects on the physical plant of a community, b) effects on the economic structure of a community, c) effects on the social structure of a community.

a) The most common effect of mobility is to build up population pressures which demand new kinds of, or additions to, the housing supply. Increased population also brings demands for more, or better, or new services, which in turn create the need for modification of existing facilities or the development of entirely new facilities. In areas of population loss, both housing and service facilities could move into a dormant stage which could lead to eventual deterioration.

Some typical results of the foregoing effects of mobility on a community's physical plant might be enumerated as follows: 1) Slums develop, sometimes more rapidly than they can be replaced. 2) Housing is subdivided into smaller dwelling units to accommodate more people than it was created to handle, and neighborhoods rapidly downgrade. 3) Land and property values respond to the impact of mobility in widely separated ways. In areas where the loss of population is serious, values are frequently depressed. In areas where population pressure creates significant demands values are inflated, sometimes very seriously. 4) Development of the community takes place. Slums are replaced by new housing, both publicly and privately financed. Downgraded sections are frequently replaced by high cost and luxury housing developed by speculators. Office buildings and light industry often move into both of these kinds of areas. Open areas are converted to housing or industry. 5) Streets are widened, parking facilities are developed, arterial highways are built at the expense of housing, business locations and open spaces. 6) New housing and facilities for other services mushroom. 7) Sources of food supply and esthetic values, as well as essential recreational areas, are pushed further into the hinterland for vast numbers of mobilites.

b) Mobility's impact on a community's economic structure is largely measured in terms of prosperity or recession. Communities which show no economic fluctuations are probably not experiencing mobility to any significant degree.

For the rural areas, mobility's prime impact is to force individual farming units to become more productive. Essential ingredients are the increasing price squeeze and the continuing out-migration of labor. Another economic impact on rural areas is their conversion from an agriculture base. This conversion may be to residential or industrial. At any rate the economy of the community undergoes a complete shift.

Mobility's effect on local economic enterprises frequently entails extensive modications. Where there is a new out-migration the quantity and scope of local business enterprises frequently decline. Where mobility changes the characteristics of a community, the nature of the local enterprises often change. Where communities expand, local enterprises expand also in quantity and scope, or are, in some instances, absorbed or replaced by larger enterprises introduced into the community.

One of the results of the above effects of mobility is that a shift from an agricultural to an industrial or mercantile base often modifies the stability of the economic structure in a community but usually increases the quantity of economic activity. Consequently, institutions and services of an area have more resources from which to draw. In such situations there usually results a much wider diversity of economic enterprises also.

c) Significant effects of mobility on a community's social structure may be enumerated as follows:

1) Areas of high mobility tend to be socially disorganized. There is also a demonstrable relationship between the socio-economic status of the residents of a mobile area and the degree of disorganization. For example, higher status areas appear to be more integrated, regardless of the rate of mobility, than lower status areas. It is true, however, that even in these higher status areas interpersonal ties tend to be dispersed beyond community boundaries more than in less mobile or stable areas.

2) Areas of high mobility appear to have higher rates of divorce, insanity, suicide, and delinquency than more stable communities. Areas with high mobility rates are also often characterized by high percentages of single persons, childless couples, and familyless households. It should be again emphasized that the mobility rate in these areas might well be caused by the families with children who find the area uncongenial and therefore rapidly move out. The persons with the characteristics dominating areas of mobility may not actually be the mobile persons. Of course, every type of household tends to be more mobile in a highly mobile area. For example, a recent study in the central city area of Philadelphia found that 82% of the full families wanted to move. Yet stable neighborhoods are characterized by high percentages of full families.

3) The residents' self-image of their area tends to be more negative in highly mobile areas than in stable ones. For example, the more mobile the area, the greater the difference perceived by its residents between themselves and their neighbors; the more unfriendly the neighborhood is perceived to be by its resident, the less likely are they to form personal ties with their neighbors; the larger proportion of persons there is feeling they have no place in the dominant class system of the area; the more the residents tend to ascribe neighbors to lower class status than themselves.

4) One of the significant effects of mobility on the community's social structure may be the undermining of the informal mechanism of social control by producing a lack of concern in the residents of the community for the general climate of public opinion in the community. That is, since

residents of mobile areas have less regard for their neighbors
and few significant personal ties within the neighborhood
they aren't particularly concerned about what either the
neighbors or the neighborhood thinks about their behaviour.

5) The impact of mobility upon organizations within the social
structure of a community is most keenly felt in member-
oriented organizations. A member-oriented organization
constitutes a social group in the population it serves; members have social relationships with each other as well as
with the leaders or key personnel. Such organizations function by maintaining organization-member relationships and
member-member relationships. Schools, churches, social
clubs are examples of such organizations which are hardest
hit by mobility and which, incidentally, are generally most
concerned and most aware of the problems mobility creates
in a community.

6) A locally oriented organization tends to be much more
vulnerable to mobility than a regional or metropolitan oriented organization. Thus a local YMCA or a German
bakery might be much more sensitive to the impact of mobility than a utility company or a real estate agency. (An
exception to this general finding might be a local organization specializing in a particular population type which remains stable in a mobile area. The impact of mobility on
such an organization would be slight.)

The following suggested results of mobility's impact on a community's social structure point up some of the most sensitive areas
with those implications with which the church should be rightly
concerned:

1. The sense of transiency. A mobile community assumes some
of the characteristics of a traditional port of entry. The newcomers, especially, tend to have their friends and personal ties
elsewhere. They turn away from personal or organizational commitment. As the older residents lose friends and neighbors in the
transition, they, too, find their interpersonal ties more widely dispersed. As the organizations to which they belong change their
character or effectiveness, they are less and less bound to the community which has been "home" for them. Restlessness, which characterizes the newcomers who may look upon the mobile community as a stop on the way to something else, now begins to
transform even the older residents into mobilites.

2. Another result is the creation of sizeable pockets of captive populations in many mobile communities. Sometimes these are long time residents of the community who for one reason or another happen to remain while many of their former acquaintances and friends move on to something better. Other times these are newcomers who arrive with the idea of getting their feet on the ground in the new community and then moving on as their resources and status improve. But something happens, and they never seem to be able to make the move. In both cases the captive populations come to resent the community as such, and their neighbors in particular. Trapped by limited skills, limited education, limited income or sometimes overpowering family ties and responsibilities, these people become frustrated and bitter. Where formerly they might have provided leadership for the organizational life of the community, they now are unable to contribute any creative leadership. Frequently they remain in control of the organizational structure of the community, largely by default, preventing the organizations from adapting to or making a creative contribution to the new needs of the community. Sometimes they succeed in completely killing the organization as a useful social instrument.

3. A weakening of social controls. Most of the effects of mobility on a community contribute to a loosening of social controls in a community—the lack of "pride in our community"; negative images of neighbors and the community; the sense of transiency; the anonymity which in part arises from the instability of mobile areas. All of these contribute to the weakening of social controls. Oftentimes this progresses to the stage where somewhat artificial controls need to be developed and/or imposed from the outside. Most common of such outside controls are city-wide, state, or federal legislation; or some kind of police or economic activity. It should be noted in passing that anonymity tends to be a more important factor in low status mobile communities than in those of higher socio-economic status. An understanding of how socio-economic status leads to anonymity may be much more fruitful than simply ascribing this phenomenon to mobility.

An implication of the foregoing results of particular importance to the church is that in mobile communities considerable popular resistance may develop into an action program designed to remedy defects as seen by an "expert." The resident's self-image of the area is pretty generally radically different from the objective facts about a particular quality of the area, or a general appraisal by some objective observer. Popular opinion is a social fact and should be used as part of the data in the planning process. This is not to say that popular opinion should dictate the program of, for example, the church. But it is to point out that popular opinion is a relative factor which aids or hinders the carrying out of such program and should be dealt with accordingly.

4. Another result of a community becoming a mobile area is the demise of mono-orientation organizations unable to adjust to mobility. For instance, an Italian bakery in an area in which the Italian population is being replaced by Southern Negroes. The bakery's products may not be of sufficient quality to justify a metropolitan orientation, and the owner does not have enough capital or "know-how" to become a local restaurant. The only solution he sees is to go out of business. Another example is the small town church, the oldest in the area, controlled by and oriented almost exclusively to farmers and local small businessmen with strong congregational polity. Postwar mobility converts the area to fast-moving suburbia. Other churches adapt and new churches arise. Unable to adapt to new population types, or to reorient the church's program to the many new needs, the church remains small, stagnant and ingrown. Frequently it closes up shop in the face of the booming competition.

5. Adjustments by organizations. As a result of the effects of mobility social organizations may change their orientation from a local one to a metropolitan one. They may concentrate their services and attention on stable population groups rather than mobile ones. Some organizations change locations to survive. Others adapt by initiating special activities designed to meet specific impacts of mobility. For example, they recognize that the organization needs to provide constant attractions for new members. Or they need to plan for rapid integration of the new clientele into the organization without disrupting the very structure of the organization. Sometimes old organizations must give way to completely new kinds in order to serve useful functions in a mobile community.

Mobility's effect on a community may be positive or negative, it may be extensive or limited, it may be constructive or destructive. Usually the effects are neither all black, nor all white. For many individuals and communities, mobility opens the door to opportunities. Sometimes it confronts both with new problems, often serious problems. For the church it is a challenge. For some particular churches, it is undoubtedly a mixed blessing. Mobility may be divisive in a community; but it may also be a unifying force. For America it is a phenomenon with which to reckon!

F. SPECIAL EFFECTS ON CHURCH MEMBERSHIP ROLLS

As pointed out earlier in this paper, neighborhoods and communities are constantly in flux as a result of rapid population increase and mobility. The churches themselves also are experiencing significant changes.

Urban congregations constantly are being confronted with a changing neighborhood picture. The tendency of the typical congregation is to perpetuate itself and its own kind even in the midst of social change. The desire to preserve the status quo and to achieve "peace at any price" further emphasizes this tendency. The result is that a church becomes selective in its outreach and ministers to but a segment of society.

Leadership in the typical urban congregation tends to be more widely scattered than does the membership. Stated somewhat facetiously, it might be said that the farther away from the church a member lives, the better are his chances for leadership in that church. Thus it easily develops that the thinking and planning of the policy-makers in a congregation are based on life in a different kind of neighborhood. This is comparable to the criticism leveled at "absentee ownership" in the business world. This makes for exploitation of a neighborhood rather than service to a neighborhood.

Another one of the stumbling blocks in a church's adaptation to its changed community is its use of leadership in a mobility situation. A typical congregation had a membership in 1944 of about 500 members. After a ten-year period of time only some 200 of the original 500 were still active in the church and living in their same residence. Another 50 or so had moved and were still active in the church. Of the 450 members of the congregation ten years later we find that over 200 are new members—received in the last nine or ten years. In summary, half of the membership is new in the last ten years.

Examining the leadership further we find that only one-quarter of the leadership of the congregation is from this new half and three-quarters is from the old half. Thus, we see that the "old timers" or the "old guard" is given a three to one preference in voting. This can easily lead to a three to one *vote for the status quo* and the gradual freezing out of the newcomer. It is important that in the light of this contemporary mobility congregations constantly relate themselves more effectively to the immediate neighborhood—including, certainly, the involvement of neighborhood people in the leadership.

In a recent study the reporting churches said that during the past ten years they have received into membership a number of persons equal to 66% of the present membership. This can be illustrated by an average of the reporting churches. The average would be a church with a present membership of 530; that church would have received into membership during the past ten years 350 persons.

It is noted that the churches in the Northeastern section of the country (New England and Middle Atlantic states) have received 56% of the number of their present membership in the last decade, while the churches in the West (Mountain and Pacific states) have received 85%. Again, across the nation as a whole, churches in small towns and open country have received 49% of the number of their present members while the churches in the new suburbs have received 89%. These variations may well reflect the impact of the mobility of the population upon the membership of the churches.

Figures from various studies warrant the suggestion that roughly, one-third to one-half of the members of the reporting churches have come from other denominations. There seems no question but that the availability in a particular community of a church of a particular denomination has a bearing on this fact.

Churches evidently deal with a membership that is continually changing. How great this change is cannot be stated with certainty, but the fact that the number of new members churches have received during the past ten years is 66% of the number of their present members would indicate a considerable degree of shifting among church members. The responding churches indicate that of the new members they have received during the past ten years approximately one-half came from churches of their own denomination.

In the light of rapid population shifts and neighborhood changes, it becomes imperative that congregations study their local situations and face up to these immediate concerns.

A pursuit of rural or suburban stereotypes in the midst of fluid urban neighborhoods spells death for many churches.

Mobility further means for the church that new programs and adaptations need to be considered carefully and prayerfully.

References

"Christ for the Moving Millions"—A conference on mobility. National Lutheran Council, 327 South La Salle Street, Chicago 4, Illinois (1955).

"Why Families Move"—Peter H. Rossi, The Free Press, Glencoe, Illinois (1955).

"Redistribution of the Population, 1940-1950"—Henry S. Shryock, Jr., *Journal of the American Statistical Association,* Volume 46 (December, 1951), pages 417-437.

"Population Pressure and Other Factors Affecting Net Rural-Urban Migration"—C. Horace Hamilton, *Social Forces,* Volume 30 (December, 1951), pages 209-215, The University of North Carolina Press.

"Selective Internal Migration: Some Implications for Mental Hygiene"—Dorothy Swaine Thomas, *The American Association for the Advancement of Science,* Publication No. 9 (1939), pages 256-262.

For one interested in the entire field of mobility there are many fruitful essays to be found in "Demographic Analysis," edited by Joseph Spengler and Otis Duncan, The Free Press, Glencoe, Illinois (1956).

APPENDIX II

WHO'S WHO

DELEGATES

Note: Numbers following names indicate Section assignments.

African Methodist Episcopal Church

Barnett, Mrs. Claude A. (Etta Moten) 6
Benn, Rev. J. S., III 12
Odom, Rev. Edward James 12
Spivey, Dr. Charles S. 1
Stokes, Dr. Rembert Edwards 9
Ward, Dr. A. Wayman 4

African Methodist Episcopal Zion Church

Brown, Dr. Frank Reginald 2
Carrington, Dr. W. O. 3
Hoggard, Dr. J. Clinton 1
Satterwhite, Dr. John Henry 12
Walls, Bishop William Jacob 7

American Baptist Convention

Handy, Dr. Robert Theodore 7
Hannen, Dr. Robert Balloch 4
Hudson, Dr. Winthrop S. 8
Leavenworth, Dr. James Lynn 2
McBain, Rev. L. Doward 7
Morikawa, Dr. Jitsuo 12
Porter, Rev. Willis Hubert 6
Rinck, Miss Suzanne G. 9
Scalise, Rev. Victor F. 10
Skoglund, Dr. John Egnar 3
Slemp, Dr. John Calvin 1
Squires, Dr. James Duane 10
Wallace, Mr. Robert Bruce 5

American Evangelical Lutheran Church

Jensen, Dr. Alfred 3
Kildegaard, Rev. Axel E. C. 2
Knudsen, Dr. Johannes H. V. 8
Villaume, Dr. William John 10

American Lutheran Church

Belk, Mrs. L. L. 5
Braulick, Rev. Roald Edward 8
Ewald, Dr. A. H. 7
Ludwig, Dr. Leonhard Michael 1
Reuss, Dr. Carl F. 9
Riensche, Rev. R. H. 4
Utech, Mr. George Walter 2

Anglican Church of Canada

Fairweather, Dr. Eugene Rathbone 8
Jellicoe, Dr. Sidney 3
Owen, Dr. Derwyn R. G. 8
Puxley, Dr. James H. L. 11
Slater, Dr. Robert H. L. 2
Watney, Rev. Canon Douglas P. 11

Augustana Evangelical Lutheran Church

Carlson, Dr. Edgar M. 2
Fjellman, Dr. Carl Gustaf 3

Baptist Federation of Canada

Aldwinckle, Dr. Russell F. 3
Davies, Dr. Emlyn 5
Levy, Dr. I. Judson 8
McDormand, Dr. Thomas Bruce 7
Thomson, Dr. Donald Morley 10

Canadian Council of Churches

Coles, Rev. Stuart Bowyer 2
Gallagher, Dr. W. J. 10
Hay, Dr. David W. 8
Millman, Dr. Thomas Reagh 1

Christian Methodist Episcopal Church

Cummings, Rev. James L. 7
Johnson, Dr. Joseph A., Jr. 1
Merriweather, Rev. Moses C. 12
Ryce, Rev. Amos, II 5

Church of the Brethren

Baugher, Dr. Norman J. 7
Groff, Dr. Warren Frederick 2
Miller, Dr. DeWitt L. 1
Ziegler, Dr. Jesse H. 5

Churches of Christ (Disciples)—Canada

Wakelin, Rev. Howard Oliver 3
Wills, Rev. Kenneth Swayze 4

Congregational Christian Churches

Buschmeyer, Dr. Fred Sherman 10
Carleton, Dr. Alford 10
Coe, Rev. Chalmers 4
Douglass, Dr. Truman B. 7
Durgin, Rev. Lawrence L. 11
Graham, Mr. Walter 10
Horton, Dr. Douglas 8
Horton, Dr. Walter 2
Hoskins, Dr. Fred 8
Hyslop, Dr. Ralph 7
Sarles, Dr. Philip W. 1

Czech-Moravian Brethren in North America

Barton, Rev. Josef A. 8

Disciples of Christ

Adams, Dr. Hampton 7
Blakemore, Dr. Wm. Barnett 6
Cartwright, Dr. Lin D. 6
De Groot, Dr. Alfred Thomas 4
Gulley, Dr. Halbert E. 11
Lunger, Dr. Irvin Eugene 9
McCaw, Rev. John E. 3
McCrae, Rev. Ian James 10
Owen, Mrs. George E. (Dr. Margaret R.) 9
Pack, Dr. John Paul 5
Rossman, Dr. G. Parker 4
Short, Dr. Howard Elmo 2
Tobias, Dr. Robert 8
West, Dr. Robert Frederick 12

Evangelical and Reformed Church

Arndt, Dr. Elmer J. F. 6
Bartell, Mrs. Vincent J. (Magdalene R.) 9
Huenemann, Dr. Ruben Henry 2
Koch, Rev. R. David 3
Miller, Dr. Allen Ott 3
Snyder, Mr. Daniel John, Jr. 10
Vassady, Dr. Bela 2
Wagner, Dr. James Edgar 8

Evangelical Lutheran Church

Eastvold, Dr. Seth Clarence 11
Nelson, Dr. E. Clifford 5
Preus, Dr. Christian 3
Quanbeck, Dr. Warren 4
Rogness, Dr. Alvin Nathaniel 1
Schiotz, Dr. Frederik A. 9
Storaasli, Dr. Olaf Kenneth 2

Evangelical United Brethren Church

Dennis, Bishop Fred L. 8
Hallman, Rev. Errol Emerson 5
Hilton, Dr. Richard McKinley 9
Kaebnick, Dr. Hermann Walter 7
Kline, Dr. Walter D. 12
Mueller, Bishop Reuben Herbert 1
Roberts, Dr. Walter N. 2
Welty, Mrs. Mervie H. (Mary E.) 6

Five Years Meeting of Friends

Jones, T. Canby 2
Newby, Richard P. 9
Purdy, Alexander C. 5
Reece, Glenn A. 12

Friends General Conference

Compter, Mrs. H. E. (Frances B.) 1
Roberts, Preston Thomas, Jr. 11
Taylor, Richard Knight 1

Greek Archdiocese of North and South America

Athenagoras, Rt. Rev. 11
Florovsky, Rt. Rev. Georges 3
Poulos, Rev. Fr. John A. 1
Stephanou, Very Rev. Eusebius A. 2

Methodist Church

Abbey, Dr. Merrill 5
Anderson, Dr. Bernhard W. 1
Beach, Dr. Waldo 12
Bollinger, Dr. Hiel D. 11
Bosley, Dr. Harold A. 5
Boyd, Dr. W. Sproule 9
Cannon, Dr. William Ragsdale 7
Clair, Bishop Matthew W. 6

Copher, Dr. Charles B. 12
Creeger, Dr. Marion James 10
Cuninggim, Dr. Merrimon 10
Cushman, Dr. Robert Earl 3
Ensley, Bishop F. Gerald 1
Hager, Dr. Wesley Harold 6
Harkness, Dr. Georgia 5
Harmon, Bishop Nolan Bailey 8
Herbert, Dr. Chesley C., Jr. 12
Howes, Rev. Allan J. 12
Kearns, Dr. Francis Emner 1
Kepler, Dr. Thomas 2
Loder, Dr. Dwight E. 5
McCulloh, Dr. Gerald O. 2
Martin, Bishop William Clyde 1
Michalson, Dr. Carl 3
Montgomery, Dr. Robert M. 7
Muelder, Dr. Walter G. 6
Mumma, Dr. Howard E. 1
Newell, Bishop Frederick Buckley 10
Olson, Dr. John Frederick 11
Olson, Dr. Oscar Thomas 6
Outler, Dr. Albert Cook 4
Parlin, Mr. Charles C. 4
Quillian, Dr. Joseph, Jr. 4
Ramsdell, Dr. Edward Thomas 8
Richardson, Dr. Harry Van Buren 12
Stidley, Dr. Leonard A. 5
Stokes, Dr. Mack B. 2
Tillman, Mrs. J. Fount (Sadie W.) 7
Tolley, Dr. William P. 11
Trott, Dr. Norman Liebman 3
Williams, Dr. Walter George 8

Moravian Church in America

Couillard, Dr. Vernon William 2
Dreydoppel, Rev. Otto 3

National Baptist Convention, U.S.A., Inc.

Ellison, Dr. John Malcus 6
Lee, Dr. J. Oscar 12

Polish National Catholic Church of America

Golawski, Very Rev. Dr. Bernard 10
Magyar, Rev. Eugene William 2

Presbyterian Church in Canada

Fowler, Rev. Louis H. 3
Lennox, Dr. Robert 7
MacNaughton, Miss Margaret E. 1
Nicolson, Rev. Murdo 7

Presbyterian Church in the U. S.

Calhoun, Dr. Malcolm Patterson 12
Fulton, Judge John Anderson 7
Hollingsworth, Dr. A. Hayden, Jr. 5
Norton, Dr. Joseph Andrew 10
Rolston, Dr. Holmes 2
Winn, Dr. Albert Curry 11

Presbyterian Church in the U. S. A.

Barnes, Dr. Roswell P. 10
Bennett, Mrs. E. Lansing 5
Biederstedt, Mr. Frederick H. 6
Blake, Dr. Eugene Carson 7
Come, Dr. Arnold Bruce 4
Davies, Mr. Richard Lloyd 1
Gill, Dr. Theodore Alexander 10
Hunt, Rev. George Laird 3
Isler, Rev. Richard D. 5
Johnson, Dr. Robert Clyde 1
Kerr, Dr. Hugh Thomson 3
Mackay, Dr. John A. 2
McCreath, Mr. David William 11
McDowell, Dr. W. Davidson 5
Rogers, Miss Isabel Wood 12
Watermulder, Dr. David B. 2
Woehrle, Mr. Thomas Herbert 11
Wright, Dr. Paul Stuart 9

Protestant Episcopal Church

Anderson, Dr. Paul B. 10
Bayne, Rr. Rev. Stephen F. 3
Coburn, Very Rev. John Bowen 11
Dawley, Dr. Powel Mills 8
Day, Mr. Peter 7
Dun, Rt. Rev. Angus 1
Gibson, Rt. Rev. Robert F. 8
Harrington, Dr. Virginia D. 11
Hirst, Mrs. Penrose W. (Derby Q.) 6

Katz, Dr. Wilber G. 10
Vogel, Dr. Arthur Anton 2
Weaver, Very Rev. John J. 9
Wilmer, Dr. Richard Hooker, Jr. 4

Reformed Church in America

De Beer, Mr. Leonard James 3
Eelman, Rev. James C. 9
Hageman, Dr. Howard G. 4
Vander Kolk, Dr. Justin 10
Wierenga, Dr. Cornelius R. 12

Romanian Orthodox Episcopate of America

Galdau, Very Rev. Fr. Florea Marin 9
Hategan, Rev. Fr. Vasile 8
Trifa, Rt. Rev. Bishop Valerian D. 1

Russian Orthodox Greek-Catholic Church of North America

Borichevsky, Rev. Vladimir Stakhy 9
Schmemann, Rev. Alexander 4

Salvation Army

Kaiser, Brigadier Paul Stephen 7
Ryan, Colonel Glenn 12

Seventh Day Baptist General Conference

Hansen, Rev. Clifford W. P. 2
Hurley, Dr. Loyal F. 8
Smith, Rev. Kenneth Edward 7

Syrian Antiochian Orthodox Church

Schneirla, Rev. William Sutfin 7

United Church of Canada

Chalmers, Dr. Ralph Carleton 2
Cragg, Dr. Gerald R. 1
Davidson, Rev. Richard H. N. 4
Fennell, Rev. William Oscar 1
Fleming, Mr. Douglas Ewart 5
Forster, Dr. Harvey George 12
Grant, Dr. John Webster 4
Long, Dr. Ernst Edgar 8
MacLean, Rev. Alexander Frank 11
Thompson, Dr. Edmund Jabez 9

United Evangelical Lutheran Church

    Larsen, Rev. William 2

United Lutheran Church in America

    Brammer, Mr. Bart Ross 9
    Fry, Dr. Franklin Clark 8
    Heikkinen, Dr. Jacob Werner 1
    Horn, Rev. Henry Eyster 11
    Kantonen, Dr. Taito Almar 2
    Kloetzli, Rev. Walter 9
    Little, Dr. Arthur Bernard 4
    Minnick, Mr. Malcolm Lee, Jr. 5
    Rilling, Dr. John William 4
    Sittler, Dr. Joseph 3
    Witzeman, Mrs. L. A. (B. Evangeline) 12

United Presbyterian Church

    Copeland, Mrs. S. B. (Margaret W.) 5
    Hutchison, Dr. Russell S. 11
    McConnell, Mr. Judson Cumming 12
    Montgomery, Dr. Frank William 1
    Turnbull, Rev. William Thomas 8

YOUTH DELEGATES

Canadian Council of Churches

    Heaven, Rev. Edwin B. 5
    McKinnon, Mr. Charles Paul 4
    Reeve, Mr. David Edward 3

Interseminary Movement

    Bosbyshell, Mr. William Allen 7
    Epperson, Mr. Sidney 11
    Hall, Mr. Philip Stanton 7
    Johnson, Mr. James L. 12
    Johnson, Mr. Wayne Everett 3
    Masters, Mr. Ralph Leeper 4
    Roessler, Mr. H. Carl 6
    Royster, Mr. James Edgar 6

United Christian Youth Movement

    Clark, Miss Carmeta Elizabeth 6
    Schrock, Mr. J. Gladden 11
    Young, Rev. Andrew 4
    Young, Mr. David Earl 1

United Student Christian Council

Allen, Mr. James 8
Ely, Miss Rebecca Ann 11
Johnson, Mr. Richard Norris 3
Jones, Mr. Bruce 1
McSwain, Mr. Holland, Jr. 9
Ward, Mr. Gordon W., Jr. 2

CONSULTANTS

Adams, Dr. John Maxwell, *Presbyterian Church, U.S.A.* (11)
Anderson, Miss Leila Warren, *Protestant Episcopal Church* (4)
Bach, Dr. George Leland, *Presbyterian Church, U.S.A.* (12)
Bodensieck, Dr. Julius H., *American Lutheran Church* (4)
Calhoun, Dr. Robert L., *Congregational Christian Churches* (2)
Carlson, Dr. C. Emanuel, *American Baptist Convention* (10)
Collier, Rev. Donald Fair, *Presbyterian Church in Canada* (11)
Cotter, Dr. Graham, *Anglican Church of Canada* (11).
Dawkins, Rev. Maurice A., *Council of Community Churches* (12)
Demaray, Dr. Donald Eugene, *Free Methodist Church* (3)
Dillenberger, Dr. John, *Evangelical and Reformed Church* (11)
Dirks, Dr. J. Edward, *Presbyterian Church, U.S.A.* (11)
Dunstan, Dr. J. Leslie, *Congregational Christian Churches* (9)
Elliott, Dr. Willis Edwin, *Council of Community Churches* (6)
Espy, Dr. R. H. Edwin, *American Baptist Convention* (8)
Fisher, Rev. Robert Cameron, *Council of Community Churches* (5)
Foreman, Dr. Kenneth Joseph, *Presbyterian Church, U.S.* (4)
French, Rev. Roderick Stuart, *Protestant Episcopal Church* (8)
Fukuyama, Rev. Yoshio, *Congregational Christian Churches* (9)
Harkins, Dr. George F., *United Lutheran Church* (7)
Harms, Dr. John W., *Disciples of Christ* (10)
Harrelson, Dr. Walter J., *American Baptist Convention* (1)
Heaton, Rev. Richard L., *Congregational Christian Churches* (7)
Heick, Dr. Otto William, *United Lutheran Church* (2)
Henry, Dr. Carl F. H., *American Baptist Convention* (2)
Hogg, Dr. W. Richey, *Methodist Church* (3)
Jackson, Dr. Gordon Edmund, *United Presbyterian Church* (12)
Jones, Dr. E. Stanley, *Methodist Church* (7)
Kazmier, Mr. Harvey F., *Congregational Christian Churches* (1)
Kennedy, Dr. James W., *Protestant Episcopal Church* (7)
Kilpatrick, Mr. Harold Cecil, *Presbyterian Church, U.S.* (6)
King, Dr. Joseph, *Congregational Christian Churches* (3)
Kirtley, Colonel Edwin Lankford, *Disciples of Christ* (10)
Knapp, Dr. Forrest Lamar, *Congregational Christian Churches* (1)

Lacy, Mrs. Graham G., *Presbyterian Church, U.S.* (10)
Lockhart, Dr. Wilfred Cornett, *United Church of Canada* (3)
Loescher, Dr. Frank Samuel, *Friends General Conference* (12)
Lowder, Rev. Virgil E., *Disciples of Christ* (7)
MacLeod, Mrs. W. Murdoch (Dorothy S.), *Presbyterian Church, U.S.* (6)
McCarthy, Mrs. Eugene Ross (Louise R.), *American Baptist Convention* (1)
McCord, Dr. James Iley, *Presbyterian Church, U.S.* (4)
Marteney, Colonel Charles W., *American Baptist Convention* (10)
Mathers, Dr. Donald Murray, *United Church of Canada* (8)
Meckstroth, Rev. Arnold W., *Evangelical and Reformed Church* (5)
Merle-Smith, Mrs. Van Santvoord (Kate G.), *Presbyterian Church, U.S.A.* (9)
Merrill, Dr. Charles Clarkson, *Congregational Christian Churches* (8)
Michaelides, Dr. George Peter, *Greek Orthodox Church* (7)
Miller, Dr. J. Quinter, *Church of the Brethren* (7)
Morrison, Dr. Charles Clayton, *Disciples of Christ* (8)
Mudge, Rev. Lewis Seymour, Jr., *Presbyterian Church, U.S.A.* (3)
Ogawa, Rev. Seido, *Congregational Christian Churches* (5)
O'Nan, Mrs. John W. (Mary M.), *Methodist Church* (12)
Osborn, Dr. Ronald Edwin, *Disciples of Christ* (8)
Rankin, Rev. Robert, *Methodist Church* (11)
Reissig, Dr. Frederick Edward, *United Lutheran Church* (6)
Ross, Dr. Roy G., *Disciples of Christ* (2)
Ruoss, Dr. Meryl H., *Evangelical and Reformed Church* (9)
Sanderson, Dr. Ross W., *Congregational Christian Churches* (9)
Shinn, Dr. Roger Lincoln, *Evangelical and Reformed Church* (1)
Skinner, Rev. Stanley Edward, *Methodist Church* (6)
Smith, Dr. John W. V., *Church of God* (2)
Stokes, Mrs. S. Emlen (Lydia B.), *Friends General Conference* (6)
Taylor, Dr. Charles Lincoln, *Protestant Episcopal Church* (9)
Terrell, Mrs. William Sale (Marjorie S.), *American Baptist Convention* (10)
Thornton, Mrs. Maxine, *Protestant Episcopal Church (Y.W.C.A.)* (4)
Wagoner, Rev. Walter D., *Congregational Christian Churches* (11)
Whidden, Dr. Evan MacDonald, *Baptist Federation of Canada* (3)
Whitman, Dr. Lauris B., *American Baptist Convention* (9)
Whittemore, Rev. B. Bruce, *Methodist Church* (6)
Whittemore, Rev. Edward L., *Presbyterian Church, U.S.A.* (6)
Wilson, Dr. Jesse Rodman, *American Baptist Convention* (4)
Witheridge, Rev. David Edward, *American Baptist Convention* (8)
Wyker, Mrs. James D. (Dr. Mossie A.), *Disciples of Christ* (12)
Wysner, Dr. Glora May, *Methodist Church* (9)
Young, Dr. Franklin Woodrow, *Protestant Episcopal Church* (4)
Young, Dr. W. Harold, *United Church of Canada* (11)

OVERSEAS CONSULTANTS

Appel, Rev. Andre, *Evangelical Lutheran Church (France)*
Barbieri, Bishop Sante Uberto, *Methodist Church (Brazil)* (10)
Chandran, Rev. J. Russell, *Church of South India*
Devadutt, Dr. Vinjamuri E., *Baptist Union of India* (2)
Ehrenstrom, Dr. Nils L., *Church of Sweden* (5)
Geldenhuys, Dr. Francis E. O'Brien, *Dutch Reformed Church (South Africa)* (12)
Graham, Rev. Ronald William, *Disciples of Christ (Australia)* (3)
Guerra, Rev. Eduardo, *Congregational Churches (Mexico)* (4)
Harms, Dr. Hans Heinrich, *Evangelical Church in Germany* (3)
Latuihamallo, Rev. Peter D., *Protestant Church in Indonesia* (11)
Lilje, Bishop Johannes, *Evangelical Lutheran Church (Germany)* (8)
Metropolitan James of Melita, *Greek Orthodox Church* (10)
Potter, Rev. Philip Alford, *Methodist Church* (5)
Visser 't Hooft, Dr. Willem Adolf, *Netherlands Reformed Church*

OBSERVERS

Amstutz, Mrs. Hobart B., *Methodist Church* (10)
Bradley, Mr. John, *Protestant Episcopal Church* (4)
Bretscher, Dr. Paul M., *Lutheran Church—Missouri Synod* (2)
Carr, Rev. Warren, *Southern Baptist Convention* (12)
Carrington, Rev. John, *African Methodist Episcopal Zion Church* (8)
Crouse, Dr. Moses, *Advent Christian Church* (1)
Dana, Mr. Ellis H., *Congregational Christian Churches* (9)
Gaines, Dr. David P., *American Baptist Convention* (6)
Geranios, Rev. John G., *Greek Orthodox Church* (3)
Gifford, Rev. Gerald G., II, *Protestant Episcopal Church* (5)
Hatch, Rev. Clarence W., *Church of God* (7)
Heebner, Rev. Harvey K., *Schwenkfelder Church* (6)
Hitchcock, Mr. Lowell Burton, *Church of the Saviour* (5)
Hogg, Rev. William, *Methodist Church* (11)
Huber, Mr. John G., *Lutheran Church—Missouri Synod* (4)
Hull, Miss Lillian P., *Presbyterian Church, U.S.A.* (5)
Johnson, Rev. Warren, *Congregational Christian Churches* (4)
Ketcham, Rev. John B., *American Baptist Convention* (6)
Koontz, Rev. Donald H., *Methodist Church* (6)
Landram, Dr. Hughbert H., *Presbyterian Church, U.S.A.* (5)
Lazenby, Professor John C., *Methodist Church* (11)
Lee, Rev. Robert, *Congregational Christian Churches* (12)
Loots, Rev. Zacharias B., *Dutch Reformed Church, South Africa* (10)
Lynes, Rev. Warren, *American Baptist Convention*
Markin, Rev. Luther E., *Presbyterian Church, U.S.A.* (6)

Marney, Dr. Carlyle, *Southern Baptist Convention* (4)
Martin, Dr. Wilbur Lee, *Presbyterian Church, U.S.A.* (6)
Nelson, Rev. F. Burton, *Evangelical Mission Covenant Church* (4)
Newberry, Dr. Gene, *Church of God* (5)
Palmquist, Rev. Herbert E., *Evangelical Mission Covenant Church* (6)
Phillips, Dr. Harold, *Church of God* (1)
Ramseyer, Dr. Lloyd L., *General Conference Mennonite Church* (11)
Royston, Rev. James M., *National Baptist Conv., U.S.A., Inc.* (9)
Saffen, Rev. Wayne, *Lutheran Church—Missouri Synod* (11)
Sangrey, Rev. Abram W., *Methodist Church* (9)
Sheerin, Rev. John, *Roman Catholic Church* (1)
Stewart, Rev. James A., *Congregational Christian Churches* (9)
Swanson, Rev. Neil H., Jr., *Congregational Christian Churches* (1)
Thorp, Rev. Almus M., *Protestant Episcopal Church* (11)
Walther, Rev. Daniel, *Seventh Day Adventist*
Weigel, Rev. Gustave, *Roman Catholic Church* (2)
Wharton, Rev. W. E., *African Methodist Episcopal Church*

STEWARDS

Bolliger, Mr. Theodore T., *Evangelical and Reformed Church*
Crews, Mr. William, *Protestant Episcopal Church*
Crow, Rev. Paul A., Jr., *Disciples of Christ*
Darrell, Mr. Chickford Bobbiee, Jr., *Methodist Church*
Davies, Mr. John D. M., *Presbyterian Church, U.S.A.*
Dixon, Rev. William John, *United Church of Canada*
Donnelly, Mr. James Ralph, *United Church of Canada*
Eiler, Mr. David Richard, *Evangelical United Brethren Church*
Flesher, Mr. Hubert Louis, *Protestant Episcopal Church*
Fountain, Mr. David B., *American Baptist Convention*
Gattis, Mr. John Wesley, *Methodist Church*
Jewett, Mr. Daniel Gordon, *Presbyterian Church, U.S.A.*
Karney, Mr. George James, *Methodist Church*
Lanou, Mr. Frank S., *Congregational Christian Churches*
Lawson, Mr. James M., *Methodist Church*
Minear, Mr. Richard, *Congregational Christian Churches*
Smith, Mr. Wesley Hugh, *Protestant Episcopal Church*

MESSENGERS

Arms, Mr. David
Harrelson, Miss Marianne
Minear, Miss Anita
Wagoner, Mr. Walter, Jr.

STAFF

Bilheimer, Dr. Robert S., *Presbyterian Church, U.S.A.*
Bridston, Dr. Keith, *Evangelical Lutheran Church*
Browne, Miss Eleanor Kent, *Methodist Church*
Bullard, Miss Anne, *Congregational Christian Churches*
Cavert, Dr. Samuel McCrea, *Presbyterian Church, U.S.A.*
Crow, Mrs. Mary, *Disciples of Christ*
Gallin, Mrs. Elizabeth, *American Baptist Convention*
Jurgens, Miss Vivian, *Methodist Church*
Lamb, Mrs. Innes, *Presbyterian Church, U.S.A.*
Leiper, Dr. Henry Smith, *Congregational Christian Churches*
Maeda, Miss Frances, *Presbyterian Church, U.S.A.*
Minear, Dr. Paul S., *Congregational Christian Churches*
Moore, Mr. Arthur, *Methodist Church*
Mudge, Mrs. Jean, *Society of Friends*
Nelson, Dr. J. Robert, *Methodist Church*
O'Dell, Mr. Robert, *Presbyterian Church, U.S.A.*
Schiller, Miss Lilo, *Evangelical Lutheran Church*
Thompson, Miss Betty, *Methodist Church*
Yamaguchi, Miss Tada, *Presbyterian Church, U.S.A.*

APPENDIX III

THE SIXTEEN STUDY GROUPS

Austin

James I. McCord, Chairman
Franklin W. Young, Secretary
Joe W. Bailey
John Barclay
T. Harold Branch
J. Chrys Dougherty
J. M. Dawson
Royal Embree
Page Keeton
Edward V. Long
Carlyle Marney
Joseph Quillian
Mrs. Lewis Speaker

Boston

William A. Overholt, Chairman
Henry E. Horn, Secretary
Leonard Clough
John Dillenberger
Mrs. Douglas Horton
George Kalbfleisch
Norman B. Nash
Miss Nancy Lewis
Samuel H. Miller
Miss Nancy Simons
Seymour Smith
Samuel Wylie

Chicago

Edward T. Ramsdell, Chairman
Paul H. Eller, Secretary
William B. Blakemore
Moses C. Crouse
Edward Dowey
Robert H. Fischer
Theodore A. Gill
Joseph M. Kitagawa
William H. Nes
Miss Suzanne Rinck
Don E. Smucker
Theodore C. Thalassinos
Jesse H. Ziegler

Durham

Waldo Beach, Chairman
R. Frederick West, Secretary
Warren Ashby

Raymond M. Bost
Warren Carr
Carl E. Devane
Neal Hughley
Mrs. Sadie Hughley
Malcolm McAfee
Gaylord Noyce
Miss Isabel Rogers
Alvin Rose
William T. Scott, Jr.
Harry Smith
J. W. Smith

Honolulu

Seido Ogawa, Chairman
Richard D. Isler, Secretary
Robert Dye
Gerald G. Gifford
Mrs. Martha Hohu
Harry S. Komuro
Donald Legg
Andrew W. Lind
Robert C. Loveless
H. B. Ramsour
W. A. Schroeder
Paul M. Wheeler
Richard Wong
Harley Ziegler

Minneapolis

Edgar M. Carlson, Chairman
Howard Conn, Secretary
John Maxwell Adams
Sjoerd L. Bonting
Anthony M. Coniaris
Edward W. Foote
Henry N. Hancock
Paul Holmer
Monrad G. Paulsen
Paul Rees
Forrest Richeson
John Rilling
Harold Ruopp
David L. Stowe
Willmar Thorkelson

Nashville

Roger L. Shinn, Chairman
Mrs. C. S. Johnson, Secretary

C. Thomas Baker
Arthur W. Braden
Hiel Bollinger
Lyman Cady
Bayard Clark
Langdon Gilkey
Joseph Johnson
John Keister, Jr.
William Lloyd Imes
Mrs. John T. McCall
Gerald McCulloh
A. C. Miller
James E. Savoy
Kelley Miller Smith
Whitworth Stokes
Bard Thompson
Andrew White
Miss Louise Young

Newark

Howard G. Hageman, Chairman
Lynn Leavenworth, Secretary
Richard N. Bolles
James Eelman
Carl Fjellman
J. Bernard Haviland
George L. Hunt
Stephen James
Hugh T. Kerr
Vernon Kooy
Carl Michalson

New York

Truman B. Douglass, Chairman
George F. Harkins, Secretary
Hampton Adams
Roswell P. Barnes
Robert F. Capon
Powel M. Dawley
Florea Marin Galdau
Robert T. Handy
Miss Virginia Harrington
Paul Hoon
Ralph D. Hyslop
John Knox
D. Ward Nichols
Alexander Schmemann
Paul W. S. Schneirla

Pittsburgh

Gordon E. Jackson, Chairman
William R. Vivrett, Secretary
Alexander J. Allen
George Leland Bach
Michael Budzanoski
Paul Erb
William J. Harvey III
Mrs. Marguerite Hofer
Alan J. Howes
Robert Kincheloe
Mrs. John W. O'Nan

George Parker
Milan G. Popovich
Miss Ruth Shinn
Charles S. Spivey, Jr.
Theophilus M. Taylor
O. M. Walton

St. Louis

Elmer J. F. Arndt, Chairman
W. D. McDowell, Secretary
Mrs. J. D. Bragg
Allen Hackett
Wesley Hager
Arthur Lichtenberger
George Loose
George Mastrantonis
Mrs. Eugene Ross McCarthy
H. Louis Patrick
Prentiss L. Pemberton
Leon R. Robison
Jesse E. Thomas
Mrs. W. W. Towle
Robert Vernon
O. W. Wagner
Mrs. Frank Lee Wright

Seattle

John Skoglund, Chairman
Donald Demaray, Secretary
Mrs. Arthur B. Barnett
Stephen Bayne
Victor Bendsen
Martin Goslin
Richard M. Hilton
Edward Hummon
Gil Lloyd
John Magee
John Paul Pack
Ralph Turnbull

Washington, D. C.

Marion J. Creeger, Chairman
Mrs. Graham Lacy, Secretary
Mrs. E. Lansing Bennett
C. Emanuel Carlson
George P. Gallos
W. M. Hale
Miss Elizabeth Lam
John F. McClelland
John R. McLaughlin
Engebret O. Midboe
Francis P. Miller
Edward M. Mize
A. T. Mollegen
William W. Parkinson
Frederick E. Reissig
Harold D. Shoemaker
Robert E. Van Deusen
Frank T. Wilson
Frank H. Yost

Saskatoon

R. C. Chalmers, Chairman
E. S. Mackay, Secretary
R. S. Dean
R. R. Dolan
Andrew G. Elliot
Vincent Goring
George McMichen
Otto Olson
A. R. Pohl
Walter Sluzar
S. C. Steer
O. K. Storaasli
T. Tatsuyama
S. A. R. Wood

Toronto

David W. Hay, Chairman
E. R. Fairweather, Secretary
R. F. Aldwinckle
W. R. Coleman
C. E. J. Cragg
Emlyn Davies
A. L. Farris

W. O. Fennell
W. J. Gallagher
O. Heick
J. Ray Houser
G. H. Johnson
U. S. Leupold
Ernest E. Long
J. C. McLelland
Derwyn Owen

Vancouver, B. C.

W. S. Taylor, Chairman
F. Temple Kingston, Secretary
J. Bishop
H. Diers
John W. Grant
G. Hollingworth
E. W. Horton
M. Nicolson
A. Schweitzer
T. D. Somerville
Hayden Stewart
C. G. Stone
D. P. Watney
H. F. Woodhouse